The Dovecotes and Pigeon Houses of
Herefordshire

The Dovecotes and Pigeon Houses of
Herefordshire

by

Robert Walker

Logaston Press

LOGASTON PRESS
Little Logaston Woonton Almeley
Herefordshire HR3 6QH
www.logastonpress.co.uk

First published by Logaston Press 2010
Copyright © Robert Walker 2010

ISBN 978 1906663 49 0

Typeset in Garamond by Logaston Press
and printed in Malta by Gutenberg Press

Contents

Foreword

Pigeon houses are very appealing buildings. Their human scale and the seemingly infinite variations of design on simple themes of form and materials that they display give great pleasure. There is a visitors' book in the pigeon house at Eardisland that records reactions to the building and the exhibition it houses. The building clearly inspires fulsome praise, and the pages of the book are peppered with exclamation marks and words like 'amazing', and 'fascinating'.

Not much more than 100 yards away, along the village street, there is an example of how this strong appeal has been translated into the design of new development. It takes the form of a sham timber-framed pigeon house, in a prominent position, in front of the new houses (Fig. 1). It appears to have no purpose other than decoration, and has been carefully designed, and built at considerable cost, simply for visual effect. It flies in the face of the 'honesty' that both modern architects and conservationists hold dear. Some might say it is the triumph of the twee, but rather it is, perhaps, the triumph of a building form which has the coherence and pleasing proportions that are lacking in much modern building but deeply embedded in our folk memory of dovecotes.[1] (Other modern examples exist at, for example, Westonbury Mill water gardens west of Pembridge.)

In my own case, as a conservation officer, I have always enjoyed

Fig. 1 Sham pigeon house at Eardisland

my encounters with dovecotes, although my involvement often arose from their poor condition, or from ruinous schemes to convert them to houses. Perhaps rock bottom was reached early on in my working life (not in Herefordshire) when I was dealing with a housing developer who offered to call his new estate 'The Dovecotes', if only he could be allowed to demolish the stately, octagonal pigeon house that stood forlornly in the middle of the site. Thirty years on, the same, now restored, pigeon house still graces its surroundings under the protection of its Grade II listing – a note of optimism at the beginning of this study which will reach some dismal conclusions about the survival of dovecotes.

When a measured drawing was needed for my conservation course back in the '70s, I spent a long summer weekend measuring the beautiful timber-framed pigeon house at Luntley,[2] which will always be in mind as a quintessentially English moment of deep green, bright blue and black and white (Fig. 55). I came to work here three years ago and explored possible writing projects as ways of engaging with the landscape of the area in my own time. I began by looking at the broad sweep of farm buildings but inevitably focused in on dovecotes – the buildings that had given so much pleasure. I will say more about why such a book is worthwhile, here it is important to say a 'thank you' to Andy Johnson of Logaston Press for agreeing, and for encouraging me.

In undertaking any survey of this type as much is learnt about people as about buildings. Of those two opposing threads in human nature – meanness and generosity – I could write much. Suffice to say that meanness, with access and with information, was not unknown but, thankfully, still eclipsed by the kindness, generosity, encouragement and interest I encountered in the great majority of places I visited. I record my thanks to all who allowed me to see their dovecotes. I also want to thank the writers of published parish histories, the staff of the Hereford Reference Library, the Herefordshire County Record Office and the Sites and Monuments Record, and the voluntary keepers of the Woolhope Club Library.

Abbreviations used in the text and endnotes

B & S	Reid, P. *Burke's and Savills Guide to Country Houses: Vol.2: Herefordshire, Shropshire, Warwickshire and Worcestershire*, Burke's Peerage (1980)
Cohen	Refers to photographs taken by Israel Cohen in the 1950s. These are small square format pictures kept in Case 20 Box 2 in the library of the Woolhope Naturalists' Field Club in Hereford
Hansell	Hansell, P. & J. *Doves and Dovecotes*, Millstream Books (1988)
HFNS	Herefordshire Field Name Survey undertaken by the Woolhope Naturalists' Field Club. The survey can be consulted in the Herefordshire Records Office. Each parish has a folder with the names and plot numbers listed. There is also a searchable database attached to the County Sites and Monuments Record
HRL	Hereford Reference Library
HRO	Herefordshire Record Office
Marshall	WNFC Library ref. 728.99 Case 20 Box 1. This is George Marshall's bound copy of Watkins' paper with his own hand written annotations.
McCann (1991)	McCann, J. 'An Historical Enquiry into the Design and Use of Dovecotes' *Transactions of the Ancient Monuments Society* 35 (1991), pp.89-160
McCann (1992)	McCann, J. 'An Historical Enquiry into the Design and Use of Dovecotes: Addendum' *Transactions of the Ancient Monuments Society* 36 (1992), pp.137-138
McCann (1998)	McCann, J. *The Dovecotes of Suffolk*, Suffolk Institute of Archaeology and History (1998)
McCann (2000)	McCann, J. 'Dovecotes and Pigeons in English Law' *Transactions of the Ancient Monuments Society* 44 (2000), pp.25-50
McCann (2003)	McCann, J. & P. *The Dovecotes of Historical Somerset*, Somerset Vernacular Buildings Research Group (2003)
McCann (2006)	McCann, J. & P. 'Dovecotes of Rutland' *Transactions of the Ancient Monuments Society* 50 (2006), pp.9-36
NMR	National Monument Record
RCHM	The three published surveys of the Royal Commission on Historical Monuments England:

	Vol. I 1931 South-West Herefordshire
	Vol. II 1932 East Herefordshire
	Vol. III 1934 North-West Herefordshire

Stainburn   Stainburn, I. *A Survey of Dovecotes in the Old County of Herefordshire*, Hereford and Worcester County Council (1979). An omission sheet was added later to include Stretfordbury and Wickton Court in the parish of Ford and Stoke Prior

(S.-)   Followed by reference number refers to numbered entries in the above. 'T I' etc. refers to the tables

SMR   Herefordshire Sites and Monuments Record

TWNFC   *Transactions of the Woolhope Naturalists' Field Club*

VCH   Victoria County History

Watkins (1890) Watkins, A. 'Herefordshire Pigeon Houses' *TWNFC* 9–22 (1890) Additional notes in 1904: 264-265.

(W.-)   Followed by a reference number refers to the page number in the above 1890 article

Watkins (1892) Watkins, A. 'A Summer Among the Dovecotes' *English Illustrated Magazine*: 45-53 (1892)

Introduction

Aims of the Book

Four past presidents of Herefordshire's learned Woolhope Club[3] have come under the spell of dovecotes. Their interest, sparked perhaps by the innate charm of the little buildings, is inevitably part of a wider, national context, and through them can be seen the development of ideas, both locally and nationally, which are the foundations of this book and the source of its purpose.

First and most important, even now, is the work of Alfred Watkins.[4] His article on Herefordshire's dovecotes, which appeared in the Woolhope Club *Transactions* in 1890,[5] was one of the earliest county surveys to be published; it was supplemented with additional notes in 1904. Watkins' survey was probably already well in hand when R.S. Furguson published a general paper in 1887, and a survey of Cumberland in 1888.[6] It is, however, likely that Watkins' interest was sparked not by Cumberland, but by Garway and the article of 1846 by Rev. John Webb, which was the first detailed account of a dovecote to be published with some semblance of archaeological accuracy. More importantly, it was a dovecote which, by its early, given date, brought great distinction to the county Watkins loved and served.[7]

Watkins recorded most of the standing dovecotes and gave a list of some which had been demolished in the preceding half century. He missed remarkably few standing buildings given that he was working at a time when travel was relatively difficult and there were no comprehensive listing surveys or computerised monuments records. He also photographed many buildings which have since been altered or demolished, but most of his pictures have not been published, even in his own seminal paper, which was illustrated mainly by line drawings. Here then is one of the aims of this book, to use Watkins' pictures to bring a number of lost buildings back to the light and to glimpse a time, now far removed from our own, when the use of dovecotes was still in living memory.

In 1902 George Marshall, another giant of local history in Herefordshire, published a paper about his local church at Sarnesfield, in the tower of which he found nesting holes for pigeons set out in the manner of the nests inside a stone pigeon house.[8] His paper was not the first about ecclesiastical dovecotes,[9] but it was the first to give a detailed account of a particular church building. Marshall's bound copies of Watkins' papers form a slim volume in the Woolhope Club Library. Bound up with it are manuscript notes which include details of important buildings, which were not included in Watkins' work, notably the now demolished building at The Moor, Clifford.

About 50 years after Marshall made his notes, Israel Cohen, who gave the Presidential Address to the Club in 1954, took a photograph of the building at the Moor which is included in the gazetteer below, and which was part of a small collection of small photographs that help to illuminate the history of some of the buildings in this book.[10] He was taking his pictures some 30 years after the publication of a national survey by Arthur Cooke, which included a chapter on Herefordshire, which might well have stimulated his interest.[11]

Another 50 years passed before Frank Pexton's (posthumous) paper on the pigeon house at Burghill Grange was published in the 2007 Woolhope Club *Transactions*. It was jointly written with John McCann, and expresses ideas and knowledge quite different from any earlier publication on the county's pigeon houses. The connection to John McCann is an important one, for most of what we now understand about the design, purpose and history of dovecotes springs from two groundbreaking papers by John McCann in 1991 and 2006, and from his accounts of buildings in Suffolk, Somerset and Rutland.

It would be difficult to overstate the influence of John McCann's writings on this book; they define its second and third principal aims, to survey the county's pigeon houses in the light of modern ideas, which are radically different from those held by previous authors and to present a more comprehensive picture and more accurate descriptions of the standing pigeon houses.

In recent times, Herefordshire has seen the foundation of a sites and monuments record and the transcription and computerisation of the mid-19th century tithe apportionment records. These resources, combined with the many parish documents and histories now available, have opened up the possibility of a much deeper exploration of the place of pigeon houses in the Herefordshire landscape: that exploration is the fourth aim of this book.

What is a Dovecote?

Previous surveys of Herefordshire state the purpose of dovecotes as providing fresh meat through the long winter months when other fresh meats were not available. They say that they were needed to make up for the poor methods of medieval farmers who could not provide winter keep for their beasts, and were consequently forced to slaughter most of them in the autumn, in the graphically named *Blodmonath*, or blood month, of the Saxon November (S.5).

John McCann provided a very different picture; it seems like common sense now but required uncommon sense to provide it. He pointed out that pigeons are not at their breeding peak in the winter and were unlikely to produce large quantities of edible young birds in that season. Also, in the winter, the large flocks of birds, which are accused throughout the literature of laying waste to neighbours' crops at other times of the year, would have little to eat. He studied medieval household accounts and demonstrated the complete opposite of the prevailing view, showing that the wealthy builders of pigeon houses did not go short of fresh meat, and actually enjoyed a rich variety of it throughout the winter – except for pigeon! In his words:

> At all periods fresh meat was to be had throughout the year – by the wealthy. The meat of pigeon squabs was just a luxurious supplement. It is impossible to appreciate the social significance of dovecotes unless their association with a luxurious way of life is understood.[12]

'Dovecote' is a collective word for structures in which doves, or pigeons (which are descendents of the rock dove), are kept. There have been many terms used in the past, embracing all possible spellings and combinations of pigeon/dove and house/cote. The most pleasing, but now archaic, terms in the literature are 'culverhouse' from the Anglo-Saxon word for a pigeon and 'columbarium' from the Latin for dove.

The main produce of dovecotes was not adult birds or eggs but young birds, called squabs, which were killed and eaten before they had flown, while they were still unexercised and tender. The design of dovecotes has varied greatly over time, as the purpose, demands and form of pigeon keeping have changed. The detailed historical account below shows that the story probably begins with large, round, free-standing buildings erected by monasteries, bishops or lords to supply food for their own tables, and to sell. The right of these privileged minorities to build dovecotes was protected by common law prerogative down to 1619, and their free standing buildings, dedicated wholly or partly to rearing birds, were normally called 'pigeon houses'.[13] That is the term which will be used in this survey for the tower-like buildings designed for pigeons, to distinguish them from other types of dovecote. When the prerogative ended, there was a spate of buildings so that most of the standing buildings today were built after 1619, including the many ambitious octagonal brick buildings which seem to put pigeon keeping on a factory farming scale.

A number of examples of small dovecotes survive from later on, with nest holes in the walls of houses or barns – called here 'gable-cotes', 'eaves-cotes' or 'chimney-cotes'. In addition, there are examples of small wooden structures, of various shapes, attached to the exterior of buildings which are called 'box-cotes' in this survey.[14]

From the 1730s birds began to be kept for their decorative, sporting or racing qualities. They were often housed in the roof of a building; I will refer to these as 'pigeon lofts'.

The parts of a dovecote can be described in common language – ledge, nest holes, revolving ladder etc. – but there is some disagreement about the naming of the upper structure on top of the roof which acts as the pigeons' entrance. Here I will use the word 'lantern' for glazed structures such as that at Hellens, Much Marcle (Fig. 2a), and 'louver' for open structures and those with sloping boards, such as that at Eardisland (Fig. 2b).

Earliest Records
The early history of dovecotes took place outside Britain, probably in the Middle East, and perhaps as long as 8,000 years ago.[15] Nearer in time, the Romans certainly had them, and

Fig. 2a 'Lantern' at Hellens, Much Marcle
which has modern glazing (left) and Fig. 2b
'louver' at Eardisland (right)

left a number of texts about pigeon keeping.[16]
They are assumed to have introduced dove-
cotes into northern Europe, but no archaeological remains of dovecotes have been found
in Britain from the Roman occupation,[17] or from the following millennium, and we must
assume that the agricultural landscape had not yet developed into a pattern that could
support flocks of pigeons to supply a luxury trade. It may be that there were smaller,
wooden dovecotes which have left no imprint, but that seems unlikely given the absence
of any written or pictorial material at all from a period of a thousand years. It is, however,
tantalising that the description of a pigeon house by the Roman writer, Verro could be a
description of our earliest dated pigeon house at Garway (Fig. 3): 'The peristerion is the
shape of a large testudo with a vaulted roof …'.[18]

The round stone pigeon house at Garway,[19] built or restored in 1326, is the earliest
dated, standing, pigeon house, not just in Herefordshire but in Britain. Documentary
sources can take us back a little further in Herefordshire. Part of the household accounts
of Richard de Swinfield, Bishop of Hereford, for 1290 survive. They record that he ate
pigeons taken from the pigeon house at Bosbury (see Gazetteer below) on, among other
days, Easter Sunday and during the subsequent week.[20] The Bosbury pigeon house, a

round stone building like Garway, survived for another six centuries, until it was demolished in the late 19th century.

The Bishop's diet is interesting (particularly as his accounts were a cornerstone of John McCann's thesis about the purpose of dovecotes). The accounts, which are among the most important of their kind, record the eating of pigeons on fifteen days in the ten month period, October 1289 - July 1290, which they cover as follows:

October 2nd	12 birds	
October 4th	12 birds	
October 9th	10 birds	3 pence
October 16th	31 birds	12 pence
October 18th	8 birds	8 pence
October 23rd	birds	1 penny
October 24th	16 birds	4 pence
October 25th	birds	3 pence
November 8th	16 birds	4 pence
November 21st	birds	4 pence
April 2nd	68 birds	17 pence
April 3rd	50 birds	12 pence
April 6th	12 birds	3 pence
July 16th	birds	8 pence
July 22nd	46 birds	11 pence

Fig. 3 Garway: The earliest dated pigeon house in Britain

The absence of pigeons from the Bishop's plate in the winter stands out, but what can be read into the rest of the pattern? The greatest peak in April corresponds both to Easter and to the first crop of squabs of the year. It is as though a great treat was being enjoyed after the winter absence of pigeons and the rigours of Lent, and to celebrate that most important of festivals. A three month gap ensued, when production in the pigeon house might be expected to have been at a high level; this must represent a time when the population of the pigeon house was being replenished and increased after the early Easter culling. The spring gap was followed by another 'treat' in July, at the feast of Mary Magdalene (22 July),[21] and a few days before it. The accounts for August and September are missing; because of this we cannot know whether the regular consumption through October was the continuation of a summer pattern or, perhaps, the eating up of the last squabs before closing down for the winter. John McCann's research into other domestic accounts, such as those for Durham Abbey,[22] found that consumption was highest during the summer months and up to the end of October, when the population of the pigeon house had built up to its greatest level. It is therefore likely that the missing accounts of the Bishop are those with the greatest number of pigeons. The price of birds in October, three or fewer per penny, is however considerably higher than the four per penny[23] pertaining through the spring and summer, which suggests scarcity and winding down.

Only ten years after Swinfield's accounts were written, in 1300, a dovecote was included in the possessions of the deceased lord of the manor of Kentchurch. That building must have been standing during the 1200s, perhaps even within living memory of the Conquest. The recently dead owner was a Norman, John de Tregoz, whose ancestor fought with King William at the Sussex landing. Alfred Watkins thought that another round stone pigeon house, at Much Cowarne, was Norman, but there is no clear evidence for that. He was however, voicing a supposition, which may be true, that it was Normans, like the Tregoz dynasty, who established the pigeon house among the manorial class in Britain. Outside Herefordshire, there are round stone buildings associated with castles, such as Manorbier, which may date from the century after the Conquest; and there are dovecotes incorporated into the fabric of castle towers, for example at Rochester Castle keep, which is thought to have been built in the 1100s, but nothing is certain about the dating of these buildings (see Richard's Castle in the gazetteer below).[24]

The Manorial Pigeon House

The history of pigeon houses in the medieval landscape, right down to the early 17th century, must focus on the manor, for the building of pigeon houses was, as noted above, a prerogative of manorial lords which was enshrined in common law until 1619. Manors varied greatly in size, and they also varied considerably in tenure over time; but the prerogative remained with the lord, so that tenants could not build pigeon houses themselves, although they could rent them.[25] At first thought this appears to be a law designed to protect the interests of lords, but it was actually to the common good. Herefordshire manors could have a large number of tenants; at Whitbourne, for example the Bishops, who held the manor, had up to 40 tenants.[26] It would have been to no one's benefit to have many tenants owning dovecotes.

There has been an assumption that 'every manor had its dove-cote'.[27] That is clearly untrue for large-scale pigeon houses (although it might be true of small box or pole cotes) simply because manors in upland areas could not have sustained them. If we ask the quite simple question as to how many Herefordshire lords of manors availed themselves of the prerogative to build pigeon houses, it is not possible to give an accurate answer. Most of the standing buildings date from after the ending of the prerogative in 1619, and there is too little documentary material readily available on the matter of manors and their possessions in Herefordshire.[28] In the gazetteer below, about 40 of the 300 sites represent potentially medieval buildings associated with medieval manors, by document, field name[29] or the presence of a round pigeon house (18 of the 23 known round stone buildings could pre-date 1619). This is a small number in relation to the number of manors which (based on the Domesday survey) was in the region of 300. This rough assessment is a base line figure, as more documentary research would probably increase it, but it suggests that at least 14% of manorial lords exercised the prerogative.

If we wanted to argue for a much higher figure than 14% we would say that it is simply a matter of survival, that the evidence, the buildings and documents, have been lost. We would also say it is naive to attribute little enthusiasm to those who could take advantage of a privilege which allowed their stock to feed on the land of others. It would also, perhaps, be perverse to conclude from a survey which has greatly increased the numbers of known sites that there were fewer dovecotes than previously thought!

Somehow we must try to look past the large number of post-prerogative buildings to the remoter past. One view is in the distribution of round stone pigeon houses, which are generally considered to be the earliest buildings, shown in Fig. 13. This shows a strong preference for the eastern half of the county, which might allow the conclusion that research would extend the 14% to 50%, but probably not much further.[30] We could also look at the manors of the Bishops about which a good deal is known (see below). Only two of their 21 manors had pigeon houses (9.5%), and they were both, on trend, in the east. If we try to look at the capacity of the land to support pigeons, calculation is almost impossible, but it is known that cereal yields in the county were very low – around 5 bushels/acre.[31] If the whole area of the county had been cultivated then the output of its 540,000 acres would have been 2,700,000 bushels. About half of the county was common or waste and about a third of what was left would have been fallow every year, so the output would reduce to 900,000 bushels. It would have been intolerable to have pigeons eating more than, say, a fifth of the crop or around 180,000 bushels. A calculation made in the 17th century suggested that four bushels were consumed by a pair of pigeon in a year,[32] so the 180,000 bushels would support 45,000 pairs. If we take the model of the round stone pigeon house with 600 nests or 300 pairs of birds (they needed two nests per bird) then our assumptions would lead to the conclusion that 150 dovecotes, or one on 50% of the manors could be supported. This can hardly be called a calculation, given the unknowns and approximations but the point is that the land had limited capacity to support a luxury trade.

Should we be surprised at what appears to be small enthusiasm in Herefordshire for dovecotes before 1619, from this provisional estimate of 14% – 50%? John McCann has consistently argued that dovecotes were producing top of the range, luxury food, and that they were not actually needed, as was previously purported, to prevent the upper classes from starving in the winter months.[33] Both of these facts are consistent with there being few rather than many pigeon houses. In addition, the stone pigeon houses of the time could only be afforded by the wealthiest lords, and the many who were absentees, renting out all but a modest demesne, would have been disinclined to invest in expensive buildings for the use of tenants.

We do not know the extent to which more ephemeral or smaller scale dovecotes were used prior to 1619 or whether they were exempt from the manorial prerogative, but the Ledbury tithe book gives an indication of a number of small-scale enterprises:

> In the tithe book pigeons are always listed, but never the huge numbers sometimes given in other parishes. The first mention of them was in 1599 when John Heyward, of Priors Court, Wellington paid two birds. There was a gradual increase, but some names were entered with the payments left blank. Andrew White of Old Lilly Hall was listed in 1600 but deleted in 1601 as 'never any'. The maximum number was 78 in 1606 paid by six persons. In 1598 Richard Hooper had been given a licence to build a dovecote but was not listed in the tithe book until 1601, and did not pay birds until 1603, building up to 18 in 1606. Hilltop was later rebuilt without a dovecote.[34]

These small numbers of birds and the way production seems to have petered out reinforce the impression that pigeon keeping was a lower key activity than has previously been assumed.

The Parson's Pigeon House

The clergy shared the right, alongside lords of manors, to build pigeon houses under the common law prerogative, and it might be thought that pigeon keeping, or renting out a pigeon house, would be an attractive proposition. In most cases, where parishes were endowed, glebe lands were of modest extent, and a pigeon house would be a way of using a small area of ground in an exceptionally productive way. It is therefore, surprising to find that very few priests took advantage of their uncommon right.

The surviving glebe terriers for Herefordshire cover most of the parishes, but only about 25% have been transcribed. Most of them date from the late 16th century or, more commonly, the first decades of the 17th century. For this survey the southern part of the county, south of Hereford, corresponding with a relatively dense distribution of pigeon houses today, was looked at in detail, and all the terriers examined.

In the area of the deaneries of Hereford, Ross and Archenfield references to pigeon houses appear in only two parishes (Eaton Bishop and Linton by Ross) of the 46 parishes with surviving terriers – about 4.3%. At this rate there may have been one other pigeon house on glebe in the south of the county, in one of the parishes for which the terriers have been lost.

Whilst other parts of the county have not been looked at in the same detail, it is possible to draw some further conclusions from the terriers that have been transcribed. In the east of the county the occurrence of dovecotes on the glebe was significantly higher. There were pigeon houses on the glebe at Withington, Ledbury, Ullingswick and Cradley, and in the former parishes of Astley and Upper Court in Bromyard. That sector of the county has, say, 66 parishes, very few of which have been investigated, but, if no more were found, the lowest possible proportion of parishes with pigeon houses on the glebe is 9.1%. The north-west, on the other hand, has a lower occurrence; the 17 terriers which have been transcribed yielded no records of pigeon houses. Overall, the proportion of parishes with pigeon houses in all of the terriers examined is (8/77) 10.3% – the gazetteer gives details of each example – but this is weighted to the south and east, where their occurrence seems to be denser, and a comprehensive reading of all terriers would almost certainly decrease this percentage.[35]

This figure, though small, is considerably higher than that found in the adjacent county of Shropshire, for which there are published transcripts of all the surviving terriers. In that county 4.7% (12) of the 257 parishes with surviving terriers had pigeon houses.[36] It is difficult to establish reasons for this; it may be simply be that a full survey of Herefordshire terriers would yield, as noted, a lower figure, closer to that pertaining to Shropshire. If there is a real difference, it could be to do with the nature of the land and the farming response to it, in which case it would be found that secular landowners in Shropshire were also less than half as inclined to build pigeon houses as their Herefordshire counterparts.

Further comparison with the few counties which have been studied in detail show that Herefordshire did not have an exceptional number of parsonages with dovecotes. In Somerset almost a quarter of the terriers record pigeon houses,[37] whilst in Suffolk only about 3% have them.[38]

In Herefordshire it appears that the clergy were less likely to build pigeon houses than the manorial land owners. There were, of course, practical difficulties and great expenses in building and maintaining pigeon houses that could be ill afforded from small holdings of land, and in many cases the way of gaining income from the glebe was by renting it out rather than farming it. It has been suggested that there was a pecking order; the lord taking precedent over the priest, yet there is an example at Ullingswick, which is probably not unique, where both glebe and adjacent manor kept pigeons. That arrangement could only have been possible in a landscape where competition for free grazing was low, and where resources were not pinched. It would have been impossible in that scene depicted in the earlier literature on dovecotes which portrayed a sky full of marauding pigeons descending on the crops of the peasants. It now appears that there may have been far fewer pigeon houses than was previously assumed. The emerging figures for all owners enjoying the prerogative in Herefordshire show no great enthusiasm by any class.

We live in a cynical age, which probably sees the medieval clergy as more like Friar Tuck than St Francis, but it may be that the clergy were simply disinclined to keep pigeons at the expense and to the disadvantage of their parishioners. It is striking that even on the manors controlled by the Bishop of Hereford, where the church was free of secular manorial control or competition, few were furnished with pigeon houses. This is seen in the late 13th century register of Bishop Swinfield which lists only two pigeon houses, at Bosbury and Colwall, on his 21 Herefordshire manors.[39] Later on, the glebe terriers for Linton by Ross and Shawbury (Shropshire) both record pigeon houses which, at the beginning of the 17th century, had been allowed to decay; perhaps further evidence of an enduring lack of enthusiasm for pigeons.[40]

Fig. 4 Sarnesfield Church: The upper stage of the tower contains nest holes like those found in pigeon houses

Herefordshire has an excellent example of the priest's alternative to the building on the glebe, which was using the church building. At Sarnesfield (Fig. 4) the upper part of the tower has nest holes, very similar in form to those in the round stone pigeon houses in this survey. Marshall thought that he had found a second church tower with nest holes at the, now ruined, church of St John the Baptist, Llanwarne, but there must be doubts about whether the holes were meant for pigeons (see the gazetteer entry). Examples outside Herefordshire are very few, and there seems to be no other in a tower of such early date as Sarnesfield.[41]

In theory, the clergy could also benefit from the pigeon houses of parishioners through the collection of the tithes.[42] In the parish of Lewknor in Oxfordshire the glebe terrier notes that a tithe of 3s 4d was to be received for every 'dovecot or pigeon house'.[43] Only two similar references have been found in the Herefordshire terriers, at Weston Beggard and St Katherine's, Ledbury (see above).[44] It is, perhaps, surprising that in parishes such as Dilwyn and Ford, where there were relatively large numbers of pigeon houses, the inclusion of pigeons in the minor tithes is not stated.

The Monastic Pigeon House
The general picture of the place of pigeon houses among the buildings of great monastic foundations is unclear. Hereford, a monastic foundation in a town, has not yielded any record, but there were pigeon houses within sight of the mother churches at the more

rural foundations of Abbey Dore and Wigmore (see the gazetteer below).[45] The round stone building at Wigmore was demolished soon after Alfred Watkins photographed it in the 1880s (Fig. 5).

It is at the granges and the remoter religious houses that the evidence suggests that pigeon houses were standard kit. Leominster Priory had granges at Stocktonbury, Stoke Prior (Bury Farm), Ivingtonbury, Bury of Hope and Lustonbury, all of which had pigeon houses.[46] Stocktonbury stands and is round; Stoke Prior is also known to have been round but has been demolished; the design of the others is not known. Two other round stone buildings in this survey are associated with religious houses. The standing pigeon house at Garway and the

Fig. 5 Wigmore Abbey (Alfred Watkins Collection)

lost building at Dinmore Manor are both associated with preceptories of the orders of knights.

As a class of landowner, the monastic foundations show a stronger inclination for building dovecotes compared to their parochial and, perhaps, to their manorial counterparts. About half of the religious houses listed on the County Sites and Monuments Record are known to have had them. It has been argued that monastic agriculture was subject to 'a more organised, intensive and perhaps technologically innovative estate management regime',[47] which would have grasped the advantage that the prerogative afforded. In addition many religious houses were sufficiently endowed to be able to build pigeon houses, and they had the human resources to manage them. They were therefore particularly well equipped to be keepers of pigeons.

After the Dissolution the manors owned by monastic estates passed to individuals. John McCann portrays the national picture: 'Therefore many new dovecotes were built in the generation after the Dissolution as a direct consequence of [the] transfer of manorial rights … Many of the lawyers, officials and younger sons of landowning families … were actively engaged in establishing their new social position. One way of asserting their status as manorial lords was to build a conspicuous dovecote near the manor house.'[48] It is difficult to see the mirror of this national trend in the surviving buildings of Herefordshire, where the urge to build and assert seems to have been delayed by a number of generations, until the framed buildings of the mid 17th century appeared and, later still, the country house builders became a significant force in the landscape.

After 1619

The ending of the common law manorial prerogative in 1619[49] resulted in an upsurge in the building of pigeon houses, clearly seen in the fact that the majority of surviving buildings in this, as in most counties, were built after 1619. In some parishes the standing and recorded remains portray considerable enthusiasm. That is seen clearly in the parish of Dilwyn, which has three standing timber-framed buildings at Luntley, Bidney and Lower Hurst, a record of a fourth framed building at Bearton, a standing masonry building at Little Dilwyn and a record of an octagonal building in the centre of the village at Great Court; all of which were built after the end of the prerogative. There are other concentrations; Stoke Prior has four pigeon houses,[50] two field name sites and a gable-cote, Burghill has four pigeon houses and two field name sites, and Leominster, a relatively large parish, has ten sites, although only the barns with gable-cotes and eaves-cotes at Brierley remain standing.[51] An examination of the statutory lists for adjacent counties reveals that there are significant numbers of parish clusters, but whether they are an accident of survival, an expression of social rivalry or a response to particularly favourable local conditions for pigeon keeping cannot be unpicked with the presently available information.[52] What is perhaps more significant for Herefordshire is the intensity of its 'hot spots' which have multiples of dovecotes, of more than two, which are not found elsewhere in the literature.

We are, of course, studying a pattern of survival – surviving buildings and documents – which means that this survey represents a baseline in the number of dovecotes which further research can only increase. However, these parishes do appear to be exhibiting a phenomenon which sets them apart from the majority of parishes across the county and the country where there is, on average, evidence of only one dovecote per parish. It is interesting that in two of the four parishes the urge to build is strong at one particular time. In Dilwyn it was the mid to late 17th century period of timber frames, while in Burghill the urge to build was strongest in the age of the octagonal brick pigeon houses. This might betray a competitive attitude between landowners, commercially in terms of competing for a luxury market, and in the sense of ensuring that 'if your pigeons are going to eat my grain then my pigeons are going to eat yours'.

There is also a hint of this attitude in the field names data. It is generally thought, particularly at a later date, that dovecotes were best located at the working centre of a farm where they could be protected and supervised, but a significant number of named fields are remote from centres of holdings as set out in the tithe apportionments. These locations appear designed to take greatest advantage of feeding on neighbouring land. That these sites are now, without exception, bare of buildings shows that they were probably not sustainable, nor were they conducive to finding new uses to ensure their survival.

Pigeons, if not their owners, continued to enjoy the protection of the law, up to a point. In 1603 an Act was passed to modernise the law relating to game. It made shooting at, killing or destroying pigeons an offence. The same law was re-enacted in 1627, 1640 and 1692 and thus kept in force throughout the 17th century. Marshall's notes refer to a case in Hereford which must have been brought under these statutes: 'In 1625 Richard Jauncey was presented in Hereford City "for shotinge in a peece at piggons within the liberties of the said Cittie." This occurs again in 1657.'

Elizabeth Taylor also reports a case in her enthralling history of King's Caple:

> 1672 John Cole of Llanwarne was bound over to appear at the next Quarter Sessions for shooting pigeons and was threatened with imprisonment if he did it again.
>
> A new edict was published in the parish churches in 1677 that a 6s 8d reward was offered for information … against any one shooting or destroying pigeons, unless they had lands of more that £100 per annum.
>
> Thus James, soon to be Duke of Chandos, had reserved for his own well fed stomach and those of about half a dozen others, all the pigeons in the Hundred of Wormelow and had made criminals of any who disobeyed the order.[53]

The underlying aim of these laws was the protection of pigeons as property, and they were strengthened and modified in subsequent centuries as pigeon racing and fancying became established. There was, however, ambivalence about whether pigeons, which are wild birds, can be considered to be personal property.[54] The thread in common law was that pigeons were not personal property once out of the pigeon house, while the thread in statute was successive Acts that tried to criminalise the killing of pigeons. The idea that a farmer should be able to protect his crops from a neighbour's pigeons by shooting them is never explicitly stated (perhaps it was assumed that there were other means of scaring birds away) but it seems to have been understood. Later on, as pigeon farming was declining, the Larceny Act of 1827 left a clear loophole which, in effect, allowed a farmer to protect his crops as he wished. John McCann suggests that this Act which 'stopped short of treating honest farmers as criminals', was a determining factor in ending large scale pigeon keeping.[55]

The Country House Dovecote
The most recently published survey of country houses in Herefordshire lists 133 'seats' which existed in the 18th century or earlier.[56] Some of them have manorial roots, but many were started following the grab of monastic lands or by the application of money earned in trade to the assembly of large estates. The builders of big houses had pretensions, and dovecotes were considered, by some, to be a status symbol. It is, perhaps, not surprising that 47 of these 133 country houses (35%) are known to have had pigeon houses, most of which were built after the mid 17th century. As a class of landowner, the builder of a country house was probably more inclined to indulge in pigeon farming than his predecessors who held the manorial prerogative. Only the monastic builders appear more enthusiastic, and it is probably significant that the monastery and the country house both required the feeding of resident and visiting establishments. It is, of course, also

significant that two-thirds of country houses did not have dovecotes – a clear indication that they were not considered to be necessary by a majority of those landowners who were most able to build them.

The country house builders preferred brick,[57] as at Shobdon (Fig. 6) but a number of stone dovecotes were built or inherited by them, for example at Cowarne Court. They exploited the full range of plan forms and were central to the development of the polygonal forms which play so prominent a part in the 18th-century history of dove-cotes. It is in the estate context that dovecotes continued to be built until the late 18th or early 19th century, and at this late date the builders were capable of reverting to square timber cotes (at Berrington – see Ashton in the gazetteer – and Burton for example) or round stone cotes (at Holme Lacy) despite the pre-eminence of octagonal brick buildings.

Fig. 6 Shobdon: The pigeon house of a great country estate set in the walled garden

The country house builder was often building his dovecote with more than one aim in mind. The roofless pigeon houses at Eywood and Staunton on Arrow are deliberately placed and made to appear like Classical temples[58] as part of grand parkland designs. The timber pigeon house (now demolished) at Broadward was re-faced in brick, on one side, to stand more elegantly alongside the façade of the big house, so too was the round building at Old Sufton faced as part of the formation of a grand walled garden. The lower part of that building was used as a summer house, and we can see similar ideas built into the cote at Hill Court, which had a garden room with a door and two windows facing across the garden to the big house. At Shobdon the pigeon house stands in the walled garden and the stone basement was used as a gardener's room. At Gaines there is an icehouse under the raised dovecote, an arrangement said to have also existed at Tyberton. Serving the needs of the kitchen of the big house was taken a step further at Foxley, which has three levels – ice house, game larder and dovecote.

A number of country house dovecotes have outlived the great houses they served. The round stone pigeon house at Much Cowarne saw a big house come and go, while those at Shobdon, Eywood and Foxley (Yazor) stand as magnificent memorials to lost fortunes and ambitions. At Holme Lacy the home farm afforded the context for what may be the last dovecote to be built in Herefordshire. It stands today, but the big house is now an hotel.

The Entrepreneurial Farmer

The distinction between the smaller country houses and the homes of the wealthiest farmers is often not clear, and the most ambitious of the squires were capable of building on a grand, country house scale. The magnificent brick pigeon houses at, for example, Eardisland, Stocks House in Wellington (Fig. 7), Burghill Grange, Poston Court, Weston Beggard and Whitwick (now demolished) express status and farming ambition in abundance. They are prominently positioned for all to admire, but it is doubtful whether their farming purpose was ever profitable or whether they were actually in full use for a sustained period. It is probable that they represent the peak in the luxury trade in pigeons and in the benefits of status which protected the birds that fed on the land of others. That they have survived is a testament of the quality of their construction and the greater adaptability of larger buildings.

Fig. 7 Wellington: The wealthy farmer's status symbol

These builders were also capable of innovation. The Eardisland pigeon house has a garden room which was entered under a fine door hood and heated by a fireplace. At Bodenham, the pigeon house is also built into the garden wall with two levels below the storey with nest holes (Fig. 8). At Hermitage Farm, Burghill (Fig. 34) and Bollitree Castle (Fig. 160), the simple vernacular design tradition was abandoned to allow display with a distinctly original architectural flavour.

The County Sites and Monuments Record has nearly 4,000 records for sites classed as farms, most of which have been identified by the Herefordshire Historic Farmsteads Characterisation Project as being present on the Ordnance Survey First Edition, pre-Second World War and modern maps. Clearly only a very small proportion of these are associated with known pigeon houses. On current evidence no more than 2% of Herefordshire's farmers built pigeon houses, and many who did indulged in small scale dovecotes forming part of a barn or other building.

Fig. 8 Bodenham: A three-decker pigeon tower with the pigeons in the upper stage (Alfred Watkins Collection)

The Broader Picture of Distribution

The foregoing discussion of particular types of owner shows that even though the right to erect dovecotes was protected, those with the right and the means were probably not as enthusiastic about building them as has previously been assumed. The survey includes 300 possible sites, which is probably a baseline figure, in that more sites are likely to be discovered. These sites were not all occupied at the same time, but it is doubtful, in simple resource terms, whether the landscape had much more capacity to accommodate pigeons.

In national terms farming in Herefordshire was backward until modern times. The few documentary snapshots available illustrate a frontier area which was notable for producing wood, wheat and wool. However in the 14th century it was 'a very poor county' and fields put to wheat yielded only 5 to 6 bushels per acre. There was a steady improvement into the 17th century indicated by the county's assessment for ship-money and land tax in which its value ranged from 12th to 18th lowest among the counties.[59] Throughout this period a form of common field system was in operation which lasted well into the 18th century. This may have been a particularly inefficient arrangement described as 'utterly unlike the order and symmetry of the Midland two or three field holdings'.[60]

In 1794, when dovecotes were probably beginning to go out of use (see below), a typical Herefordshire farm would have had about a fifth of its area given over to cereals.[61] There was a local tendency to sow different cereals together, which must have been very attractive to pigeons; as Camden notes, 'About Leominster they sow wheat and rye together and call it "munk corn" and with the addition of barley "blend corn"; and they make excellent bread of the two mixtures.'[62] It is unlikely that a greater area was given over to cereals prior to 1794, so this marks, perhaps, a high point in cereal production in the period when pigeon houses were probably most numerous. If we take this as the basis of calculation, and err again on the side of maximum production by taking the whole of the area of the county as being farmed, and also assume that productivity has risen to 20 bushels per acre[63] then Herefordshire would yield 540,000/5 acres x 20 = 2,160,000 bushels or, dividing by 300, then 7,200 bushels per dovecote. As noted earlier, a calculation made in the 17th century suggested that four bushels were consumed by a pair of pigeon in a year[64] which suggests that the landscape could support 1,800 pairs in each dovecote if they consumed all of the grain. Clearly, a situation where the pigeons share exceeded, say, a fifth of the crop would have been intolerable, so that 360 (1,800 ÷ 5) pairs would be a tolerable, average population for each of 300 dovecotes. The fact is that there were probably more dovecotes, significantly less land in cultivation and a significantly lower yield than this estimate allows for; yet it must be unlikely that there were many more dovecotes, or that those we know from this survey, with many hundreds of nest holes, ever worked at maximum capacity. Even if we see the figure of consumption of four bushels per pair as an exaggeration by a campaigning, anti-dovecote writer, the errors in the assumed variables probably cancel out and might not change the overall picture that 300 dovecotes was not far off the capacity of the Herefordshire landscape at that point in time.[65]

The examination of different landowners showed that there could be distinct differences between adjacent areas. The analysis of glebe, for example, showed that in Herefordshire the proportion of clergy building dovecotes was about twice that of the adjacent county of Shropshire. It would be interesting to make broader comparisons with surrounding counties but this is almost rendered pointless by the huge number of variables at work and by the disparate nature of the information available.

The statutory lists of listed buildings, now on the Internet, offer one way of comparing different areas in some detail, but the lists are a very incomplete medium. The 46 listed pigeon houses[66] in Herefordshire represent only a fraction of the sites identified in this survey, and that low level of representation would probably be found in all areas; the lists do however present a consistent selection of surviving buildings of higher quality construction based on standard listing criteria. If it is assumed that survival is influenced by a common set of factors[67] then quantitative comparisons should betray real differences between counties, if they exist. Considering the adjacent and nearest English counties:

County	Listed pigeon houses	Area of county. km²	Area per pigeon house. km²
Shropshire	50	3197	64
Worcestershire	67	1741	25
Warwickshire	32	1951	61
Gloucestershire	87	2653	30
Herefordshire	46	2180	47

In the counties over the Welsh border the numbers of pigeon houses become very small, which is not unexpected given the sharp change to upland farming. In Powys, which covers a huge area, there are only eleven listed dovecotes (all but one of which are pigeon houses), including the matching pair at Felindre. In Monmouthshire, Sir Cyril Fox, one of the pioneer recorders of vernacular architecture, noted: 'The Hygga affords a good example of a dove-cot [pigeon house] and there is also one at Llantellen, Skenfrith: these are rare in Monmouthshire. Provision for doves is, however, not infrequently made in the Renaissance house gables … or in farm buildings as at Trevella, which is dated 1674.'[68]

In terms of density of distribution in the table, Herefordshire is in the middle of the range. Comparing with Shropshire, the significantly lower density corresponds with the analysis of glebe. Shropshire landowners as a whole *were* significantly less inclined to build dovecotes, which is probably, at least in part, a reflection of the greater upland and urban areas in that county. Comparison with the denser counties of Worcestershire and Gloucestershire is more difficult. In the case of the latter, the availability of good limestone has assisted the survival of buildings, and the quality of building may also be a factor in Worcestershire, where the pigeon houses have a grander, better-built feel to them compared to Herefordshire buildings.

If Herefordshire were also the average dovecote county nationally, then the 300 sites in this survey would, at the same density, correspond to about 12,000 in the whole of

England.[69] This is about half of the figure of 26,000 which has been suggested as the number of dovecotes existing in England in the 17th century.

The overall distribution of dovecotes within the county is shown in Fig. 9. The immediate impression of the map is that most of the county supported pigeons. The densest area is in the fertile central plain around and to the west of Leominster and stretching south across the Wye to the south-west of Hereford. The sparsest area is the western, upland fringe. There are smaller blank areas which are probably the result of the loss of evidence

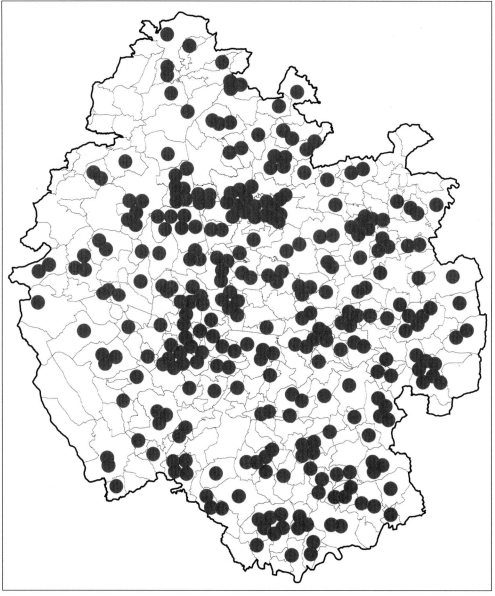

Fig. 9 Map of Herefordshire showing the distribution of the sites included in the gazetteer

rather than a lack of sustaining topography. Kingsland, in the north, has only the one record at Street Court, but is otherwise rich lowland, and Much Dewchurch, Dewsall, St Devereux and Kilpeck in the south are similarly lowland parishes with a predominance of arable but no known dovecotes.

Decline and Fall

Pigeon houses, if not dovecotes, probably had their heyday in the middle of the 18th century. After that the number of new buildings tailed off until the first decades of the 19th century. Watkins, writing in 1890, said of Herefordshire that dovecote building 'suddenly stopped in the beginning of the present century, for none appear to have been built since about 1810'.[70] This local trend is reflected in the national scene where there are very few dovecotes associated with the development of the model farms which are characteristic of the industrial age. John McCann refers to the building and running of a new pigeon house in Wakefield in 1846,[71] but this is an unusual record. The causes of decline are delineated by John McCann:

> The high wheat prices of the Napoleonic Wars induced many landowners to farm their own newly-enclosed land.[72] The articulate progressive farmers, whether tenants or landlords, became more aware of the depredations of pigeons because the losses were their own. Increasingly from 1800 the keeping of pigeons was reduced to a small-scale operation in which the birds were fed in the yard like poultry.
>
> The change in attitude … can be seen in the farming literature of the time … In 1825 J.C. Loudon wrote that pigeons were 'scarcely admissible in professional agriculture, except in grazing districts, where the birds have not so direct opportunity of inuring corn …'. These excerpts describe the end of traditional pigeon keeping on a major scale – relatively earlier in corn growing regions, later in pastoral regions.[73]

Locally these sentiments were voiced by John Duncumb, in his observations on Herefordshire's agriculture in 1805; 'Pigeons are not generally kept by the tenants of farms in this county, nor is their increase a desirable object, where so large a proportion is occupied by grain.'[74] Duncumb was writing in the hard-bitten time of great price inflation which was followed, at the end of the Napoleonic Wars, by a slump – who then could afford to keep, let alone build for, pigeons for a luxury trade?[75] Duncumb's survey came only ten years after the publication of a more thorough agricultural survey by John Clerk[76] which did not mention pigeons at all, presumably because they were already of no consequence.

The decline of industrial scale production in pigeon houses did not, however, lead to the removal of pigeons from the Herefordshire scene. Watkins said that a third of the buildings he visited in the 1880s were still in use. Smaller scale production, which had always existed in parallel with the big pigeon houses, continued in a number of ways, for example in the eaves and gable-cotes that are considered in more detail below. Some pigeon towers were built after Duncumb was writing. That at Pencoyd, with a box-lined upper chamber and distinctive overhanging eaves, is probably of the first quarter of the

19th century. Upton Bishop with its distinctive open nest boxes, the Italianate Hermitage Farm, Burghill, and Holme Lacy, with its beautifully fitted-out upper loft, are also likely to be late in date.

The Management and Design of Dovecotes

The Yearly Round

The purpose of dovecotes was, as already noted, to provide luxury food in the form of young birds called squabs. The raw materials, the pigeons, were descendents of the native rock dove which had certain characteristics that assisted their domestication in dovecotes; they were social and they could breed all year round. They could also adapt to buildings (something of a problem in modern cities). However, like bees in hives, they were free to fly, which meant that the keepers of dovecotes had to make their buildings and their management regimes attractive to the birds. They also had to protect them from their natural predators such as birds of prey and, later on, from the immigrant brown rat.

There is a good deal of folklore about the ways of attracting birds and keeping them. The most important task must have been providing them with sufficient food. Pigeons survive in the wild on a wide variety of foods, including insects, but their state of health and breeding success are variable and below the level required by farmers. It was therefore impossible to rely on their foraging abilities alone, nor could the fields and gardens of neighbours be relied upon throughout the year. Pigeons were fed, and well fed at that; hence the proverbs that 'pigeons find cherries bitter' and 'the pigeon never knows woe but when she does a benting go'. The latter refers to the time of feeding on bents (grasses) after the harvest of field crops. There are many examples, but none in Herefordshire, of feeding platforms inside pigeon houses, usually associated with the revolving ladders described below, but the birds could also be fed outside in the farmyard like hens.

Pigeons were given a variety of seeds, peas, lentils and beans.[77] John Moore, an 18th-century apothecary, recommended that tares were the best food and that, 'pease, wheat and barley are apt to scour your pigeons too much'.[78] He also recommended a delicacy called a salt-cat: 'a mix of sand and lime and loam and saltpetre and stale urine and cumin keeps pigeons at home and lures strays … By this means therefore you keep 'em from pecking the mortar of your own, or your neighbours' houses.'

In their survey the Hansells note:

> There were many recipes for this concoction, but it consisted basically of a sort of cake made up of lime, grit and salt which are essential mineral requirements of the bird and are still provided by competent owners today. If deprived of these substances, pigeons have been known to peck at the mortar on walls … lime is needed to harden the eggshell and grit aids digestion.[79]

At the beginning of the yearly cycle of husbandry, in January, the dovecote would have been occupied by the relatively few birds spared from the late-autumn cull. Some would still be breeding, and the young would be allowed to mature. The much quoted advice of Thomas Tusser written down in 1580 sets out the winter programme:

> Feed doves but kill not,
> If lose them ye will not.
> Dove house repair,
> Make dovehole fair.
> For hop ground cold
> Dove dung is worth gold.[80]

The almost magical properties of dove dung,[81] which is exceptionally rich in nitrogen, potash and phosphorous,[82] must have been important in Herefordshire, where hops have been a significant crop:

> Besides being used for hops, pigeons' dung was valued for other purposes. It was a useful addition to other supplies of animal excreta, but supplies must always have been small. The largest dovecote can hardly have produced enough of this material to fertilize more than an acre or two. Its scarcity made it precious. Gabriel Plattes roundly declared that he had known a load of pigeon dung fetched sixteen miles, and a load of coal given for it, a story that sounds too good to be true. He estimated that the effect on the land was worth double the charges.[83]

In some pigeon towers with a ground-floor room given over to another purpose and no door at the upper level, mucking out must have been a difficult and unpleasant activity. A further part of mucking out and making fair was limewashing. There is evidence of both interior or exterior limewashing in most types of pigeon house, in accordance with the view held by some experts that a white building attracted pigeons.

In addition to fertilizer, there were other by-products of the pigeon house that had value. Old birds and eggs were eaten, feathers were used in bedding and saltpetre was got from the dropping for the making of gunpowder. The dung was also used in tanning.

Breeding began in earnest in late February/early March. Pigeons are very fecund, as the Hansells say:

> The pigeons' steady cycle of breeding ensured a regular supply of meat … Each pair of birds produces two chicks eight to ten times a year for about seven years and during this time the parents fatten the squabs on their own regurgitated 'pigeons' milk'. The young birds were generally culled at the age of four weeks when still covered with down …[84]

The first generation of squabs was usually left to mature, and would itself be ready to breed by the end of July. Some birds were taken for special occasions, as seen above in the Easter accounts of the late 13th century Bishop of Hereford. In many household accounts, as with the Bishop's, June and July tended to yield few birds as the first brood reached maturity. At that time there was much for them to eat beyond the walls of the dovecote, so that the pigeon keeper was little occupied with his flock.

The squabs that were bred from the first generation and from the second breeding of the older birds would have been ready by August, and in that month and the next two, the greatest harvesting of squabs took place. Relatively small numbers of birds would be taken throughout the spring and summer, but the evidence of accounts shows that the whole enterprise was focused on the late-summer/early-autumn quarter of the year. One question which is difficult to answer is about the intensity of use of the pigeon houses. In general, they would have been only half full because of the need for the parent birds to have two nesting places, but whether they were otherwise full to capacity is unknown. There must have been variations through good and bad weather and harvest years, and it is likely that the more spacious interiors maintained a higher occupation rate because they were more attractive to the birds.

After the grain harvest came 'the time of bents', when there was less to eat in the fields and the pigeons had to resort to the tiny seeds of bents (*Agrostis*). During this season, until the end of October, the keeper would feed the birds to maintain production at a high level. After that came the culling of the older birds, which tended to become ill-suited to communal life and regular breeding, and finally the winding-down of breeding for the winter.

Location

The first decision for the pigeon house builder was where to keep his pigeons. Pigeons are sensitive to disturbance and like a quiet place; they prefer to be away from trees, where there are good lines of sight to see approaching birds of prey. They also like to be near to water which, like most creatures, they need for drinking and bathing. The great stone pigeon house at Garway was provided with its own water supply, and a stone cistern was found inside by its first recorder in the 19th century. John McCann has detected the earthworks of moats and ponds formed to serve pigeon houses, but no clear features of this nature were found in this survey.[85] There are few cases where the ideal location is achieved. The demolished building at Tyberton which was in open parkland close to a lake probably exemplified it.

The requirements of the pigeon keepers were often dominant in the matter of location. They usually preferred their cotes to be near their centres of farming activity, where they could be more easily operated and secured against predators and thieves.[86] This safer location had the cost of disturbance, and may have implied disregard for the need for water close at hand. There is evidence of remote locations, from field names, for example, but they are not typical. Of the standing buildings those at Staunton on Arrow and Eywood (Titley) are remote. They are country house estate pigeon houses and their locations were dictated by the requirements of picturesque landscape design.

Some pigeon house towers serve more than one purpose and this influences the decisions of their builders about their location. When the pigeons shared with a garden room, gazebo or garden shed they had to be located in the garden, as at Eardisland, Hill Court Walford or Bodenham.

There is also a sense that dovecotes, particularly those of the squirearchy, were more than occasionally located to proclaim the status of their owners. This appears obvious in a number of cases, for example, at Eardisland, Luntley, Burghill Grange, King's Pyon, Wellington and Pencoyd where the preeminent farmers gave visual expression to their position in the village community.

Louvers and Lanterns

The crucial design challenge of the pigeons' means of entry and exit at the top of the tower roof is how to allow the birds easy passage while keeping out predators such as peregrines, sparrow hawks and tawny owls. Some examples, such as Richard's Castle, Stocktonbury and Foxley (Yazor) are open structures, but the design of louvers usually incorporates broad sloping boards for perching with a restricted vertical gap of about 6 inches or 0.15m for entry. There are excellent examples at Eardisland and Great House, Stoke Prior.

The same principle is used for lanterns, which almost always have a slot of similar depth at the base, sheltered by a sloping board fixed between the slot and the glazing. The lantern was the first choice of the 18th-century country house pigeon keepers so that the great majority of octagonal buildings have lanterns rather than louvers.

The less common approach is to have a solid structure with shaped pigeon holes as at Barton Court and Netherwood (Figs. 40 and 148).

Almost all of the lanterns and louvers in this survey have been altered, boarded up or renewed. Most are probably a reasonably good attempt at copying the original form, but many are crudely detailed or simply ill-informed replacements.

Some pigeon houses have a hinged trap door just inside the lantern or louver. The best surviving examples in Herefordshire are at Canon Frome and Barton Court, Colwall. The trap could be operated remotely by a cord and was pulled shut to keep the birds inside or outside the pigeon house. The birds would be shut in to be collected[87] and culled, or to spare newly sown seed in surrounding fields. They could be shut out when maintenance and cleaning of the interior were needed.

Another device associated with louvers and lanterns was the 'pipe', an inverted box, open at the top and bottom and suspended below the louver. It is explained by John McCann:

> This was an ingenious protective device against sparrow hawks, which could some-
> times penetrate to the inside of a dovecote. Pigeons can fly vertically so that they
> could pass through the pipe without difficulty, but sparrow hawks could not. A
> sparrow hawk which managed to drop down into the building would be trapped
> there until it was found and destroyed by the pigeon keeper.[88]

A small number of pigeon houses have small groups of holes, usually with ledges, set in the wall below the eaves of the roof (Fig. 10). In most cases these are arranged to be in view of the owner's house and were intended to exploit the decorative qualities of the birds. There are examples at Staunton on Arrow, Llangarron Court and Foxley. They

Fig. 10 The stump of Staunton Park showing the three flight holes and the brackets for the alighting ledge on the elevation facing the house

might also be part of closing the dovecote down for winter, serving as the front door to the reduced numbers of birds in winter residence and allowing the louver/lantern trap to be shut against the weather.

Doors and Windows

The most usual arrangement in pigeon houses with a full height interior was to have a single small door at ground level with a very low lintel (Fig. 11). In this survey, no clear preference was found for the direction that the doors face. It appears to be dictated by the location of the pigeon house relative to circulation routes in the farmyard.

A number of reasons have been advanced for having a small doorway; it reduced the disturbance to the birds caused by light and shadow as the keeper entered, and it allowed the keeper to block the opening with his body so that birds could not get by him. In addition, a small door takes less wall space that could be occupied by nests, and may have impeded a thief with a bag full of birds.[89]

Where the pigeons are confined to an upper loft a door is required at that level for access and to allow mucking-out to be done without having to contaminate the lower

Fig. 11 Low doorways at Barton Court, Richard's Castle and Hellens, Much Marcle

chamber. Watkins' picture of Bodenham (Fig. 8) shows the ideal arrangement with an access ladder fixed in place. A surprisingly large number of pigeon towers do not have an external door at the upper level, for example at Hill Court, Walford and Eardisland. It is possible that this indicates that the floor is a later insertion, and even that the intention was to abandon the upper floor and the nests at that point.

Only about half of the pigeon houses have windows. Of the round stone buildings only Barton Court and Stocktonbury have them. The former has very small openings just below the eaves, while the latter has lancets on all four quarters. A majority of the square masonry buildings have them – Upper Bache, Kimbolton is probably the best furnished with one (now) slatted window on each face (Fig. 90). The square timber-framed buildings are windowless, but Luntley has shuttered openings in the gables for the birds to come and go. The octagonal, estate buildings are windowless except where they have chambers for occupation by humans; it was probably felt that the glazed lanterns that these buildings disport gave sufficient light and air.

The Interior and the Nests

There are two approaches to the provision of nests in the pigeon houses in this survey; they are either incorporated into the fabric of the walling or formed as a secondary timber lining of nest boxes.[90] All of the timber-framed buildings in this survey had nest boxes – there is no other way of building nests with timber framing because the walls are thin. Those that survive are similar to the layout described by John Moore early in the 18th century:

> To make your breeding places, you may erect Shelves of about 14" broad, allowing 10" betwixt shelf and shelf; for other-wise your tall powters, by being forced to crouch for want of height, will get a habit of playing low, and spoil their Carriage: In these shelves erect partitions at about the distance of 3ft fixing a Blind by a board nail'd against the Front, on each side of every partition; by this means you will have two nests in the length of every three feet, and your pigeons will sit dark and private. You may if you wish fix a partition between each nest …. For in breeding time when the young ones are about 3 weeks old, the hen, if a good Breeder will lay again and leave the Cock to take care of, and bring up the young ones.[91]

The best surviving boxes, at Kings Pyon (Figs. 12a and 94), have shelves about 16in (400) broad with 10in (250) 'betwixt' shelf and shelf. In that example the partitions are set at an angle, forming a nest with a lozenge shape on plan, each tier going in the opposite direction, so that, as Watkins put it, 'The bird might not be cramped for tail room when sitting on her eggs.'[92] The nests are built almost like a house of cards, there is little nailing, and the whole mass of boards depends on the front frame to hold it all in place. It is probable that the diagonal boards were also preferred because they gave greater stability in this arrangement. The shelves which form the floor and roof of every nest are in some other places projected forward of the front board to provide a perching and alighting ledge, as at Holme Lacy (Fig. 83).

Later masonry buildings, which tended to be built with thinner walls, also used wooden nest boxes. The very pretty interior of Holme Lacy, the upper loft at Eccleswell and the, now derelict, nests at Moor Abbey, Middleton on the Hill are the principal examples. At Holme Lacy the interior is given decorative charm by the use of round arched entrances to the nests.

In stone and brick buildings the most common arrangement of nests on elevation is to be staggered from tier to tier (Fig 12a). This is almost always accompanied by the holes being 'handed' from tier to tier as shown in Fig. 12a and Fig. 12c, which shows L-shaped holes in brickwork.

In the earlier, thick-walled, stone buildings the nests are formed in the thickness of the wall. There are some common features; the openings are usually 6 or 7 inches square and are staggered from tier to tier, albeit quite imprecisely in some cases. The holes are usually horizontal but enter the wall at an angle and this skewing is alternated to left or right from tier to tier. The shape and depth of holes varies, but the most common is a club shape, widening into the depth of the wall and penetrating about 14 inches (350). Garway is untypical in Herefordshire, although not nationally, in having quite good quality facing stonework which allows the formation of square, L-shaped holes which is not possible with rubble stone.[93]

The other variable in stone build-ings is the provision of alighting ledges,

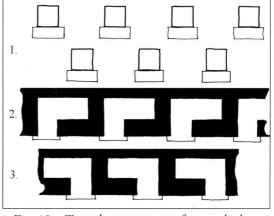

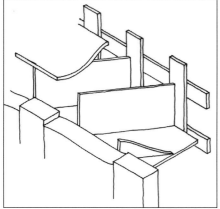

Fig. 12b Nests at King's Pyon viewed from outside

Fig. 12a Typical arrangement of nests which are 'staggered' and 'handed' from tier to tier
1. 'Staggered': Elevation of typical arrangement of holes staggered from tier to tier
2. & 3. 'Handed': The plan on tier 2 shows nest holes turning right, whilst on tier 3 they are 'handed', i.e. turn the opposite way

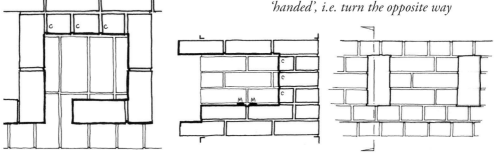

Fig. 12c Nests at Eardisley Park

which normally take the form of a continuous stone course projecting by about 2 inches. In the broader description of stone pigeon houses below it will be seen that these ledges can be provided for every tier of holes or for as few as every third tier.[94] The nest holes in stone buildings tend to penetrate the walls by less than half their depth; this, combined with alternate skewing and staggering from tier to tier, appears to be designed to give maximum stability to rubble stone structures. Even so, the resulting honeycomb is sensitive to movement and long vertical cracks can be seen in some buildings. Those that are rendered externally, for example Netherwood in Thornbury and Barton Court, Colwall may well be displaying a remedial measure intended to consolidate fragile masonry.

Most of the brick buildings have nest holes formed in the thickness of their walls. The most common arrangement is tiers of nests four brick courses high in which the nests are three courses and the separating floor/ceiling one course (Fig. 46). The entrance holes are most commonly two courses deep, but there are more than a few examples where a slot, three courses deep, is formed as at Eardisley Park for example (Fig. 12c). In brick buildings the holes most often have individual ledges for each nest hole, formed of one or two brick headers or specially shaped bricks or stones. Continuous ledges, as at Great House (Ford and Stoke Prior), are exceptional. It is also the only brick cote with arched nest holes (Fig. 69). The nests are almost always L-shaped with the inner chamber extended to one side or the other, and these extensions are alternated (handed) from tier to tier (Fig. 12). In most cases the holes are staggered from tier to tier as well – handing and staggering gives a stronger wall than one where, as at Eardisland for example, the holes are aligned vertically.

Revolving Ladders or Potences

Attention to the nests and squabs required the use of ladders. In round pigeon houses it seems obvious that ladders could be fixed to a frame rotating on a central pivot, and that this would make the keeper's work easier. Not all the earlier round stone buildings in Herefordshire have them, but there are surviving examples at Court Farm in Richard's Castle, Stocktonbury in Kimbolton and Netherwood in Thornbury, which may be later additions. John McCann discovered a reference in the writings of Roger North in 1698 extolling their virtues[95] and they were adopted in many later buildings. Evidence, often only the upper bearing of the post in the eaves tiebeam, exists in 17 cases in the gazetteer, although many of these have been lost. The ensemble of nest boxes and revolving ladder at Holme Lacy is therefore a particularly precious survival.

Some of the octagonal estate pigeon houses of the 18th century were made octagonal outside but cylindrical inside so that the revolving ladder would work most effectively – Eywood, Titley and Stocks House, Wellington are good examples. At Wellington, Watkins found a two tier revolving ladder (W19) standing on 'a circular mass of brickwork, with nesting holes',[96] but all that remains of it is the pivot in the crossed beams at eaves level. There are many variations of form in other counties: double frames with two ladders are not uncommon, but Herefordshire's only known examples at Whitwick and Bromtrees Hall, Bishops Frome have been demolished. The pivot post may have supported feeding platforms, but none now survive.[97]

There are three examples of revolving ladders in square pigeon houses.[98] That at Brockhampton Park (Fig. 30B) survives intact, while only the post remains at Wormbridge. At Upper Bache, Kimbolton only the cross beam and pivot are evident. In these cases it would have been possible, but quite difficult to reach into the corners, and an assistant would have been needed to steady the ladder as the manoeuvre was made.[99]

Rats and other Pests

Among the copious household papers from Hill Court, Walford[100] are the bills of the rat-catchers, Richard and Thomas Nash, rendered in neat copper plate in 1704-1709. They charged a guinea a year (with no inflation!). If they wrote their own bills, the small rectangles of foxed paper portray educated and trusted men, earning good money for what was clearly considered important work – one might almost say professional work. The rats that they were catching would have been black rats (*Rattus rattus*), a species that is predominantly vegetarian. The black rat is a good climber but 'there is no convincing evidence that they have ever done any harm to pigeons except by eating their food and possibly disturbing them'.[101]

About 20 years after the period covered by the Nash bills a rather more unpleasant relative of *Rattus rattus* began to appear in Britain having come out of Central Asia. This was *Rattus norvegicus*, the brown rat, which was to have serious implications for pigeon house keepers. The brown rat is much more destructive than the black; it can burrow and it will eat eggs and young birds, but it cannot climb vertical masonry walls or jump to any great height. David Plummer in his memoirs of a rat-hunting man said:

> Another great untrue about rats is the story that if a rat is cornered it will leap for one's throat … Alas, formidable as they are, they lack the biological equipment to enable them to leap as high as a man's throat. When I did a great deal of live rat catching, I kept my captives in barrels only three feet high, and I found that no rat could escape.[102]

Despite this simply observed truth, a legend persisted that the string courses or ledges found on some pigeon houses were intended to prevent rats from climbing up to gain entry at the eaves.

When Watkins described the square stone pigeon house at Dairy Cottages, Weston under Penyard (W16) he said, 'plates of sheet iron bent round outside angles of walls 18ft up to keep rats from climbing.' In his introduction he refers to an 18th-century text which suggests that iron spikes should be set in the ground to impale the rats which fell while attempting to negotiate this obstacle (W13). He says that 'Rats have always been a source of danger to pigeons, and seem able to climb up the walls and gain entrance at the top. A number of Herefordshire dovecots are provided with a projecting string course on the outside, which baffles the climbing rats.' Stainburn elaborated and attributed all forms of projection and decoration, including panelling and cornices, to the need to 'hinder the climbing animals'.[103]

This was the prevailing view until John McCann, in his 1991 essay, pointed out that the black rats that could climb were not dangerous to pigeons, while the brown rats that are dangerous cannot climb vertical masonry walls. He showed that many 'rat ledges' were on buildings constructed after the non-climbing brown rat had taken over, and that some were placed above windows that rats could enter if they were able to climb. Some were placed on buildings with roof openings that were either protected or, as at Garway, that would not allow rats easy access and escape if they reached them. He argued that the ledges are simply there to allow the pigeons to perch on the sunny or sheltered side of the pigeon house.[104]

The part of masonry pigeon houses which was at risk from the brown rat was the lowest tiers of nests up to about 4ft (1.2m) from the ground floor. This led to the blocking up of nest holes where rats were a particular problem. Very few examples were found in Herefordshire. This suggests that active means of control by the successors of Messrs Nash were successful. The now demolished 'cote at Bromtrees Hall, Bishops Frome had blocked lower nest holes, and the upper loft at Croft Castle has the holes blocked to 4ft above the upper floor (Fig. 46), but no other examples were found.[105]

Timber-framed buildings were much more vulnerable than masonry buildings because brown rats could burrow and gnaw through wattle and daub. In almost all framed pigeon houses, the nests are at first-floor level. Burton Court (Eardisland) and King's Pyon are good examples where the frames were raised on tall masonry plinths. Both have (or had) flimsy framing which suggests a date after the arrival of the brown rat; at Kings's Pyon the nests survive in an upper loft high above ground level. An alternative found elsewhere in England was to replace the wattle and daub infill panels with brick,[106] but none of the Herefordshire buildings have this adaptation. Perhaps pest control was sufficient in some places. That was the approach at Luntley where a dog hole was formed, against which a kennel would have been placed. This allowed the nests to be retained to ground level. Another approach was to move framed buildings closer to working farmyards. This was done at Ashton and Bidney – the former was raised on staddles and the latter was placed on top of a stone cart shed.

Building Forms

The almost universal form adopted for large enterprises was the pigeon house tower with an entrance and perching place for birds on the roof. This apes the cliff-ledge home of the rock dove ancestors of the domestic pigeon. Along this strand of evolution pigeons have developed a way to escape from birds of prey by plunging downwards, a tactic which takes them rapidly to top speed, and the tower form allows them to use this adaptation. A tower roof provides a place for perching, to rest and bask, and has the advantage of always having a side more sheltered from the wind or more exposed to the sun. These advantages could be enhanced by design, for example by the addition of dormers, as at Richard's Castle (Fig. 140) or, in the case of square towers, by folding the roof into the four-gabled form, as at Upper Bache, Kimbolton (Fig. 90). Additional places for sheltered perching could be provided on the exterior of the walls by string courses or pentice boards, which were usually placed immediately below the eaves.

The plan forms are considered in detail next. The plan forms of 122 pigeon houses are known from standing buildings and records. The four principal forms – round, timber-framed, square masonry[107] and octagonal – are almost equally represented, with square masonry buildings forming the largest group. Only the hexagonal plan is rare, with two examples at Staunton on Arrow and Foxley, Yazor. The square plan accounts for more than half of the buildings because the timber frames are also all square.

Round Stone Pigeon Houses

The distribution of the 24 known round stone pigeon houses is shown in Fig. 13. They are widespread, except that they are predominantly close to or east of the line of Watling Street, the Roman road which bisects the county. These early buildings are in, what was at the time, the more settled, more agriculturally advanced eastern half of the county, away from the troubles of the March. Only the pigeon houses of the Knights of Garway and the monastic protectorate of the Mortimers at Wigmore were established far west of that line.

Comparing the features of the buildings – wall thickness, ledges and nest shape – there is no clear pattern in the dimensions in the table below which might be attached to the date of the buildings. The assertion that walls are thicker with earlier buildings is difficult to test since we are only sure of the date of one of them (Garway). It would be less tendentious to say that walls get thinner with decreasing internal diameter. That pattern is visible in the table and makes sense as, conversely, wider spans create a greater thrust from the roof or vault and need thicker walls to resist it.

The sample is too small to make assertions about the pattern of ledges, although it does appear that the smaller buildings are more likely to have a ledge for every tier.

The following table lists the round stone buildings in order of known dimensions, those in italics are demolished.

	Internal Diameter	Wall Thickness	Ratio D/T	Number of nests	Tiers between Ledges
Garway	17ft 6in	3ft 9in	4.7	610	2
Old Sufton, Mordiford	17ft 6in	3ft 9in	4.7		2
Richard's Castle Court	17ft	4ft	4.25	580	2
Much Cowarne Court	16ft 3in	3ft 9in	4.3	500	3
Aldersend, Tarrington	*16ft*	*2ft 9in[108]*	*5.8*	*576*	
Instone, Bromyard	15ft	3ft 3in	4.6		
Barton Court, Colwall	15ft	3ft	5	430	2
Netherwood, Thornbury	15ft	2ft 6in	6	698	2
Richard's Castle Town Wall	*14ft 6in*	*4ft 3in*	*3.4*		*3*
Stocktonbury, Kimbolton	*13ft 6in*	*3ft 1in*	*4.4*	*510*	*1*
Bury Farm, Stoke Prior	*13ft 6in*	*3ft*	*4.5*		*1*
Holme Lacy	12ft 9in	1ft 6in	8.5	462	Wooden boxes
Other round stone buildings of unknown dimensions were at Wigmore Abbey, Adforton; Bosbury Bishop's Palace; Tillington Court, Burghill; Derndale, Canon Pyon; Court House, Eardisland; Dinmore Manor; Amberley Court, Marden; Wisteston Court, Marden; Pigeonhouse Farm, Ross Rural; and Showle Court, Yarkhill (the only brick cylinder).					

Table 1: Round pigeon houses

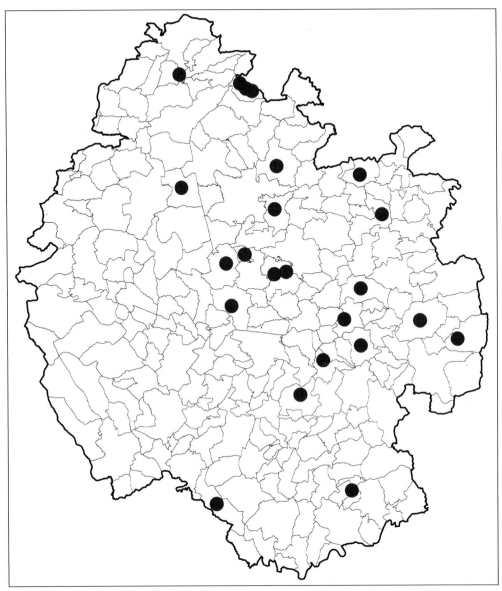

Fig. 13 The distribution of round stone pigeon houses across Herefordshire

It is difficult to compare the range of sizes of round pigeon houses in Herefordshire with those in other counties because few have been surveyed. Comparison with Somerset shows that there is a much wider range of sizes in Herefordshire which has buildings both bigger and smaller than any found in Somerset.[109]

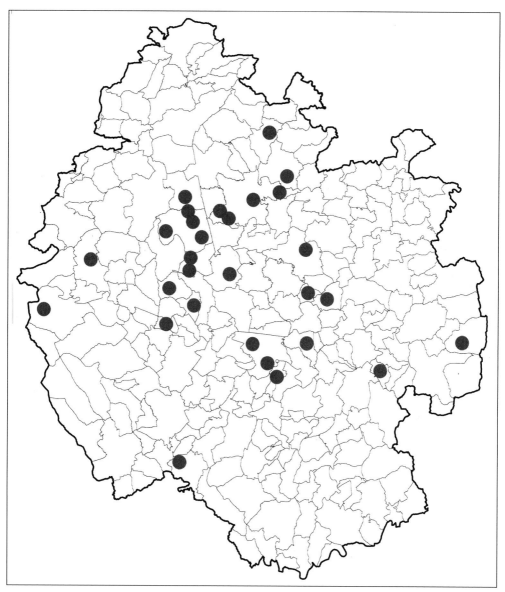

Fig. 14 The distribution of timber-framed pigeon houses across Herefordshire

Timber-framed Pigeon Houses

The distribution of 30 known timber framed buildings is shown in Fig. 14. They are mainly buildings of the central plain and the valleys of the rivers Arrow and Lugg.

The following table orders the buildings by their largest dimension. All but three of the buildings for which the nesting arrangements are known have or had their nests in a raised loft. The roof forms are equally divided between four-gabled (two of which are in Dilwyn parish), pyramidal and two gabled. Demolished buildings are in italics.

	Dimensions	Framing panels Wide x High (excluding gables)
Lower Farm, Ashton	20ft x 18ft	Tall panels
Pontrilas Court	17ft x 17ft	4w x 6h
Byford	16ft x 16ft	5w x 3h
Lower Hurst, Dilwyn	15ft x 13ft 6in	4w x 3h
Brook House, King's Pyon	14ft 3in x 14ft 3in	Tall panels
Bidney, Dilwyn	13ft 6in x 13ft 6in	4w x 3h
The Moor, Hereford	*12ft 6in x 12ft 6in*	
Luntley, Dilwyn	11ft 3in x 11ft 3in	4w x 4h
Burton Court, Eardisland	11ft 3in x 11ft 3in	Tall panels
Wilcroft, Lugwardine	*11ft 3in x 11ft 4in*	
The Buttas, King's Pyon	11ft 2in x 10ft 10in	Tall panels
Bereton, Dilwyn	*11ft x 11ft*	
Putley Court	*10ft x 10ft*	
Bollingham, Eardisley	9ft x 9ft	Tall panels
Mansell Lacy	*9ft x 9ft*	
Broadward Hall, Leominster		*5w x 4h*
Other known timber framed buildings were Upper Maund, Bodenham; Lawson's Hope, Canon Pyon; The Moor, Clifford; Brockbury Manor, Colwall; Putson, Hereford; Lower Hamnish, Kimbolton; Knoakes Court, Leominster; Upper Wintercott, Leominster; Lower Bullingham; Old Post Office, Mansell Lacy; Stretford Court, Monkland; Norton Canon; Lyvers Ocle, Ocle Pychard and Preston Wynne.		

Table 2: Timber-framed pigeon houses

Square Masonry Pigeon Houses

The distribution of the 43 known square masonry buildings is shown in Fig. 15. Only about a third are built wholly of stone and it is only in the very far south of the county that stone building has any majority. Almost all brick buildings have stone plinths but only two may be described as half and half – at Little Dilwyn and King's Caple. There is no discernible pattern of distribution on the plan, but to the west of Hereford, and in the far south there are distinct clusters of buildings of similar form (and possibly date) – perhaps further indication that, after 1619, the building of pigeon houses followed a social imperative rather than an economic one.

The dominant roof form for these buildings is the pyramid with only about a quarter taking the four-gabled form. Only eight were built with nest holes down to ground level.

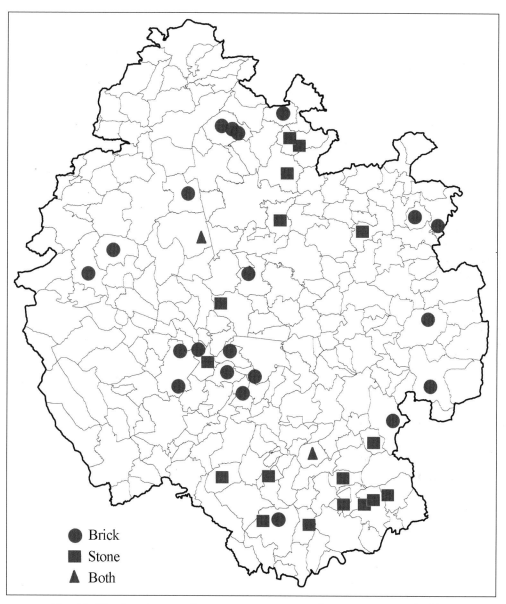

Fig. 15 The distribution of square masonry pigeon houses across Herefordshire

	Stone: S Brick: B	Dimensions	Number of Nests	Nest holes: Square: S Slot: O
Breinton	B	22ft x 22ft		s
Eardisland	B	20ft x 20ft	884	o
Wickton	S	20ft x 20ft		s
Field's Place, Madley	B	20ft x 20ft		
Much Marcle Vicarage	B	20ft x 20ft		
Nurton Court, Middleton	*S*	*20ft x 20ft*	*850*	
Moor Abbey, Middleton	S	20ft x 18ft 6in	Wood boxes	
Alton Court, Ross	S	19ft 3in x		
Croft Castle	B	19ft x 14ft 6in	500	s
Eardisley Park	B	18ft 9in x 18ft 9in	250	o
Great House, Stoke Prior	B	18ft x 18ft	470	Arched
Little Dilwyn	B & S	17ft 3in x 14ft 3in	200	s
Brockhampton Park	B	16ft x 16ft	350	s
Upper Bache, Kimbolton	S	16ft x 16ft	640	s
Haywood	*B*	*16ft x 16ft*		
Kipperknoll, Wellington	B	15ft 5in x 15ft 6in	380	s
Kings Caple	B & S	15ft x 15ft		
Bosbury House	*B*	*15ft x 15ft*		
Gaines Hall, Whitbourne	B	15ft x 15ft	490	o
Hermitage Farm, Burghill	S	14ft 3in x 14ft 3in		
Old Barn Court, Bircher	B	14ft x 14ft	380	s
Green Court, Eaton Bishop	*S*	*14ft x 14ft*		
Webton Court, Madley	*B & S*	*14ft x 14ft*		
Eccleswell Court, Linton	S	13ft x 13ft	Wood boxes	
Pencoyd Court	S	13ft x 11ft	Wood boxes	
Croft Old Rectory	B	12ft 3in x 10ft 6in	150	s
Llangarren Court, Llangarron	B	12ft x 12ft		
Orcop	S	12ft x 12ft		
Ledbury	B	12ft x 9ft 9in		
Canon Bridge, Madley	B	11ft x 11ft	200 (?)	
Lower Drayton, Brimfield	*B*	*11ft x 11ft*		
Dairy Cottages, Bollitree, Weston	S	10ft 6in x 8ft 6in		
Upton Bishop	S	10ft 3in x	Open boxes	
Glewstone Court, Marstow	S	10ft x 10ft		
Kilreague, Llangarron	S	9ft x 9ft		
Bollitree Castle, Weston	S	9ft x 9ft	150	s
Other square pigeon houses were at Nieuport House, Almeley; Rudhall, Brampton Abbotts; Rowden Abbey, Bromyard; Clehonger Court; Newton Farm, Hereford; Rock's Place, Yatton				

Table 3: Square masonry pigeon houses

Octagonal Pigeon Houses

The distribution of the 25 known octagonal pigeon houses is shown in Fig. 16. As with the other plan forms they follow no distinctive pattern but there appears to be a linear cluster to the north and west of Hereford. This form of pigeon house is associated with country houses and squires, and that part of the arable plain, close to Hereford would

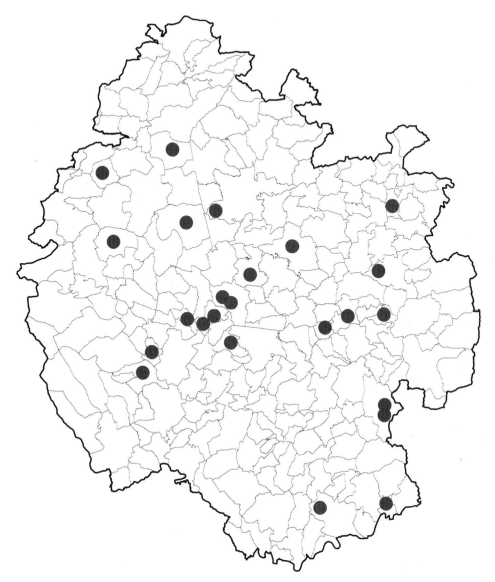

Fig. 16 The distribution of octagonal pigeon houses across Herefordshire

have been a particularly attractive area in which to build a country house or capital farm.

Table 4 sets out the dimensions of the buildings; again, demolished buildings are in italics. The largest by far was the building at Whitwick which is now demolished. The measurement of the building, which was recorded by Watkins, must be in doubt given Watkins' inaccuracies and the significant gap between it and the next group of buildings in the table.

Only one of the buildings in the table, at Lea, is built of stone, the rest are brick except that almost all have stone plinths of varying depth. Generally, as with round stone buildings, the walls get thicker as the buildings increase in size. Six of the buildings have cylindrical interiors, but only Canon Frome (octagonal inside) retains its revolving ladder.[110]

	Facets	Wall	Number of Nest Holes	Shape of Holes Square: S Slot: O	Interior Round: R
Whitwick, Yarkhill[111]	*13ft 4in*		*432*		
Great House, Dilwyn	9ft 10in				
Shobdon Court	9ft 9in	2ft 4in	424	O	
Poston C't, Vowchurch	9ft 9in	2ft 2in	780	S	R
Hill Court, Walford	9ft 9in	2ft 3in	600	O	R
Eywood, Titley	9ft 6in	2ft 4in	760	S	R
Weston Beggard	9ft 4in	2ft 8in	720	S	
Nieuport H'se, Almeley	*8ft 9in*	*2ft 0in*			
Burghill Grange	8ft 6in	2ft 3in	614	O	
Tyberton Court	*8ft 6in*				
Buckenhill, Norton	8ft	2ft 4in	440	S	R
Stocks House, Wellington	7ft 9in	2ft 8in	550	S	R
Canon Frome Court	7ft 4in	2ft 3in	520	S	
Hellens, Much Marcle	7ft 4in	2ft 3in	wood		
Homme House, Much Marcle	7ft		wood		
Bromtrees, Bishops Frome	*7ft*				
Credenhill	6ft 11in	1ft 9in	530	S	
The Old Weir, Kenchester	6ft 9in	1ft 6in	475	S	
Bodenham	6ft 9in	1ft 9in	160	S	
Bishopstone	6ft				
Lea	5ft		180	S	R
Other octagonal buildings have been recorded at The Hyde, Hyde Ash, Leominster; Warham House, Breinton and Burghill Court.					

Table 4: Octagonal pigeon houses

The octagonal buildings display a significant difference from the square buildings in terms of the arrangement of the nests. The great majority (18) of the octagonal buildings had nests down to ground level, whilst almost all of the square buildings had nests in raised lofts. This could be explained simply by the fact that, if the builder's intention was to have a two-storey building with the ground storey in a different use, then a rectangular building would be an easier shape in which to make an upper floor. It might also be significant that the octagonal estate buildings appear to be of the earlier part of the 18th century when there were no brown rats to contend with. If true, this would suggest that the square buildings, as a group, are generally later in date and therefore built with the idea of protection from brown rats in mind.[112]

Game keeping might also have something to do with the practice on country estates. Hill Court, Walford, as was shown above, could afford to employ rat catchers. Most estates would also have had game keepers skilled at keeping down the numbers of pests. With these active measures, rats would be less of a problem both at the design stage and in the decision as to whether to block up lower nest holes.

Gable-cotes, Eaves-cotes, Chimney-cotes, Lofts and Boxes

Eaves and gable-cotes replicate the cliff face of the ancestral rock dove to great effect. The most impressive examples are like pigeon houses turned inside-out, complete with alighting ledges and L-shaped holes staggered and handed between tiers. There is a very fine example at Pencombe, in which the stone barn is furnished with nests on three elevations (Fig. 17). The barn at Brierley Court also impresses with both gable and eaves-cotes on a large stone barn (Fig. 99).

Fig. 17 Gable-cotes at Court Farm, Pencombe

Again, there is no distinct pattern of distribution; the 35 examples of gable-cotes and eaves-cotes are widely spread, although there is a slight bias toward the north-east of the county both in terms of numbers and the scale of the 'cotes.

In Somerset, John McCann found examples of gable and eaves-cotes on buildings that could be confidently dated to the 17th century[113] and, as noted above, Fox and Raglan found one on a house dated 1674 in Monmouthshire. The earliest dated example in Herefordshire is at Upper Penalt, King's Caple; which bears the date 1701. The more famous Herefordshire example at Mansell Lacy (Fig. 115) is usually given a 17th-century date, but the part of the building in question might well be later. At the other end of the time scale, there are examples such as the brick gable-cote at Upper House, Little Hereford which appear to be built around 1800. Most of the examples that are attached to listed buildings are given as 18th century in the statutory lists: that cannot be certainly stated but it is within the known limits of dating.

The external 'cotes are probably all later in date than the ending of the manorial prerogative in 1619. They are associated with farms of middle to large size and, with one or two exceptions noted above, they are small-scale structures for small-scale husbandry. The squabs from them were probably more for consumption by the household than for sale – a chance for that lower class to eat the food of medieval Bishops and enjoy the sight of doves in the yard. For the keeper, the external 'cote must have had the great advantage of being more or less self cleaning, and who would not have preferred working outdoors to working inside a pigeon house producing at full output?

In two places, Kipperknoll, Wellington and Moor Abbey, Middleton, there are exterior 'cotes on a range of buildings which includes a pigeon house. This may represent two possible cases: in the first, the enterprise started small and was successful, so that investment

was made in a pigeon house; in the second the pigeon house came first and was so successful that additional accommodation had to be made.

In a few cases, the external holes in a gable or wall were not themselves the nests but gave entrance to a pigeon loft inside the building. The examples at Dulas Mill[114] and Huntsham Court are of this type. The interior boxes are ephemeral, but the modern example at Almeley Malthouse[115] shows an arrangement which is probably not untypical of the arrangements used in the past (Fig. 18).

Fig. 18 Modern loft at Almeley Malt House

Nest boxes on the exterior of buildings were advocated by the agricultural theorist J.C. Loudon in his work of 1825, (Fig. 20).[116] There a few examples which may be of some age, for example Broadfield Court, and a few more in the photographic record are noted in the gazetteer. There were, no doubt, also numerous pole-cotes (Fig. 19), but these were ephemeral and no ancient examples have been found.

Fig. 19 Top of pole-cote, about 50 years old (Hereford Museum Collection)

Fig. 20 Design for a box-cote from Loudon's Encyclopaedia of Agriculture, *1825*

Fig. 21 Chimney-cote at Yarkhill

Strangest of all are the chimney-cotes at Green Lanes, Yarkhill (Fig. 21) and Kynaston House, Hentland (Fig. 79) which seem to have no peers in other counties. It was thought that pigeons would benefit from heated accommodation, and there are examples of pigeon houses with fireplaces.[117] Placing nests in a chimney is an unusual but logical extension of the idea.

Pigeon Houses with Ice Houses

Four of the county's country estate pigeon houses were built over ice houses – at Foxley, Yazor; Gaines, Whitbourne; Whitwick, Yarkhill and Tyberton. At Whitwick, the house was started *c.*1690; Gaines (Fig. 22 overleaf) is quite reliably dated to 1718, and the house at Foxley was being finished about the same time. At Tyberton the house was being finished around 1730. In each case the chosen location was close to a lake or pond. In the winter, ice would be harvested from the lake and packed into the ice house. The ice was not itself consumed, it was there to act as a refrigerator.

As a group, the buildings are probably quite close in date, although they are widely spread geographically. They are remarkable as examples of a very rare type of dovecote that is only found in one other place outside Herefordshire, at Harewood Park, near Leeds.[118]

Field Names

The transcription and computerisation of the tithe maps of the 1830s and 1840s is a remarkable resource and has revealed about 121 likely locations for pigeon houses. There are numerous examples where field names and known buildings can be associated, for example at Bishops Frome, Little Dilwyn, Eaton Bishop and Upper Bache, Kimbolton. These are sufficiently numerous to leave little doubt that a 'pigeon house' field name does betray the site of a pigeon house. It is difficult to see how such names could arise in another way except from the name of an owner. The surname 'Pygynhouse' is found in 16th-century tax returns for Marden,[119] but it is its only occurrence in a book containing many thousands of names. The name 'Pygyn' and variations of it occur more frequently but there is only one field name, Pigeons Knap in Clehonger, which might indicate the possessive use of the name.

There are 100 'pigeon house' field names and 121 'pigeon' field names[120] including names like 'pigeon plock' and 'pigeon orchard'. The words 'culver', 'culverhouse', 'dovehouse' and 'dovecote' are with a single exception absent from the record. 'Dove', 'cote' and 'Pigeonhouse' occur only once each.

The age of these named fields is elusive; there is an example of a 'Colverhouse Close' in Abbey Dore (see the gazetteer) which is recorded on the tithe map as 'Pigeon Close' which suggests that its roots could be deep in the past. If that were so the 100 field name sites in the gazetteer could represent the majority of the estimated 150 manorial pigeon houses in the pre 1619 landscape (see above).

Herefordshire Pigeon Folklore

There is a dark tone to English pigeon folklore, much of which is associated with death. It was thought that a request for pigeon from the sick bed meant impending death and, more macabre, that 'He who is sprinkled with pigeon's blood will never die a natural death.'[121] One traditional remedy holds that as a last resort the patient in extremis might be cured by the application of the halves of a cleaved pigeon to the soles of the feet.

Ella Mary Leather, the first and best known Herefordshire folklorist, recorded the local lore that the fluttering of a dove or pigeon against the window of a sick room indicated impending death.[122] It was also believed that a pigeon's heart stuck with pins was an effective love charm.[123] On a lighter note, she says that on April Fools Day a boy would often be told to go to a chemist and ask for strap oil or to the farmhouse for 'a pennorth of pigeon's milk'.[124]

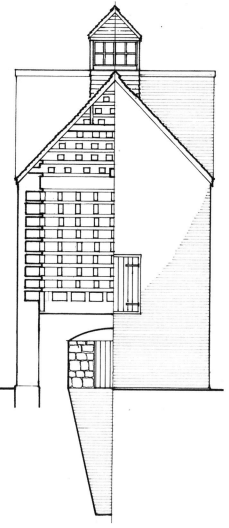

Fig. 22 The pigeon house at Gaines, near Whitbourne showing the ice house which forms a basement. The plan of the brick tower is 15ft (4.55m) square

Conservation

This book began with the pigeon house in the village of Eardisland – a positive story of a fine building being enjoyed by the public. That story has a new chapter with the ground floor of the pigeon house becoming the village shop, in an excellent and unusual scheme that will give sustainable use to a building whose original purpose ceased a century or more ago. It is, however, not far to travel to the other end of the conservation spectrum, in the same parish, to a field near Burton Court, where a complete pigeon house has disappeared since the county council's 1979 survey, despite having been a listed building, and in the absence of any application for permission to demolish it. Here then, in one parish, the conservation problem and its solutions are defined.

Most buildings in this survey are towards the positive end of the spectrum outlined in Eardisland. A very few are open to the public and in good condition; those at Luntley and Stocktonbury stand out, but many buildings which are not open to the public have also been preserved at some considerable cost to their owners. The round 'cotes at Garway, Barton Court, Netherwood and Richard's Castle are examples in excellent condition and are clearly cherished by their owners, despite having limited utility. It is however significant that they are buildings of high listing grade and therefore qualify for repair grants from the national scheme administered (today) by English Heritage. Only one building of high grade is considered to be at risk by inclusion in the English Heritage published book of buildings at risk, and that is Much Cowarne. It is to be hoped that this inglorious designation will lead to the building's repair.[125]

The picture of the less distinguished farmyard buildings is far from optimistic. Many have repair problems of varying degrees of seriousness and virtually all need some expenditure on repairs. Until recently Herefordshire Council could offer small grants for modest, but essential repair schemes, but that help is not presently available. There are grants for farm buildings through the Higher Stewardship[126] scheme, and the pigeon houses at Upper Bache, Kimbolton and Little Dilwyn are benefiting from substantial assistance from this source. These grants, as welcome as they are, cannot help the majority of owners whose circumstances do not allow them to submit applications or meet the requirements of a complex stewardship scheme application. The overall picture is one of steadily declining condition.

There is a saying in conservation that 'poverty is the greatest preservative'. It is a half-truth wholly applicable to the country cottage bought by the bonus-bloated banker, but not to the farm building in a working farm or garden. Here, use is the greatest preservative. If a building has some use – the housing for the circuit boards, the garden store or even the place for pigeons – it will be kept in repair, but many of these small buildings have no valued purpose. It seems therefore essential for Herefordshire Council to restore its modest grant scheme, and to be evangelical about it, if these important buildings are to survive. It is also

Fig. 23 Pigeon house converted for human occupation at Much Marcle

to be hoped that it will find the resources to repair the very fine building at Holme Lacy which is in its ownership.

Herefordshire has cultivated the conversion of farm buildings as a way of 'saving' them. Pigeon houses are relatively small and therefore difficult to convert, but there are examples where conversion has taken place in connection with attached buildings. This happened at an early date at Much Marcle (Fig. 23) and Breinton, but more recently at Field's Place in Madley and Glewstone Court, Marstow. In most cases dovecotes cannot be converted without damaging their special character, and conversion should be considered to be a last resort. At Brockhampton Park, the conversion of the pigeon house as part of a group of buildings has allowed it to be retained as a single volume in an exemplary scheme.

The saving of Eardisland's pigeon house was as much about people as the building. It was vested in a Trust founded in the village, so that the building and its problems became a 'demanding common task'[127] for the local people. That collective success hints at another possible way in which the owners of dovecotes might join together in a Dovecotes Association or Trust to share information and skills, to mobilise voluntary work and to act as a conduit for grants from, for example, the Heritage Lottery Fund. Some might also wish to share their buildings with the public through a dovecotes trail which would add to the tourism initiatives in the county.

Perhaps knowledge, understanding and interest are the best preservatives? If so it is to be hoped that this book will be a part of keeping the dovecote heritage of Herefordshire into the next millennium.

Postscript

I was driving to Wormbridge, the last visit in this survey, and saw the sign for Kilpeck. When I was an undergraduate, I had worked on a project about the Herefordshire School of Romanesque Sculpture as part of the liberal studies programme. It occurred to me then that the decorative schemes at Kilpeck and elsewhere held many images of birds.[128] It was difficult to see through the veil of memory and the distortions of style to the species of birds being depicted – were they the earliest of Herefordshire's pigeon house pigeons fossilised in rich red stone?

It was not a great detour to the little church, and there, low down on the eastern jamb of the south door, I found them.[129]

The Gazetteer

ABBEY DORE: Outbuilding at Tan House Farm (Private)
This small, rubble stone outbuilding has ten nest holes in a four tier brick gable-cote in the north wall. The tiers have continuous, thin stone alighting ledges.

ABBEY DORE: Township
A survey of the abbey's demesne[130] lands in the township[131] of Dore in 1540 includes, 'at least one watermill, barns, sheephouse, oxhouse, and dovecotes.'[132] The locations of these buildings within the demesne, which extended over nearly 600 acres, are not known, but it is likely that the names of fields adjacent to the abbey in the following entry identify one of the buildings referred to in the demesne survey.

ABBEY DORE: Upper and Lower Pigeon Close
Field names of adjacent plots numbered 773 and 774 in the 1839 tithe award, in the holding named 'Abbey Dore'. These plots are in the long tapering area between the abbey ruins and the River Dore.[133] A survey of the demesne which passed into the hands of the Scudamore family refers to a pasture called 'Colverhouse Close' which may be an older name for these fields.[134]

ACONBURY: Court Farm
A view of Aconbury chapel and the site of the Augustinian nunnery published in 1787 shows what appears to be an oblong box-cote attached to the west facing gable of the old Court.[135] This is a rare, relatively early illustration of an attached box-cote. Cotes of this type, either of wood or stone, must have been easy to make and were probably commonplace in the 18th century – see, for example, Llanrothal Court; Bannut Tree Farm, Kentchurch; and Cwmmau, Brilley.

ACONBURY: Pigeon House Meadow
Field name in the 1852 tithe award, consisting of plots numbered 308 and 309, in the ownership of Aconbury Court. The meadow was in a prominent position, hard by the road, to the west of the Court.

ADFORTON: Barn east of Paytoe Hall (Listed Grade II, Private)
This gable-cote forms part of a late 18th-century stone and timber-framed barn. 'In the gable are nine nesting holes arranged in three rows of three.'[136]

ADFORTON: Wigmore Grange (Wigmore Abbey)
Site of round stone pigeon house demolished in 1888 (W21). The buildings at Wigmore Grange are the remains of Wigmore Abbey, the house of Victorine Canons which was founded in 1179.

In 1878 Alfred Watkins photographed a round stone pigeon house with a conical stone slate roof and a square, slatted louver (Fig. 5).[137] He found that it was built of dressed stone, and concluded that the presence of re-used carved corbels indicated that it was built from material robbed from the abbey after it was surrendered in 1538 (W11 and W22). There was, however, an earlier period of destruction and rebuilding, in the late 14th century, after an attack by the Welsh.[138] The 1878 picture (Fig. 5) offers no sure dating evidence, so the pigeon house could be part of this 14th-century re-building campaign, rather than a work of post-suppression salvage. Marshall took the view that it was a 14th-century building in his notes:

> The round pigeon house is shown in a print by LeVeux (*c*.1800) 'from an old Painting' (?*c*.1750) lying to the north of the entrance way against the Abbots Lodgings and beyond the great barn burnt in the '70s. It has a vane or what appears to be a two tier circular (wooden?) top. No doubt the stone building proper is much earlier than the top, may be 14th cent. Top probably 172- date of vane. I have a photo of this print. The drawing is however different to Watkins' photo. Comparison might suggest the roof had been lowered, upper part taken down which looks as if it had been domed like Garway, and a stone sloping roof put on. There is a suspicion in Watkins' photo of the truncated square windows shown in the old painting.

Fig. 24 Drawing c.1800 of the Wigmore Abbey pigeon house by LeVeux, based on an earlier painting

The drawing by LeVeux (Fig. 24) referred to by Marshall is, like many topographical drawings, probably at least partly true; the problem is to know where truth stops. The shape of the pigeon house and its location in relation to the claustral buildings are substantiated by other evidence, but the proportions and scale of the drum and the style of masonry in the print are clearly incorrect in comparison with Watkins' photograph. If the scale of the pigeons is correct, this picture shows a very modest building. It is also difficult to know what reliance can be placed on the representation of the roof and louver. Taken at face value, it shows a vaulted stone top, probably of early date, and an unusual, arrangement of ironwork for the birds to alight and perch on (see Home Farm, Holme Lacy (Fig. 82) for a similar, more recent, arrangement).[139]

Although the scale is difficult to judge, the Watkins photograph suggests a building with an exceptionally low door and relatively low eaves compared to the other similar round stone dove-cotes, which might support the theory that the building was reduced in height and re-roofed in the 1720s.

ALLENSMORE: Allensmore Farm

Among Cohen's photographs is one, taken in 1957, showing a two storey, rectangular stone barn with a louver and vane in the centre of its hipped tin roof.

ALMELEY: Barn at Meer Farm (Private but visible from the lane to Wootton)

The south-facing stone gable of the barn to the west of the farmhouse shows the remains of a gable-cote, partly covered by a later building.

ALMELEY: Nieuport (Newport) House (Site of two demolished pigeon houses)

A 17th-century picture of the great medieval house at Newport, drawn by the antiquary Thomas Dingley,[140] shows a pigeon house in a prominent position, immediately to the east of the principal façade of the house (Fig. 25). The construction materials are not clear, but it can be seen that it was square with a gable on each elevation, and that the louver was surmounted by a vane in the form of a cross.

Fig. 25 Newport House, Almeley: Part of a drawing by Thomas Dingley

The many-gabled, many-chimneyed house was demolished by the Foleys, who commenced building a new mansion in c.1718.[141] They built an octagonal pigeon house on the site of the old one, which can be seen in a painting of c.1718 and an estate plan of 1767.[142] Watkins also recorded an octagonal, brick dovecote at Newport (W20); it had 8ft 9in (2.67m) facets, 2ft (0.6m) thick walls and nest holes down to the ground. It also had an octagonal lantern surmounted by a ball on a pole. These features, similar to the pigeon houses at Eywood and Burghill Grange for example, suggest an early 18th-century date. It must have been a grand design, worthy to be set alongside the principal façade of the house. It was demolished 'before 1939' (S.TII.18).

ASHTON: See Eye

AVENBURY: Hackley

In her history of Avenbury, Phyllis Williams refers to an inventory for Hackley Farm (south-west of Bromyard): 'There is a late 17th-century timber-framed outside kitchen opposite the back door … The upper storey of this multi-purpose building provides nesting boxes for doves.'[143]

AVENBURY: The Heath

Phyllis Williams also found a description of The Heath in 1733 which includes, '… and all dovecotes barns stables gardens orchard lands … to the said messuage.'[144]

AVENBURY: Pigeon Hopyard

This is the name of a field, behind Avenbury Court, numbered 217 on the tithe award of 1839.

AYLTON: Barn at Yew Tree Farm (Listed Grade II, Private)

The east gable of this barn has five tiers of nesting boxes in its weatherboarding.[145]

AYMESTREY Yatton: Pigeon Orchard

The name of a small field numbered 374 on the tithe award of 1839 lying behind Nos. 1 and 2, The Village, Yatton. The map also shows a group of four other fields, in the ownership of Yatton Court, numbered 435-438, with variations of the name Pigeon Bottom Bank.

BARTESTREE: The Pigeon Orchard

The name of field numbered 4 on the tithe award of 1839 (on the site of the Gateway Centre).

BIRCHER: See Croft and Yarpole

BIRLEY: Pigeonhouse Farm[146] and Pigeon House Croft

Farm east of the Ivington Road in Upper Hill. Pigeon House Croft is the relatively large field across the road from the farm, field number 509 on the 1845 tithe map for Hope under Dinmore.[147]

BIRLEY: Pigeon House Orchard

Field numbered 256 on the tithe award of 1841 at Thorn Farm, north of Birley church.

BISHOPS FROME: Bromtrees Hall

Site of octagonal brick pigeon house demolished after 1945. Watkins recorded an octagonal brick dovecote with 7ft (2.12m) facets, two revolving ladders, and nest holes down to the ground (W20, S.TII.20). Marshall made a more detailed description in 1910:

> Circular inside. Alighting ledges of bricks, half circular projecting. The inside of holes are built up of special bricks about twice the length of an ordinary brick and of the same thickness and width. There are 18 tiers of holes and about 35 in a tier making about 630 holes. When I inspected it on Oct. 23 1910 the lantern was in imminent danger of collapsing and the roof in very bad repair. The ladder on one arm was gone.

The ladder remaining is upright. Some of the tiers at the bottom are blocked up.[148] A few pigeons were kept in it a short while ago, but none now. The walls have several cracks which have been filled up but are quite sound otherwise. The door is in N.East side at ground level.

Watkins noted that the louver was octagonal with a lead top and had a vane decorated with a claw. He also recorded, 'On vane E S 1721', and noted that the rainwater heads on the house were dated 1723. Marshall corrected this, 'I read the initials on the vane as R S and I find Richard Stephens built the house so no doubt this is correct.'

The site of the pigeon house is also recorded in the field name 'Pigeon House Croft' in the tithe award of 1843. The tithe map shows the dovecote in the field numbered 87, and this correlates with the first edition of the Ordinance Survey, which shows the building clearly. This is pleasing confirmation that 'pigeon house' field names may refer to the presence of buildings at some point in the past.

The Royal Commission reported in 1932 that the building was 'partly ruined'.[149] It was demolished just after 1945 (S.TII.20).

BISHOPSTONE: Bunshill and an unknown site

Watkins referred to Bunshill in his table of demolished pigeon houses and notes its shape was not known (W22). A search of the surroundings of Bunshill, a substantial three-storey brick house of the second half of the 18th century,[150] on early editions of the Ordnance Survey do not reveal a likely building.

Watkins included another site in his list of demolished octagonal brick pigeon houses, but the precise location is not given. This one was relatively small with facets of 6ft (1.8m) and nest holes down to ground level (W20, S.TII.19). The obvious locations are Bishopstone House and Bishopstone Court, but earlier Ordnance Survey editions reveal no likely candidates.

BODENHAM: Pigeon House (Listed Grade II, Private)

All that remains of this pigeon house is the octagonal brick drum standing on a low brick plinth. On plan it is one of the smallest of its type, with 6ft 9in (2.06m) facets and 1ft 9in (0.54m) thick walls laid in a mixed bond, with randomly spaced header courses. The building was a fine sight in its day (Fig. 8); it is built into the garden wall and its three storeys give impressive scale. The top of the brick drum was finished with a deep cornice with six courses of corbelling and dentils. The pyramidal roof was stone slated with lead hip rolls and surmounted by a very tall octagonal lantern. The lantern roof was elegantly curved and finished with an elaborate vane. The upper two thirds of the lantern were vertically boarded leaving a deep slot for the birds.[151]

The ground storey is entered from the walled garden and has a window on the opposite side. It is plastered inside, and each facet has a recessed panel with a shelf; it seems designed as a garden room. The upper level was entered by a ladder, also from the garden. There is no floor dividing the upper two storeys but the walls are in two distinct stages. The lower part

Fig. 26 Bodenham, Pigeon House: Interior showing the unusual arrangement of nest holes in the upper two storeys

is blank except for the unusual feature of two columns of seven nest holes immediately to the side of the door (Fig. 26). The upper part is lined with six tiers of nests arranged one above another, but handed from tier to tier, and with two brick headers for alighting. There are 158 holes in all. The lower nest holes are puzzling, but were probably intended to give some readily accessible nests in case squabs were wanted at short notice.

The building has been described as 'early 18th century', and that date is supported by the narrow bricks.

BODENHAM: Upper Maund Common
Site of demolished square timber framed pigeon house. Watkins recorded a square timber-framed pigeon house as having been pulled down in about 1875 (W21). Early editions of the Ordnance Survey show a small rectangular building on the southern edge of the common to the west of the mere. The site is also preserved in the name of Pigeon House Farm at Upper Maund.

BOLSTONE: Cote Close
This is the field name of plot 33 in the 1840 tithe map, north of Bolstone Court.

BOSBURY: Bishop's Palace, Old Court Farm
Site of round stone pigeon house demolished *c.*1884. Watkins (W11) said, 'The dovecot which stood on the site of the ancient palace of the Bishops of Hereford at Bosbury, was only pulled down in 1884, but I can hear of no description of it.' It seems possible that it existed when Bishop Swinfield's Roll of Household Expenses (see p.5 above) was written in 1298, for this mentions 'pigeons from the columbarium of the manor of Bosbury', and Rev. John Webb describes it as like the one at Garway'. The gatehouse of the Palace is now part of Old Court Farm. The dovecote stood between the gateway and the house, to the north of the church.[152]

BOSBURY: Bosbury House
Site of demolished square brick pigeon house. Watkins (W18) recorded this 15ft-square brick building which had nest holes down to the ground. The roof was two-gabled and surmounted by a square lantern without a vane. Earlier editions of OS maps clearly show

the pigeon house in a prominent position to the north of the house, close to the road. It was demolished *c.*1939 (S.TII.10).

BOSBURY: Cold Green Farm Barn (Listed Grade II, Private)
This 19th-century barn has a triangular wooden box-cote hung on its east gable.[153]

BOSBURY: Pigeon House Field, Swinmore Farm
This is the field name of plot 579 in the 1840 tithe award. It is just to the west of Swinmore Common and at a considerable distance from the centre of the holding at Swinmore Farm.

BOSBURY: Pigeon House Meadow, Little Catley Farm
The field name of plot 1111 in the 1840 tithe award. It is very close to the neighbouring farm at Note House and quite far from the centre of the landholding, of which it forms part, at Little Catley. This site and the previous one appear to have been chosen to get maximum benefit from the land of neighbours.

BRAMPTON ABBOTTS: Sites of Pigeon Houses at Rudhall
Watkins recorded a square stone pigeon house at Rudhall which he thought had been demolished *c.*1875 (W21).

Duncumb's *History* suggests that there were more than one dovecote:

> The next heir being of tender years, in ward to the crown, and his mother having taken another husband, a Royal Commission was issued to obtain particulars of the family estates. At an inquest held at Ross on 6th December 1532 (it was found that) William Rudhale was also seised of one capital messuage 60 acres of arable and pasture and two water mills in Brampton called Rudhall, with dovecots, orchards, gardens, meadows…'[154]

It is likely that at least one of the 'dovecotes' was on the field in the following entry.

BRAMPTON ABBOTTS: Pigeon House Field
The field north of Rudhall House numbered 539 in the tithe award of 1838. This field is split between two parishes; the other part appears as the field numbered 709 in the 1839 tithe award for Upton Bishop.

BREINTON: Pigeon House Farm
Watkins recorded a square brick pigeon house, which had been converted into a farm-house (W22) – probably one of the earliest conversions of an agricultural building in the county. Stainburn included it in his table of 'demolished' buildings (S.TI), but there is still a tall square-plan brick building on the site which is almost certainly the building

Fig. 27 Breinton: Pigeon House Farm

recorded by Watkins. It is a large building, 22ft (6.67m) square and 28ft (8.53m) to the eaves. It is built in English Garden wall bond with relatively thin bricks, suggesting a late 17th or early 18th century date (Fig. 27). Two brick string courses divide the façades into unequal 'storeys'. During recent alterations two tiers of nest holes were found high up in the 'attic' space above the living accommodation.[155]

BREINTON: Warham House
Marshall's notes include the following:

> A drawing of about 1840 in the possession of Capt. Wegg Prosser of Warham House shows at a point about 20 yards from the SE corner of the present house (this was entirely remodelled in 1856 …) what is evidently a lofty octagonal pigeon house entered from a lantern at the top. It is not possible to say from the drawing if of brick or stone, but probably the former as stone is not plentiful in this district.

BRIDGE SOLLERS: Pigeon House Close & Pigeon House Meadow
The names of fields numbered 49 and 96 on the tithe award of 1842 that are separated by the Wye. The former was at the centre of the Marsh Court estate, to the north-west of the Court itself. The latter was on the west bank of the Wye immediately south of the crossing.

BRIDSTOW: Barn north of Benhall (Listed Grade II, Private)
The statutory list notes, 'West gable has tallet stairs rising from south to ledged doors above which are nesting boxes'.[156]

BRIDSTOW: Wilton Castle
An inquisition post mortem of 1324 records, 'And they say there is a certain castle with an outer court with two gardens, one courtyard and one pigeon house which are worth per year 16s 8d.'[157]

BRIERLEY: See Leominster

BRILLEY: Cwmmau Farmhouse (Listed Grade II*, National Trust; open eight days a year)
The south-east side of the cross-wing has 40 nesting boxes in two tiers under a pentice

Fig. 28 Brilley: Nesting boxes below the pentice roof at Cwmmau farmhouse

roof at first floor level. The holes are shouldered. John McCann considered pentice roofs in his 1991 essay, suggesting that they were not 'weatherings', as generally held at that time, but places for pigeons to perch. Cwmmau extends the idea by combining sheltered nest boxes below the roof and a south-facing basking place on the roof. In the exposed hillside position of Cwmmau, the main roof would often have been untenable. The form and position of this dovecote is very well matched to the local conditions.

BRILLEY: Pigeon Meadow
The name of field numbered 500 on the tithe award of 1840, close to Brilley Court.

BRIMFIELD: Lower Drayton
The site of a square brick pigeon house demolished *c*.1958 (S.TII.13). Watkins recorded and photographed (Fig. 29) a four-gabled pigeon house built of brick on a rubble stone plinth.[158] It was 11ft (3.33m) square and had nest holes to the ground. The roof was covered

Fig. 29 Brimfield: Demolished pigeon house at Lower Drayton (Alfred Watkins Collection)

with stone slate and surmounted by a square louver with a pyramidal roof and a spike finial supported on four posts. The outline of the pigeon house can be seen on earlier editions of the Ordnance Survey, within the garden enclosure to the south of the farmhouse.

BRINSOP & WORMSLEY: Pigeon House Orchard
The name of a field south of Wormsley Grange numbered 4 on the Wormsley tithe map of 1846.

BROCKHAMPTON BY BROMYARD: Brockhampton Park
(Listed Grade II,[159] Private; part of a residential conversion scheme)
The big house at Brockhampton Park was started some time after 1731.[160] The pigeon house is part of a courtyard of outbuildings, stables and cottages which probably date from the second half of the 18th century. The whole range of buildings was converted to private housing in 1967 (Brockhampton Mews).

The building is 16ft (4.85m) square with 2ft (0.6m) thick walls of English bond brickwork. The top of the brickwork is finished with a brick dentil cornice, and the courtyard elevation is given further pretension with an oculus and a central doorway under a basket arch. A string course runs into the springing of the arch. This archway is intended to provide visual harmony with the arches of cart shed and other buildings round the courtyard (Fig. 30A).

The roof is a truncated pyramid covered in slate. The louver has been removed, but evidence

Fig. 30A Brockhampton Park exterior, and Fig. 30B interior showing the revolving ladder which is unusual in a square building

in the remaining timber structure suggests that there may have been an octagon – possibly intended to complement the octagonal lantern over the stables. The roof consists of stout hip rafters and common rafters spanning between the plate and a square collar. Additional support for the louver is provided by a pair of full span joists and trimmed cross joists, from which rise posts. The space enclosed by the posts may have been boarded to form a 'pipe'.

The dovecote is at first-floor level only. There are twelve tiers, holding a total of about 350 holes. The tiers are four brick courses high and the holes two courses. The holes are 1ft 3in (0.38m) deep, L-shaped and handed from tier to tier. They are not fully staggered from course to course and are relatively widely spaced; hence the low number of holes for such a large building. Each hole has its own single brick header alighting ledge (Fig. 30B).

The unusual feature in this dovecote is the revolving ladder.[161] Such ladders are rare in square pigeon houses and here it is possible to see why – the nest holes in the corners cannot be reached from the ladder without stretching to a dangerous extent or having to step off and use the nest holes as a ladder.

BROCKHAMPTON BY BROMYARD: Lower Brockhampton House
The moated timber-framed house, with its picturesque gatehouse, is one of the best known medieval houses of Herefordshire. 'There are signs of a planned landscape around this building, including a separate moated enclosure which may have contained a dovecote or summer house.'[162]

BROCKHAMPTON BY ROSS: Fawley Court
A survey of the house in 1603, prior to it being divided between five sisters, lists a 'pigeon house'.[163]

BROMYARD AND WINSLOW
Phyllis Williams's history of Bromyard[164] mentions nine pigeon houses which are not in earlier surveys, two of which are standing buildings, at Buckenhill (see Norton below) and Brockhampton (above). The seven sites which have disappeared are:

Astley
The land now occupied by the Station Trading Estate is called Pigeon House Meadow (field number 118) on the Linton tithe map of 1841. In the glebe terriers of 1589 and 1637 account is given of 'on[e] dovehouse' belonging to the rectory.

(Winslow): Hardwick Manor
Included in the 1575 survey of Winslow.[165]

(Winslow): Instone
The long meadow between the road and the old course of the railway is called Pigeon House Meadow, field number 736 on the tithe map. This name probably relates to the pigeon house that was included in the 1575 survey of Winslow.[166] During the digging of

the railway line the lower part of a round stone dovecote was uncovered, which could have been the one described in 1575. The Woolhope Club *Transactions* reported, 'The diameter is 15 feet, the thickness of the walls 3 feet 3 inches, the alighting ledges 3 inches … The lower tier is about 12 inches from the ground, and there is a distance of about 11 inches between tiers.'[167] The holes were staggered and handed from tier to tier (Fig. 31).

Fig. 31 The remains of a round stone pigeon house uncovered by railway navvies at Instone, Bromyard

(Winslow): Munderfield Harold
A pigeon house is included here in the 1575 survey of Winslow.[168]

Rowden Abbey
A pigeon house, since demolished, was included in the 1575 survey of Winslow.[169] There was a square stone one still standing in 1870 that carried the inscription, 'Anthony Rowden, Gent 16-' (W21).

Stewarts Hyde
A pigeon house is included here in the 1575 survey of Winslow.[170]

Upper Court (north of the church)
In the glebe terriers of 1589 and 1637 account is given of 'on dovehouse' belonging to the rectory. In 1637, 'on[e] barne and on[e] dovehouse with a fould or close called Mill Hill Court where in the said barne and dovehouse standeth.'[171]

BUCKENHILL MANOR: See Norton

BURGHILL: Burghill Court
Site of octagonal brick pigeon house demolished *c.*1926 (S.TII.15). Watkins said this had an octagonal lantern with a domed lead top.[172]

BURGHILL: Burghill Grange (Old Manor House)[173] (Listed Grade II, Private)
This is a fine example of an octagonal brick pigeon house, and the more important for having been dated. Watkins (W19) recorded the date stone, which can no longer be read:

E

I   I

1717

The initials are those of James Exton, who is known to have been the second wealthiest man in the parish.[174] That wealth was applied to building a well-crafted, prominent and prestigious pigeon house.

Each facet of the exterior of the brick drum is 8ft 6in (2.58m) wide, 2ft 2in (0.66m) thick (W19) and stands 22ft (6.67m) high to the eaves cornice. The brickwork, laid in Flemish bond, is of high quality; each facet has a recessed panel, and over-burnt bricks are used to decorate the panels, the segmental panel arches and the pilasters to either side. The wooden eaves modillion cornice is an uncommon refinement (Fig.32). Cohen's picture (Fig. 33) shows, on the east side, facing the house, a perching or display ledge and entrance hole about 2/3rds of the way up the wall. This may have been an addition which accompanied the full glazing of the lantern (see below) and became the pigeons' front door (it has lately been removed).

Fig. 32 Burghill Grange: Detail of the brickwork and cornice

The interior is octagonal, with the nest holes in 19 tiers rising from ground level. Each tier is four courses high; the holes are vertical slots, three courses high on the face, which is the less common form. Each hole has its own brick stretcher, rather than header, alighting ledge; a unique detail in the county. There are 614 nest holes in all; they are precisely staggered and handed from course to course. Wooden bonding timbers make floors and alighting ledges for three of the tiers – a refinement which is not common in Herefordshire. The upper and lower pivots for the revolving ladder remain but the pivot post and ladder were removed when timber floors were inserted.

Fig. 33 Burghill Grange photographed by Israel Cohen in 1957

The roof structure is formed of eight stout oak hip rafters spanning between the wall plate and the collar which supports the octagonal lantern. Purlins are butted to the hips to form a ring, and two tiers of butted common rafters span between collar and purlin and purlin and eaves plate. The 'former louver has been converted to a lantern by the insertion of a glazing bar in each facet'.[175] It is covered with a copper roof with a ball finial, which is a disappointment after the richness of the modillion eaves cornice, and it is probable that a grander, corniced and shaped cap has been replaced. There is evidence of a trap.

This description is based on a detailed account in the Woolhope Club *Transactions*.[176] One of the authors, the late Frank Pexton, a former Woolhope Club President, successfully campaigned to save this stately pigeon house from a damaging conversion scheme.

BURGHILL: Field names

Pigeon House Field is the name given to two fields numbered 946 and 947 on the 1847 tithe map. These, relatively large, fields are immediately north of Burlton Court (called Great Burlton on modern OS maps).

Pigeon House Corner is a group of four small strips numbered 911, 912, 914 and 945 to the north of Pigeon House Field.

It is likely that all six of these field names relate to a single pigeon house associated with Burlton Court.

BURGHILL: Hermitage Farm (Private, converted to residential use)

This dovecote was built as part of a grand design, in the Italianate style, for a house and landscape centred on The Hermitage, the house which stands up the hill above Hermitage Farm. It was probably built between 1832 and 1885[177] using the local purple hued stone off the hill. The plan is 14ft 3in square with a tall, rusticated plinth rising to a substantial string course. Above the string course there are pairs of smooth-faced recessed panels under semi-circular arches, and a dramatic eaves frieze and cornice. The slate roof is pyramidal with a square lantern finished with a tented lead roof and an arrow vane. This was not simply, if ever, a working building but one carefully designed to impress (Fig. 34).

There is no evidence of the original interior arrangements, but the walls are thin and suggest that there would have been wooden nest boxes. The ground level has been changed significantly in course of the conversion scheme so that the building now has very different and even more impressive proportions than those in earlier photographs.

Fig. 34 Hermitage Farm, Burghill:
The pigeon house as architecture

BURGHILL: Tillington Court

The present house of *c.*1815 is on the site of a much earlier mansion. 'There was also a dovecote on the site of a chapel founded in 1341. The *Hereford Journal* advertised the court to let on 2nd March 1796. The dove house is mentioned together with two large gardens …'.[178] Watkins recorded a round stone pigeon house in his table of demolished buildings (W21).

BYFORD: Byford Court (Listed Grade II, Private)

The Byford Court pigeon house is the second largest timber-framed example after Pontrilas Court. The timber frame is 16ft (4.85m) square[179] and 12ft 3in (3.71m) tall from the plinth to the eaves. There is a regular pattern of framing on each façade of five panels wide and three high, with braces in most, but not all, corners (Fig. 35). The lowest row of panels is square but those above are taller oblongs. The frame stands on a stone plinth with the floor inside being level with the top of the plinth walls. In Watkins' photograph[180] the infill panels are brick, but this has been replaced with cement render on metal lath. The door is off-centre to the south side of the east wall. There are no nest boxes; Watkins noted that they were 'in loft only'. The trap remains in place (Fig. 36).

Fig. 35 Byford Court

The roof is pyramidal and covered in Welsh slates; these replaced plain tiles which in turn replaced the original stone slates. The square lantern has also changed; earlier images show twelve panes over a gap for exit and entry which was sheltered by a sloping board. There is a variety of detail now with two, four or nine panes on different faces. The curved lead roof of the lantern follows historical precedent but previously had a ball finial. The roof structure appears to be much renewed and consists of stout hip rafters and common and jack rafters rising from the eaves to a collar below the lantern.

The Court has late medieval fabric, but this pigeon house is probably of the second

Fig. 36 The trap below the lantern at Byford Court

half of the 17th century. In earlier photographs, the adjacent stone-built farm buildings extended right up to its south and east walls.

CANON FROME: Court[181] (Listed Grade II,[182] Private)

There was a 'dove-house' at Canon Frome in the 16th century, probably on the site of the existing one.[183] Today's dovecote has characteristics of the country house dovecotes of the first half of the 18th century, which means that it may have been a companion to the earlier house known as Gable House[184] which pre-dates the present Court built in 1786 to the design of the architect Anthony Keck. That is confirmed by the 1720 estate plan which shows the dovecote.[185] The Wren-style lantern, seen in Cohen's picture of 1957 (Fig. 37),[186] suggests that an earlier, late-17th century date is possible, but a detailed inventory of the property made in 1702 does not mention it.

This is one of the smallest of the octagonal brick estate dovecotes, with 7ft 4in (2.22m) facets and 2ft 3in (0.68m) thick walls, but lack of stature is unimportant because its proportions and details, and the pleasing shade of brickwork, create a particularly attractive picture. The brickwork is of fine quality, laid in Flemish bond with a course of headers every fourth course. The top of the brickwork is finished with a brick dentil cornice, and there is a low door, with a segmental arch, on the east side, over which there is a two-light window. The roof is slate covered with lead hips, surmounted by an octagonal louver, glazed with small panes in timber 'sashes'. Originally the birds came and went through slots below each 'sash' which were sheltered by a continuous sloping alighting board. The louver is roofed by an ogee-shaped lead dome. Watkins' article says that he found a vane with a cock, as now, but the present ironwork may not be the original.[187] At one stage, in Watkins' lifetime, there was a ball finial.[188]

The roof structure is composed of stout hip rafters and trimmed common rafters spanning between the cornice and collar on which the lantern sits. A

Fig. 37 Canon Frome Court photographed by Israel Cohen in 1957

pair of cross beams support four posts taking the weight of the lantern. Where these beams cross is the pivot for the revolving ladder. The interior is octagonal with 522 nest holes with individual, single brick header alighting ledges. The holes are two courses tall on the interior face and are staggered. The tiers each rise four courses.

The survival of some of the working equipment is important. An inclined, revolving ladder remained in 1979 (Fig. 38) and the wooden frame for a trap was still there in 2005.[189]

CANON PYON: Derndale
Watkins noted that a round stone pigeon house was demolished at Derndale in 'about 1872' (W21). It is likely that the demolition took place earlier since the pigeon house is not plotted on earliest editions of the Ordnance Survey.

CANON PYON: Coach House at Derndale (Listed Grade II, Private)
The late 18th-century brick barn has 'Nesting ledges and holes above loft opening which is flanked by a pair of vent loops'.[190]

Fig. 38 The revolving ladder at Canon Frome as illustrated in Ian Stainburn's book of 1979

CANON PYON: Lawton's Hope
There is a substantial, late 17th-century, timber-framed house at Lawton's Hope.[191] Watkins recorded a 14ft square, timber framed pigeon house, which could have been of similar date, with a two-gabled roof and a square louver. The nest holes were 'from the ground' and there was a large stone raised on wood blocks in the middle of the floor (W17). It is surprising that none of the usual sources, including the Royal Commission, hold photographs of the building, and it seems likely that it was demolished before the Royal Commission began surveying the county's buildings in 1930.[192]

CANON PYON: Pigeon House Farm, Westhope Hill
Watkins recorded a pigeon house of unknown shape in his table of demolished buildings (W21).

CASTLE FROME: Barn at New Birchend (Private, house conversion)
A large stone barn with an eaves-cote on the south side. The upper part of the wall has been rebuilt with red brick to form the nest holes. There is a continuous tier under the eaves with a row of individual brick perching ledges two courses below. There is a lower

tier but only across the eastern half of the elevation. The conversion has involved cutting windows through the brickwork, much to the detriment of the visual impact of this very good example.

CLEHONGER: Stables at Belmont House
These late 18th-century brick stables have been demolished. The statutory list recorded: 'Attached to the right hand side is a low brick extension [with] three nesting holes either side of an exposed king-post.'[193]

CLEHONGER: Field names
Field number 244 on the tithe map of 1839, to the north of the church, is described as 'cow pasture, pigeon house, barn etc.' 'Pigeons Knap' is also recorded as field 372 north of the road to Broomy Hill.

CLEHONGER: Clehonger Court
Watkins recorded this building which was demolished *c.*1875 (W22). The first epoch Ordnance Survey shows a small rectangular building, which could be the pigeon house, to the north-west of the house, adjacent to a small pond.

CLIFFORD: The Moor
The substantial Gothic house and the farmstead at The Moor were demolished in 1956.[194] They stood between the club house of the Summerhill golf course and the B4348, just to the north of the most easterly of the fishponds.

Fig. 39 The Moor Clifford photographed by Israel Cohen in 1956
shortly before it was demolished

The pigeon house was audaciously mounted astride the parallel roofs of a large stone barn. Fortunately there is a photograph (Fig. 39), because a description alone would be difficult to believe. The picture, taken by Israel Cohen,[195] shows a square timber-framed building[196] with a pyramidal roof and a square louver surmounted by a vane. This is confirmed by George Marshall's notes from a visit in August 1935:

> The cot is of timber, roughcast over, not stone. It is built over the centre of the driving way of a very large and lofty stone barn. The pigeon holes are wood boards. I did not go up into the cot but could see the holes, so cannot say how many there are or if they reach the floor. There is a weather vane with a dragon or cockatrice which is the crest used by the Penoyres … The barn and cot are, I should say, about 1750.

The Penoyres were the leading local family and created an impressive structure which displayed their status. This arrangement of parallel stone barns with the pigeon house slung between their roofs is unique, although a logical extension of the idea of the upper loft at, for example, Moor Abbey (see Middleton).

COLWALL: Barton Court (Listed Grade II*, Scheduled Ancient Monument, Private)
The round, stone pigeon house (Fig. 40) stands alongside a large, 17th-century, timber-framed barn, and at some remove to the west of the Court, which was rebuilt in the late 18th century.[197]

The interior has a diameter of 15ft (4.55m) and the walls are 3ft (0.91m) thick (in the part of the wall above the low plinth). The nest holes are in 16 tiers, from 1ft 5in (0.43m) above the floor, with continuous alighting ledges at every second course (Fig. 41). The

Figs. 40 and 41 Barton Court Colwall exterior, and its nest holes

holes are irregular, but tend to be enlarged to one side; they are staggered and handed from tier to tier. There are 28 holes in each full tier giving a total of about 430. There is a low (3ft 6in (1.05m) high) doorway on the east side (Fig. 11) and two small openings under the eaves. The stonework is made of roughly coursed small stones which give a quite rough appearance inside. The exterior has been rendered and limewashed; earlier photographs show a patchwork of smooth render and roughcast.[198]

The roof structure is formed by 16 stout rafters spanning from the eaves plate to the collar of the louver. At about mid span there are butt purlins forming an irregular ring, and trimmed common rafters span between them and the wall plate. Additional cross beams have been provided at eaves level, with props to some of the rafters, but there is no extant beam which might suggest the previous existence of a revolving ladder. The roof is covered in plan tiles and surmounted by an octagonal, lead-topped, timber louver in the form of the box on a pole-cote, with two tiers of individual, arched entrance holes separated by a sloping ledge. This louver was built between Watkins' first visit *c*.1890,[199] at which time the louver was missing, and a later visit, when he took a photograph which was

published in 1921;[200] it is not known if its design was based on a pre-existing lantern. The trap remains, hanging on its hinge, below the collar.

The Royal Commission surveyor noted: 'The structure is possibly mediaeval but there is no very definite evidence as to this. The roof appears to be of late 17th or early 18th century date; the wall on which it rests finishes abruptly with somewhat rough edge.'[201]

COLWALL: Brockbury Manor
An estate plan of 1758 (Fig. 42) shows a square timber-framed pigeon house with a pyramidal roof and square louver.[202]

Fig. 42 Estate map of Brockbury Manor, Colwall showing the timber-framed pigeon house

CRADLEY: Glebe
Cradley's glebe terrier is written in a late medieval hand on parchment.[203] In 1589 it records a 'culverhouse' – a sadly rare word for the subject of this survey. It was also extant in 1607 ('dovehouse') and 1635 ('dovecoate').[204]

CREDENHILL: Dovecote Lane (Listed Grade II, Private but visible from public spaces)
This octagonal brick pigeon house is said to have belonged to Credenhill Court.[205] Interestingly it is placed not in the park but in the village, and it is more likely that it was

Figs. 43 (above) Lower House Farm, Credenhill (Alfred Watkins Collection) and 44 (below) today

built for the adjacent Lower House Farm. Certainly, it is a modest effort with facets of 6ft 11in (2.11m) which could indicate that it was built for a yeoman rather than a gentleman. This example is so similar to the one in the adjacent parish, at Old Weir, that the same hand must have been at work at both (Figs. 43 and 44).

The brick drum is built in English garden wall bond, 1ft 9in (0.58m) thick, and is finished at the top with a simple dentil cornice. The roof is slate (now modern artificial slate) crowned with a recently constructed octagonal louver. The original square louver had a tented lead roof with a ball finial (Fig. 43).

The entrance door, of normal height, is on the south side. Inside, the nest holes, which are staggered and handed from tier to tier, rise in 19 tiers from ground level, providing 530 nests in all, each with an alighting ledge formed by two brick headers. The central post of the revolving ladder is extant, still marked by the ivy that invaded the dovecote in its years of dereliction.

CROFT AND YARPOLE: Croft Castle (Listed Grade II,
part of the stable block of Croft Castle, in the care of the National Trust)
This seems a curiously unpretentious building given the association with a very grand
house (Fig. 45). The pigeon house is formed in the end of a range of service buildings of
the early 18th century.[206] It is only betrayed outside by two arched pigeon holes in a most
unusual sliding sash arrangement of traps in the rendered gable end, under a half-hipped
roof. The roof, which is a simple purlin and rafter roof, does not show any evidence that
a lantern once existed, so that the gable opening must have always been the entrance for
the birds.

The interior (Fig. 46) measures 19ft (5.76m) x 9ft 6in (2.9m). The holes, which are
staggered and handed from tier to tier, with individual brick header alighting ledges, start
3ft (0.9m) above the ground floor level and reach up into the gable and party wall apexes;
there were about 500 originally. An upper floor has been inserted and the holes blocked
for 4ft (1.21m) above it.

*Figs. 45 and 46 Croft Castle with its vertical sliding shutter
and interior of upper level of the pigeon house*

CROFT AND YARPOLE: Old Barn Court, Bircher (Listed Grade II, Private)
The four-gabled form of square brick pigeon houses is only represented here and at
Eardisland. Both are probably of the early 18th century. This one at Bircher is the smaller
at 14ft (4.24m) square (with 2ft 3in (0.68m) thick walls) and is without any form of
embellishment (Fig. 48). The walls, in a rough kind of English garden wall bond, stand on
a stone footing. The roof was originally covered with stone slates which have been replaced
by plain tiles. The louver too has been changed recently; the square form with segmental
arches and the pyramidal lead roof have been repeated, but Cohen's picture shows that it
previously had three tiers of sloping boards (as at Eardisland).[207]

Figs. 47 and 48 Old Barn Court, Bircher and the nest holes – the most common arrangement in brick buildings

Inside, the nest holes start about 1ft (0.3m) above the brick ground floor and finish in the gables, numbering about 380 in all. Each hole has a single brick header for alighting (Fig. 47). Lower down, the holes are staggered but not handed from tier to tier. Higher up, the more usual arrangement of staggering and handing is used. The original low door survives on the west side, and a window has been inserted on the east side. The attached privy completes a very pleasing picture.

CROFT AND YARPOLE: Croft Old Rectory (Private, but visible from public road)
This rather modest building is oblong, 10ft 6in (3.18m) x 12ft 3in (3.71m), and built in red brick laid in Flemish bond on a plinth of local stone (Fig. 49). There is a three brick string course just over half way between plinth and eaves and a number of blocked openings and openings made in the cause of later adaptations. The pyramidal roof is covered with stone slates and surmounted by a lead clad square louver topped by a pyramidal cap and a wrought iron vane.

Fig. 49 Croft Old Rectory

The ground floor has been converted to a privy, and the walls have been plastered, covering over any nest holes. It is more likely however that this was always an upper loft judging by the presence of original doors at ground floor (now blocked) and first floor. In the upper storey are nest holes which are staggered and handed from tier to tier. There are about 150 holes; each hole has a projecting brick header perch.

It is likely that this dovecote was built in the second half of the 18th century – a pleasing example of the more modest pretensions of a clergyman in the age of precautions against the brown rat.

DILWYN: Bidney (Listed Grade II, Private)

The Royal Commission reported that 'The pigeon house … is said to have been brought from elsewhere and stands on modern walling.'[208]

A field called 'Pigeon House Meadow' is shown on the tithe map of 1837 (number 753), immediately north of the house, which might reasonably be expected to be the original site of the pigeon house. The map shows farm buildings in clear detail, including a very small square building to the west of the house (in field 746). Given the map's level of resolution, it would be reasonable to expect the pigeon house to be shown, but no building is visible in the eponymous field. This suggests that the pigeon house had been moved before 1837.[209]

The repositioning and hoisting up of the pigeon house may have been a response to the depredations of brown rats, to which a timber-framed building would have been most vulnerable. Removal to a site nearer to the farmhouse and its dogs and cats, and raising the pigeons up on a plinth of stone, are obvious defences.

The timber frame is 13ft 6in square on plan and the walls are formed of square panels, which are decorated with half-round frets (Fig. 50). This is the only example of the decoration of a timber-framed pigeon house in this survey[210] and was, no doubt, intended to set this building above the other framed pigeon houses in the parish, at Lower Hurst and Luntley. It shares with them a similar arrangement of framing,

Fig. 50 Bidney, Dilwyn: the pigeon house was moved closer to the farmhouse

of four panels to each side, but has a saddleback roof rather than four gables. Otherwise, the form of the framing suggests that it is of similar age to Luntley, which is dated 1673.

The stone slate roof is supported on two trenched purlins on each slope which span from gable to gable; there is a central tie beam but no central truss. The louver is square with a pyramidal roof and a simple arrangement of slats. Extensive modern repairs, notably in the replacement of the infill panels with cement render on metal lath, mean that there are no remnants of the nesting boxes. The floor frame is quite flimsy (unlike Lower Hurst, Dilwyn) and must date from the time of the reconstruction.

DILWYN: Bereton Farm

This square timber-framed pigeon house, now demolished, was described by Watkins as being at 'Barton Court Pembridge' (W17). It was at Bereton to the north-west of Dilwyn. Bereton is called Bearton on the 1st edition OS map, which shows a small building east of the house.

The 11ft (3.33m) square timber frame was rendered externally and stood on a stone plinth about 2ft 6in (0.75m) high (Fig. 51). It was two gabled with a slate roof and a square, closely slatted louver with a pyramidal roof which, unusually, had no slot for the birds. The entrance was instead formed in the west-facing gable which was divided into three panels by raking struts. At the base of the gable (at eaves level) was a sloping perching board. The low door with its sill on top of the plinth was also in the west wall. About 3ft (0.91m) below the eaves was a continuous perching board round all four walls. The nest holes were in an upper loft only.

This rather pretty example must have been demolished before the Royal Commission survey in 1934 since it is not mentioned.

Fig. 51 The demolished pigeon house at Bereton, Dilwyn (Alfred Watkins Collection)

DILWYN: Great House

Watkins recorded and photographed this since demolished pigeon house at Dilwyn (Fig. 52).[211] It was the second largest in his table of octagonal brick buildings, with 9ft 10in (3m) facets. The nest holes started at ground level and it had a revolving ladder. This was a most unusual building in that it had no louver. Instead the birds came and went by rectangular 'entrances under gables'. The roof was covered in decorative tiles, above which was a vane with a dragon.

There is a cottage called Dove Cottage to the south of the church, but that was not the site of the pigeon house. A search of early editions of the Ordnance Survey reveals the actual site, in what was once the farmyard of Great House (now called Karen Court and all converted). The date of demolition is not known but it must have been before the Royal Commission survey in 1934 since it is not mentioned in the Commission's description of Great House.

Fig. 52 *The demolished pigeon house at Great House, Dilwyn (Alfred Watkins Collection)*

DILWYN: Little Dilwyn (Private, but adjacent to the Stretford to Weobley road)

The pigeon house is part of a substantial farmyard (belonging to Manor Farm) which is bisected by the road. It is rectangular, 14ft 4in (4.37m) to the road and 17ft 3in (5.26m) to the side, with a high rubble stone plinth and upper, brick part which holds the nest holes (Fig. 53). It is built in English garden wall bond, which corresponds with the four course depth of the nest holes and perching ledges inside. The holes have been blocked, probably in an attempt to strengthen the walls which are showing extensive vertical cracks.[212]

Fig. 53 *Little Dilwyn*

The nest holes are staggered from course to course and each hole has a pair of projecting headers for alighting. The front wall has no nest holes, the other three hold about 200 in total. The large openings on the front and west sides appear to be part of the original design, presumably to make mucking out easier. The slate-covered roof is hipped, and formed only of common and jack rafters. Prior to 2010 there was a short ridge where the roof framing suggested that there was a louver. A new louver was added when the building was repaired.

The field immediately to the east of the pigeon house is numbered 1237 on the tithe map of 1837 and called, 'Pigeonhouse Meadow'.

DILWYN: Lower Hurst[213] (Listed Grade II, Private, but visible from public road)
This timber-framed pigeon house has some similarities with Luntley and Bidney, in the same parish, but has a number of peculiarities. The buildings are broadly similar in scale and form but there the common characteristics end.

Lower Hurst is oblong; the side facing the road is 15ft (4.55m) and that to the farm-yard is 13ft 6in (4.1m). The framing is less coherent than other framed pigeon houses. It is broadly in two lifts, rather than the more typical three or four square panels high, and the framing above the rails is out of alignment with that below (Fig. 54). The corner posts have jowls, again a unique feature, and on the long side there are five panels above the rail and only four below. These features, combined with the use of second-hand timber[214] and the

Fig. 54 Lower Hurst, Dilywn

variety of infill panels and boarding, give a rather cobbled-together appearance, and probably betray at least one major reconstruction to convert it to a granary.[215] The wattle and daub infill panels were replaced with brick to contain the grain, the more exposed upper frame was given the additional protection of external weather boarding, and a door was inserted on the side facing the road at the level of a cart.

Inside, the floor over the basement is made of substantial timbers and a further floor, of lighter construction, has been inserted to make two storeys within the frame. The roof consists of two long purlins spanning between the east and west gables from which 'jack' purlins span to the north and south gables. The louver is supported on the long purlins. None of the nesting boxes survive,. They were probably confined above the upper floor and framed up in wood boards, as at Brook House, Kings Pyon (Fig. 94).

The exterior has changed little since 1895;[216] the upper storey was boarded on all sides in Cohen's picture of 1957. The louver is square with a pyramidal roof to which a modern vane has been added since 1895.

DILWYN: Luntley[217] (Listed Grade II, Dated 1673, Accessible)

Cycling along the little lanes between Pembridge and Weobley is pure pleasure, made more so by coming upon the pigeon house at Luntley. Everything is just right; the building is complete, the setting is Herefordshire exemplified and the handsome, timber-framed Court forms a fine backdrop (Fig. 55).

The frame is 11ft 3in (3.4m) square on plan and the walls are made of square panels – four wide and four high to the base of the gables. The posts are braced down to the ground plate and a sloping perching board is fixed at the top of the second panel. Each face is gabled, and each gable has a shuttered entry with a perching board. Where the barge boards meet there is a decorative turned wood pendant. The louver is also gabled on each face but shows no means of entry. It has been in this form since the late 19th century.[218] The roof is stone slated and, like Lower Hurst, consists of two long purlins spanning between the north and south gables from which 'jack' purlins span to the east and west gables. The louver is supported on the long purlins.

Fig. 55 Luntley with the Hall behind the pigeon house

Figs. 56 and 57 The interior of Luntley (left) showing the framework which supported the nest boxes and the terrier hole (right)

The door is only 4ft 8in high, and on the lintel is carved the date 1673. Inside, the framework, which once supported the nest boxes, remains (Fig. 56) although much renewed (see Brook House, Kings Pyon). Marshall visited in 1894 and noted: 'Mr Burlton of Leominster the present owner informs me the vane was put up about 50 years ago and was taken off this year [1894].' In 1903 he further noted: 'The framework of holes [is] *in situ*, though the nest boards are gone. There is a thick board about half way up (supported on brackets), and the upright strips are let into this. The cross strips are rougher and simply nailed on. The pigeons entered by little windows on the gables, the original alighting ledges outside these are, in some cases, still *in situ*.' Marshall visited only two years after the Woolhope Club visited and reported 'nest holes for about 500 pigeons, tier above tier, the nesting places in each tier being entered alternately from the right hand in one tier and from the left on the upper tier.'[219]

At the base of the west wall, the southern infill panel has been replaced with brick-work which forms a small, arched opening (Fig. 57). This is probably a cat or terrier hole, provided as a means of pest control in the age of the brown rat.[220] A kennel could have been attached at this point. This means of control allowed the nests to be retained to ground level despite the vulnerability of framed buildings to the attack of brown rats.

Extensive repairs were carried out after 1987. At that date the listing inspector noted that the roof was felted and the south-west corner was supported by timber shores.[221]

DINMORE: Dinmore Manor

Watkins recorded a round stone pigeon house, which was pulled down *c*.1790 (W21). Richard Hollins Murray wrote that 'The field to the north of the tithe barn is named Pigeon House Meadow and until the end of the 18th century there existed a circular stone pigeon house resembling, with little doubt, the one still extant but somewhat ruinous at Garway.'[222] The 'little doubt' comes from the conviction that, as Garway was a dependent house of Dinmore, the building of dovecotes in the two places would be done in the same fashion. The Preceptory at Dinmore was founded in 1186 and the dovecote was probably older than Garway's. Certainly it was in production in 1338 (Garway is dated 1326) when an account refers to 'a dovecote, of the yearly value of 6s 8d.'[223]

DORSTONE: Brynsard Farmhouse (Listed Grade II, Private)

The 18th-century house has a 'five opening pigeon loft (three blocked) with alighting ledge'.[224]

DOWNTON: Hay Mill

A photograph of 1887[225] shows a triangular wooden box-cote fixed to the gable of a building to the east of the mill. It had four tiers separated by ledges. The building has since been demolished, and the nearby mill is derelict.

DULAS: Home Farm (Private)

Fig. 58 Home Farm Dulas

The gable-cote at Home Farm is, uniquely, part of a water mill.[226] It is one of a relatively extensive range of 19th-century red brick buildings planned as a model farm.

The cote is in five tiers with 25 entrance holes arranged one over another (Fig. 58). The projecting brackets for perching ledges remain. The holes are not nest holes but give access to a loft which is separated from the stone floor of the mill by a wooden boarded partition. The nest boxes have been removed.

EARDISLAND: Court House Farm

Watkins refers to a pigeon house in Eardisland in his table of round stone pigeon houses 'now pulled down' (W21). It stood at the south-eastern end of the Court House farm-yard, roughly on a line drawn between the pigeon house at the Old Manor House (see below) and the parish church.[227] It is possible that this site was within the bailey of the motte and bailey castle, and that the dovecote was of early date. Archaeological investigations in advance of the development of the modern houses which now occupy the site did not find the foundations of the pigeon house.[228]

EARDISLAND: Field names at Hinton

It is possible that this site is associated with the ancient Hinton Manor. Hinton was one of three Domesday manors in Eardisland parish, and remained distinct until 1929. There are two 'pigeon' fields in the 1842 tithe apportionment, Pigeon House Meadow (numbered 762) and Pigeon House Croft (numbered 764 and 764a), at the southern tip of Badger's Wood, to the north of Eardisland village.

EARDISLAND: Sham dovecote at Orchard Green

This is a timber framed eye-catcher which could only have been thought up by a conservation bureaucrat.

EARDISLAND: Home Farm by Burton Court

The pigeon house at Burton has the sad distinction of being the most recently demolished dovecote in Herefordshire. Its ghost still haunted the statutory list of listed buildings which had not been amended at the time of this survey.

Fig. 59 Cohen's photograph of the demolished pigeon house near Burton Court

Old photographs and descriptions recall a timber-framed building on an 11ft 3in (3.41m) square[229] stone plinth. The proportions were tall and thin, and the framing, consisting of thin vertical studs, appeared to be late 18th or even 19th century. Stainburn thought that the timbers had come from the remodelling of Burton Court (S31). The RCHM surveyor noted, in 1933, 'Of old timber framing covered with roughcast, having two gable ends. The roof is covered with stone tiles and has above it a glazed lantern. Inside are some old timbers, but the roof mostly restored: there are no nests. The building is probably of the 17th century.'[230]

The RCHM photograph of 1933, and Cohen's of 1957 (Fig. 59), show a building in sound condition. Its proportions and the striking, glazed lantern with its continuous timber perching ledge, make an elegant impression. By 1979, the building was in a poor state: the louver skeletal, the roof full of holes and the render falling away from the timber frame – proof indeed of the need to 'Watch an old building with an anxious care; guard it as best you may, and at any cost, from every influence of dilapidation'.[231]

Fig. 60 Eardisland: The Old Manor House

EARDISLAND: The Old Manor House[232] (Listed Grade II, Accessible – open every day)
While the Burton pigeon house was sliding into ruin, the other surviving one in the parish was being repaired and given new life in the heart of the village, despite quite serious repair problems. Conservation is as much a matter of will and vision as over-vaunted enterprise – the result is a thing of beauty saved, not an empty field, and a community united in a demanding common task.

The owner of the Manor House in the early 18th century had pretensions. The most prominent wing of the house was given a brick and sash window makeover, and a walled pleasure ground was formed. In the most prominent and public position he built a handsome, four-gabled pigeon house raised up on a summer house (Fig. 60). It is 20ft (6.05m) square with 1ft 8in (0.51m)[233] thick walls but the quality of the brickwork does not match the builder's pretensions. The Flemish garden wall bonding is poorly worked out and the walls are thin, leaving only half a brick between the nests and the outside (Fig. 61). This is made worse by the way the nests are piled up one over another and not handed from tier to tier. When the Trust formed to care for the building began its task with the architect Jacqueline Demaus, there were severe vertical cracks in the brickwork.

The entrance from the garden was adorned with a pedimented door hood on moulded brackets, and the elevations facing the garden, road and river each had two tall windows. One of those facing the road has been made into a door to allow public access (this

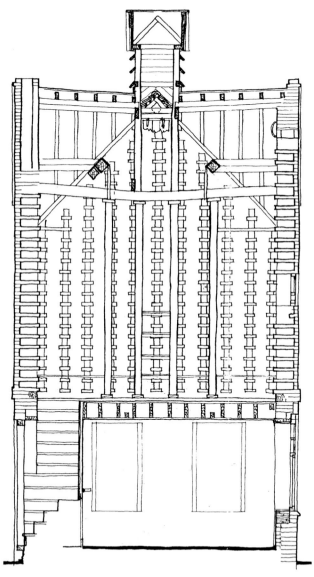

Fig. 61 Section through the pigeon house drawn
by Jacqueline Demaus
who oversaw the major repair scheme in 1999

Fig. 62 Eardisland: the nests

has required the turning of the foot of the staircase inside). Outside, at the floor level, there is a three brick deep string course but no further embellishment until the copings of the parapet gables are reached. On the road side is a small opening with a projecting perching ledge high up in the gable apex. Two modern windows have been inserted on the south and west sides. The roof is tiled and surmounted by a square louver with four gables. The sloping boards on the sides of the louver and the vane with its fish were in place in Watkins' time and are probably original features.

Inside, the ground-floor garden room has a fireplace which was served by an internal chimney terminating at the north gable apex. The nest holes line the upper chamber from the floor to the gable apexes. They number a staggering 884, each served by its own specially moulded brick perch and are, as noted above, piled one above another (Fig. 62). The roof structure is like other four-gabled buildings with two principal purlins (in this case running north-south) and trimmed purlins spanning to the other gables. This is undergirded by two steel beams which carry the weight of the louver (Fig. 3B), but all of this has had to be further strengthened with steel in the recent repair scheme. Below the louver is a trap.

The pigeon house was opened to the public in September 1999 and houses a museum with displays about dovecotes, the home front in the Second World War and motoring in the decades between the wars.[234] In 2010 the ground floor was turned into the village shop.

EARDISLAND: The Staick House (Listed Grade II*, Private, but visible from the road)
This exceptionally fine timber-framed house has a small gable-cote in the wall facing the road. Four holes are formed in a plank which sits on a perching board supported on brackets.

EARDISLEY: Bollingham House (Private, but visible from the adjacent chapel yard)
The pigeon house stands on a mound, which is thought to be a tumulus or a motte (Fig. 63),[235] in the grounds of a house which has early origins. It is, however, the later, Victorian phase of the house which corresponds with its present appearance. When Watkins visited Bollingham he found a 9ft square brick building with the 'upper part of wood' (W18). This structure, of Flemish bond brickwork with a timber-framed upper loft, is founded

on a 2ft 6in high plinth of squared stones; there is a ground-level door in the west side. He says that it was 'single span' (two-gabled) with the 'entrance in gable'. The nests were formed in wooden boxes in the upper stage only which was reached by a door (which still exists) at that level on the north side. The interior of the lower floor is plastered and painted and was either conceived as, or converted to a garden room or gazebo. There are pairs of small lunettes facing the house and the chapel to the east, which give light to this ground-floor room, although little view. A winding cinder path ascended the mound,[236] which suggests that the building was part of the perambulation of the garden providing a resting place at its highest point. The first floor form, and the used of relatively large bricks, suggest a later 18th century date for this example.

Fig. 63 Bollingham House

At some time after Watkins' visit, *c.*1890, the roof was changed to the present slate pyramid with a sloping board at the eaves. A water tank, filled by a hydraulic ram, was inserted to serve the house and associated workers' cottages.

Fig. 64 Eardisley Park photographed by Israel Cohen in 1956

EARDISLEY: Eardisley Park (Listed Grade II, Private)

The house at Eardisley Park, first built in *c.*1700, stands very proud in its setting of ancient trees and parkland.[237] The pigeon house is hard by and is of commensurate scale and quality. It stands on a rubble stone plinth which gives enhanced stature on the side facing the park, where the drive approaches the courtyard of the house. The raised brick part, at 18ft 9in (5.68m) square, is in the upper size range of square pigeon houses (Fig. 64).

Photographs down to 1979 show a pyramidal stone slate roof with a square, partly-glazed lantern with its own pyramidal roof surmounted by a vane.[238] These features are now either

81

removed or covered with tin, although much of the original material has been preserved against the day when restoration can be attempted. The timber floor, above the level of the entrance arch, is almost completely decayed, but the brick parts are in sounder condition, as is the roof, which consists of jack and common rafters supported on stout hip rafters and a ring of butt-purlins about a third of the way up the roof.

The outer brickwork is laid in a form of English garden wall bond. Inside, the brick nest holes are confined to the upper level, and are of unusually generous proportions. The holes are three courses high, but each tier occupies five courses, including a continuous string course of headers for perching under each row of holes (Fig. 12c). The priority here was clearly outward show rather than production capacity and there are fewer than 250 holes. Where the brickwork has collapsed, a rare insight is given to the interior of the nest holes which, as is most usual, are staggered and handed from course to course. The bricklaying within the wall thickness is quite confused and wooden strips were required in the 'ceilings' of the nest holes to support the ends of header bricks (Fig. 12c).

The lower part is served by a double doorway which opens into the farmyard, rather than the garden. It was probably used as an implement shed. The upper loft, combined with the low intensity of nest provision, suggest a later 18th century, post brown rat, date for this example.

The field to the north of the pigeon house, numbered 812 on the tithe map of 1840, is called 'Pigeon House Field'.

EARDISLEY: Field name at Lemore Manor
The long field running north-south along the east side of Holywell Dingle is called 'Pigeon House Croft' and numbered 262 on the tithe map of 1840.[239]

EATON BISHOP: Pigeon House Meadow
This is the name of the long field (now subdivided) north of the lane to the Sugwas Ferry, between Lane Head Farm and the Wye, numbered 506 on the tithe map of 1840.

EATON BISHOP: Pigeon House Plock and Green Court
The 1617[240] glebe terrier lists 'One Dovehouse, one garden, one little close behind the barn with a little Plocke where the Dove House doe stand.' The dovehouse is listed in a later entry for 1630, but more permanently preserved in the name of the field, immediately north of the church, numbered 436 on the 1840 tithe map. Pigeon House Plock abuts the garden of Green Court where Watkins recorded a 14ft square stone pigeon house, the upper part of which was brick and timber framing. It was already semi-derelict when he saw it, the roof and louver had gone.[241] The nests were down to ground level. The Royal Commission survey of 1931 does not include this building, which was probably demolished before that date, but early editions of the Ordnance Survey show a number of small rectangular buildings which are possible candidates.

EVESBATCH: Upper and Lower Pigeon House Orchard

The names of fields 135 and 136 on the tithe map of 1839, immediately south-west of Evesbatch Court.

EWYAS HAROLD: Pigeon House Meadow

The name of field 87 on the tithe map of 1844, south of the village between the B4347 and Dulas Brook. The field has been divided into house plots.

EYE, MORTON & ASHTON: Lower Farm, Ashton and Pigeon House Orchard

in Berrington Park (Private, but visible from the A49)

Watkins noted that this building was '… said to have been moved bodily from Berrington'.[242] The tithe map of 1844 shows Pigeon House Orchard (field 222), in the park of Berrington Hall, adjacent to the Ashton - Eye lane, just to the east of the present drive. This location, close to the road and not far from the present site, would present a relatively easy removal task. The combination of possible source and the practicality of the task support the suggestion that this building was moved.

When the building was listed, it was described as a granary.[243] Certainly, the boarded exterior, the half-hipped roof and the way the building stands on brick piers, give an appearance unlike the other timber-framed Herefordshire pigeon houses, and more like a granary (Fig. 65). Inside, there are no nest boxes to show that this building was used for keeping pigeons. In addition, the design of the unusual, hexagonal louver is not quite right; in its present form it appears far too open to be safe from birds of prey and, inside, the apex of the central truss obstructs the opening. The original design of the louver, if this was a pigeon house, must have been more enclosed without, and more open within.

There are, however, enough reasons to include the building in this survey. Considering the building itself, it is, at 20ft (6.06m) x 18ft (5.46m), a good size for a pigeon house.[244] In the 1887 sale particulars of the Berrington Hall estate,[245] only two of the many farms for sale had buildings for pigeons. Lower Farm's buildings included 'poultry and pigeon houses'; while at Stocktonbury (see Kimbolton below) the 'Dove Cote' is mentioned. This

Fig. 65 The pigeon house at Ashton said to have been moved from Berrington Hall

suggests that the original purpose of these buildings was being recognised, whether or not pigeons were being kept, and that there was a pigeon house at Ashton before 1887.

The timber frame is formed in two bays with a central truss supporting two tiers of trenched purlins. The walls are two, relatively large, panels high but the studs do not line up either side of the rail throughout, and the gable rails are higher than those in the side walls. This, combined with the lack of any provision to retain infill panels, indicates that the building has always been boarded. Floor joists are supported on the gable rails and a chamfered beam that is joined into the posts supporting the central truss. This framing is probably of the 18th century, and the deal floor structure later.[246]

The hexagonal, lead-domed louver is especially fine – a design befitting a country house, rather than a 'lower' farm (Fig. 66). Watkins recorded a ball finial (W17); today there is a simple spike.

Fig. 66 The louver at Ashton

Eyton: Pigeon House Close
The name of field 99 on the tithe map of 1843, immediately south of Hill Farm.

Eyton: Barn west of Eyton House (Private but visible from the road)
Brick gable-cote of 18 holes in five tiers. The holes are two courses deep with individual alighting ledges formed by two plinth bricks laid on their sides. The holes go through the wall, rather than providing nests in its thickness, and the birds were kept in a loft in the roof of the barn.

The literature refers to a change in pigeon keeping towards the end of the 18th century to provide birds for shooting matches. The Hansells say, 'This sport depended upon a steady supply of dovecote birds, often six to ten dozen being required for each match.' This led to a good deal of stealing from dovecotes. 'During these nocturnal exercises the birds were flushed from their nests by rattling the door and were then trapped as they emerged from the dovecote by nets secured over the exits.' I have not found any references to such matches in Herefordshire but the owner of Eyton House told me that the birds there had been raised for sport. Inside there are the remains of sliding shutters which could be closed to keep the birds in while the keeper captured them.

Ford and Stoke Prior: Bury Farm
The Bury, east of the parish church, is thought to have been the site of a grange belonging to Leominster Priory. Little surprise then that Watkins recorded a round stone pigeon house, since demolished (Fig. 67). He noted that it was rudely built, 13ft 6in (4.09m) diameter inside and had 3ft (0.91m) thick walls. There was an alighting ledge for every

Fig. 67 The demolished pigeon house at Bury Farm, Stoke Prior. (Alfred Watkins Collection)

tier of holes, which were in the full height of the wall. His photograph shows a building of relatively stout, squat proportions with an octagonal slate roof which is unlikely to be the original roof, and may have been accompanied by the lowering of the wall tops. The louver was square with a pyramidal top and two tiers of sloping boards.[247]

The circular outline is clearly visible on earlier editions of the Ordnance Survey but it appears to have been demolished before 1934 because it is not included in the Royal Commission survey.

FORD AND STOKE PRIOR: Great House Farm (Listed Grade II, Private) This 18ft (5.53m) square brick pigeon house is built into a bank and raised on a stone-built semi-basement (Fig. 68). The entrance to the basement is on the west side facing the farmhouse; the entrance to the pigeon house is at the east end of the north side with the sill about 2ft 6in (0.75m) above the ground level at that point. The brickwork, of relatively thin bricks (4 courses rise 10.5 inches (0.27m)), in Flemish bond, is of high quality, and the west elevation is articulated with sunk panels above the basement door and windows. Both the openings and the panels are under segmental arches which, in the case of the panels, are

Fig. 68 Great House, Stoke Prior

decorated with over-burnt bricks. Just below the eaves, on each elevation, there are two putlog holes. The stone basement walls have numerous brick patches with straight sides which, if this were not below ground, would suggest old openings. This basement could be part of an older building from a time when ground levels were lower, but this seems unlikely.[248] The chamfered, pegged door frame and iron hinges appear to be original.

The pigeon house floor is timber, supported on two parallel, chamfered spine beams. The nests are unlike any others in this survey (Fig. 69). There are thirteen tiers, starting from just above the floor, with a total of 470 holes, each of which has a triangular head. Each tier sits on a continuous stone ledge and the nests are L-shaped, staggered and handed. The nests penetrate the 2ft (0.6m) thick wall by 1ft 3in (0.38m).

Fig. 69 Nest holes at Great House, Stoke Prior – the only arched masonry holes in Herefordshire

There are crossed, chamfered beams at eaves level and, above, a well-carpentered, pyramidal roof. The hip rafters and two full rafters on each side are jointed into a square collar which is deeply chamfered on the inner corner. These and the remaining trimmed rafters are of square section oak. The covering for both the main and louver roofs is stone slate with modern, iron hip flashings. The louver has modern timber slats, but had a single sloping board about half way up the posts as late as 1977.[249]

This exceptionally fine pigeon house probably dates from the first half of the 18th century, judging by the fine, narrow bricks. Building over a semi-basement is reminiscent of the nearby pigeon house at Upper Bache, Kimbolton which was dated 1747.

FORD AND STOKE PRIOR: Pigeon House Close, Upper Wickton
The name of field 575 on the Stoke Prior tithe map of 1843, immediately south-west of Wickton Court (see below).

FORD AND STOKE PRIOR: Pigeon House Orchard, Ford
The name of field 39 on the Ford tithe map of 1843, immediately east of Ford Bridge and south of Ford Farm.

FORD AND STOKE PRIOR: Pigeon House Orchard, The Luce
The name of field 179 on the Stoke Prior tithe map of 1843, immediately south-east of The Luce (Steen's Bridge).

Fig. 70 Stretfordbury

FORD AND STOKE PRIOR: Stretfordbury (Listed Grade II, Private)

This is one of a small number of single storey buildings (Fig. 70) assumed to be pigeon houses in previous surveys.[250] The building is oblong, 18ft (0.55m) x 12ft 6in (0.39m), with three walls of the local rubble stone and one, at the rear, of flimsy timber framing with red brick infill panels. There are central doors to the 'front' onto the farmyard, and the 'rear'. The pyramidal roof is covered with clay tiles and supports a boarded square louver with a pyramidal lead roof. In 1979 the louver was an open four poster.[251] The walls are 1ft 6in (0.46m) thick; this would have required a lining of wooden nest boxes, but none survive.

It is possible that this building was a combined granary/dovecote of a type found at, for example, Home Farm, Fen Ditton, Cambridgeshire (Fig. 71); but the building seems too low (little more than a door's height to the eaves) to have been of that type. It may simply have been a granary, feed store or slaughterhouse for the adjacent pig sties.

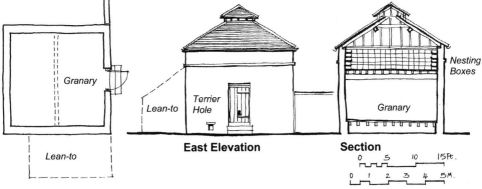

Fig. 71 Granary and dovecote at Fen Ditton, Cambridgeshire,
surveyed by Beth Davis and David Grech

FORD AND STOKE PRIOR: Wheelbarrow Castle (Private, but visible from public road)
Gable-cote at south-west end of a stone barn. There are three tiers of nest holes below the eaves level and diminishing tiers up the gable apex, all have continuous alighting ledges. This example is unusual in that it faces into a narrow gap between the gables of two barns.

FORD AND STOKE PRIOR: Wickton Court[252] (Private)

The remains of a square stone pigeon house stand between the 17th-century Court and Pigeon House Close (see above).

Two of the walls stand to a height of about 10ft (3.03m) and suggest that the building was 14ft (4.24m) square inside and 20ft (6.06m) outside. There is a low doorway on the east side and on that same side the nest holes are not hidden by ivy (Fig. 72). They are generally about 6 inches square and are skewed and widened out in different directions from tier to tier. They are roughly staggered and there is a continuous alighting ledge to every tier, about 9 inches (0.23m) apart. This building has the same dimensions as the building recorded by Watkins at Nurton Court, Middleton (Table 3) (Fig. 120). Both buildings have exceptionally thick walls compared to other, smaller square stone buildings.

Fig. 72 Wickton Court, Stoke Prior

Fig. 73 The inscription stone at Garway

FOWNHOPE: Demesne Lands
An inquisition post mortem of 1353 records '… one dovecote 40d. …'. It is not mentioned in a similar document of 1375.[253]

GARWAY: Church House Farm (Listed Grade I, Private)
The Knights Templar were given an estate in Archenfield in 1187, and it is probable that they founded their preceptory at Garway soon after that. They built a church with a round nave and they also built a round pigeon house. This is known from the accounts made by John de la Haye in 1312, at the suppression

of the Templar order, which say that the Templar dovecote was 'yielding nothing as it was broken down'.[254]

The Knights Hospitaller took possession of the Garway estate in 1324, and gave their attention to the matter of restoring the production of pigeons early in their tenure. By 1326 the present pigeon house had been built, or formed by the restoration of the Templars' building. This is recorded in an inscription on the tympanum, now illegible, over the low (5ft (1.52m) high), south-facing doorway which defines the Garway building as the oldest dated pigeon house in Britain (Fig. 73):

A Dni Mmo CCCmo
XXVI fact fuit id co
lubar per fratre
Ricm
'1326AD this pigeon house was made by Brother Richard.'[255]

There are also inscribed stones inside naming 'Gilbert' which have led to the suggestion that Gilbert was the mason working for Richard de Bire, the brother in charge of the work.[256]

The drum has an internal diameter of 17ft 6in (5.30m) (the second largest of the circular pigeon houses)[257] and the walls are 3ft 9in thick (1.14m) (Fig. 74). The stone is in relatively large blocks giving an even more monumental impression, although there is evidence of the exterior having been plastered. The walls rise to a string course or perching ledge about 16ft (4.85m) up, above which the drum is tapered over the vault up to a vertical parapet (Fig. 3). Within the ring of the parapet the roof is a shallow dish, in the centre of which is a stone-built louver which has a stone roof shaped like a beehive (Fig. 75). This depression collects water into a

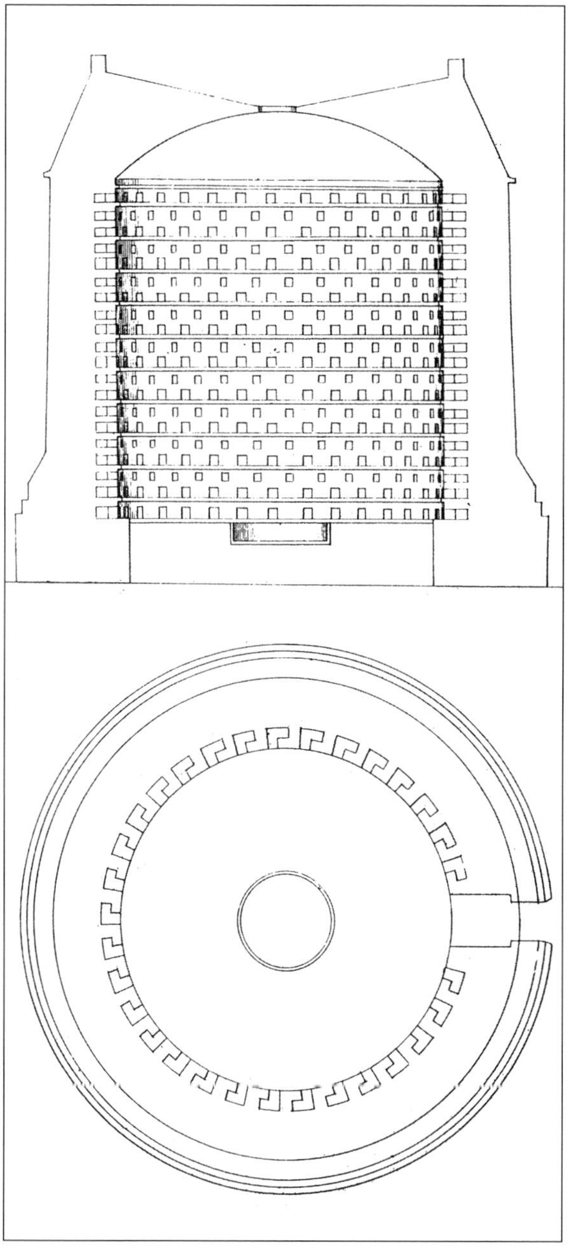

Fig. 74 Section drawing of Garway from John Webb's paper in Archaeologia, *1846*

Fig. 75 *The stone louver at Garway*   Fig. 76 *The nests at Garway*

pipe which discharges beyond the outer walls. A second doorway has been cut in the north side; this linked the pigeon house to an enclosed stockyard and barns (now demolished)[258] and allowed its use as a byre.

Inside, the nest holes rise in 20 tiers with a continuous ledge every second course. The stonework is dressed so that the nest holes are L-shaped rather than the sock shape seen in the more ragged stone at, for example, Richard's Castle. The holes are staggered and handed from tier to tier (Fig. 76) and number 610 – probably 630 before the second doorway was formed. There is an often repeated myth that there are 666 nests,[259] a number with mystical significance, which has been linked to some theories about the Knights Templar.[260] It is plausible that a religious order operating in an age of symbol would take some delight in using 666, 'The Number of the Beast', in the design of a building which housed doves whose biblical and symbolic values are peace, sacrifice and renewal. Fortunately the truth is simpler and duller.

In the centre of the stone floor is the outline of a circular stone structure on which has been placed the base stone or sump from an apple press. The earliest record shows a large stone basin, 5ft (1.52m) in diameter and 6in (0.15m) deep, said to have been provided for the birds to drink and bathe in. However, the floor of a dovecote with over 600 nests was hardly likely to be sanitary enough for either unless this cistern was sheltered in some way.

GARWAY: Cwm Maddoc Farm (Listed Grade II, Private)
The north-facing gable of a single storey, rubble stone barn to the west of the farmhouse has a gable-cote with 14 nests in five tiers with continuous stone alighting ledges.

GARWAY: New House Farm (Listed Grade II, Private)
The statutory list described a gable-cote on a 'granary and wainhouse' which is dated 1811. The 'South-west gable has central segmental-headed opening flanked by three rows of (two) nesting ledges and holes for pigeons'.[261]

GOODRICH: Cider Mill at Flanesford Priory (Listed Grade II. Private, converted to holiday accommodation)
The Cider Mill is part of an impressive range of buildings made of the local red stone. It has an eaves-cote consisting of a single row of irregularly spaced nest holes.[262]

GOODRICH: Barn at Huntsham Court (Private)
The gable over the threshing bay of the great stone barn has a gable-cote with ten holes arranged in a triangle (Fig. 77). Stainburn says there is a 'timber loft within gable'. (S.70)

Fig. 77 Huntsham Court, Goodrich

GRENDON BISHOP: Westington Court[263] (Private)
This outbuilding has a gable-cote on each gable and an eaves-cote, with a total of about 180 nest holes. It is one of the largest of the dovecotes with external holes. The nest holes are in brickwork built on the masonry of an earlier building. The gable-cotes have continuous brick ledges but the eaves-cote has none.

HATFIELD AND NEWHAMPTON: Barn at Lower Nicholson Farm (Listed Grade II, Private)
The 18th-century stone barn has a gable-cote on the west gable.[264]

HAYWOOD: The Haywood
Watkins recorded and photographed a 16ft (4.85m) square brick pigeon house rising from a chamfered stone plinth.[265] Watkins' picture captures a unique building in a setting of trees and weathered walls. There can be few more moving images of our lost past. The louver had a vane dated 1690, which means that it was the earliest dated masonry building after Garway. The narrowness of the bricks, four course only rose 10.5 inches,[266] is consistent with the late 17th century date on the weather vane.

The walls were decorated with a moulded string or perching course (bead, cavetto, chamfer) about three quarters of the way up the walls (Fig. 78).[267] The truncated pyramidal roof of stone slates was laid in diminishing courses with lead hips, and was surmounted by a tall, square, boarded louver which also had a pyramidal stone roof. The louver was entered by two slits, the higher one of which was covered with an alighting board. The vane was decorated with a 'serpentine claw'. The interior had pigeon holes to the ground and was entered by a low door under a segmental brick arch. It was demolished *c.*1940 (S.TII.12).

Field 36 on the tithe map of 1820, immediately south-west of The Haywood, is named Pigeon House Orchard. Early editions of the Ordnance Survey mark the 'Pigeon Cote' between this field and the house.

Fig. 78 The demolished pigeon house at Haywood which was dated 1690
(Alfred Watkins Collection)

HENTLAND: Kynaston House (Private, but visible from the public road)

Kynaston House displays one of two examples of chimney-cotes (Fig. 79). A triangular pattern of ten square holes with stone alighting ledges is formed in the face of the stack, and there are two holes in each flank. (See also Yarkhill, Green Lanes).

HEREFORD: Litley Court

Watkins noted this square timber-framed pigeon house with a pyramidal roof, which was probably demolished in the 1860s (W21).

HEREFORD: The Moor

Watkins reported that 'The picturesque square dovecote at the Moor Farm, Hereford, did not survive the nineteenth century. It collapsed from sheer age and decay in October 1900. An eyewitness told me that he chanced to be walking past at the time – a perfectly still evening, about 6 o' clock – and, hearing a noise, he saw it collapsing in a cloud of dust, only the low stone foundations remaining.'[268] Moor Farm now gives its name to an area of modern development to the north-west of the city centre. Part of the farmhouse has survived; the pigeon house stood just north-west of it (Fig. 80).

Fig. 79 Chimney-cote at Kynaston House, Hentland (Photograph by Chris Partrick)

Watkins recorded this dovecote and said it was, 'same date evidently as Luntley (1673)' (W17). He does not say it was actually dated, and was probably relying on the similarities of form between the two buildings. The dovecote's timber-framed walls stood on a tall, partly rendered stone plinth, which had a doorway in the south side, facing the house, and the timber frame appears to have been entirely covered in lath and plaster on the outside. It was 12ft 6in (3.79m) square and four-gabled. The roof is obscured by snow in Watkins' photographs[269] but was probably covered with the stone slates typical in the Marches. The louver was square, four-gabled and boarded with sloping boards with gaps between

Fig. 80 The demolished pigeon house at The Moor, Hereford (Alfred Watkins Collection)

them. The entrance for the birds was at the bottom and the top had a ball finial. Watkins says that the nests were 'in loft', and Stainburn in 'upper loft' (W17, S.TII.6) but it is not known if this meant that the holes were immediately above the stone plinth or at some higher level as at Kings Pyon.

HEREFORD: Newton Farm
Watkins includes this building at 'Newtown' Farm in his table of demolished buildings. (W21). The first edition Ordnance Survey shows a small square building to the north-west of the farmhouse.

Fig. 81 The demolished pigeon house at Putson, Hereford (Alfred Watkins Collection)

HEREFORD: Putson[270]
The pigeon house at Putson was two-gabled (Fig. 81). The framing was in square panels; each elevation was four panels wide by four high to the eaves, with down bracing from the corners to the sills all round. Watkins says it was 16ft (4.85m) square, but this is probably an overestimate. Byford is five panels wide and measures 16ft (4.85m) and the panels at Putson appear to be of similar size, which would make Putson about 13ft (4.24m) square. Like Bereton Court, Dilwyn, there are perching boards above the third panel all round, and across the gables at eaves level. The roof was covered with plain tiles and the louver was, uniquely in this survey, made of brick. Watkins said that there were wooden boxes 'to floor'. It was demolished in 1889.

HOLME LACY: Cote Ground
The name of field number 184 on the tithe map of 1840, to the south of Lower Bogmarsh.

HOLME LACY: Pound Farm[271] (Listed Grade II, Private, but visible from public path)
The pigeon house stands just to the north of Wilsley House among later farm buildings, which are now part of the agricultural college. Its round drum is made of large squared blocks of the local purple stone, giving a monumental feel to a relatively small building, with an internal diameter of 12ft 9in (3.86m) and 1ft 6in (0.45m) thick walls. The eaves have a marked overhang with a plaster soffit forming the base of a steep, conical slate roof.

The lantern has collapsed. Old photographs show what a very sad loss has been bought by its neglect.[272] It was round, and rose from a timber gallery with a low balustrade. The drum was divided into four panels, each of which had 16 panes over an entrance slot at the gallery level. The lantern roof was a lead cone surmounted by a vane with an arrow.

The interior is divided by a floor, above which the walls are lined with very pretty wooden nest boxes. There are 11 tiers of 42 round-topped holes (462 in all) separated by continuous wooden ledges. The nest boxes are 9 inches (0.225m) from front to back, 10 inches (0.254m) tall and 10 wide. The revolving ladder also survives, but probably not for long unless the lantern is restored.

Figs. 82-84 Holme Lacy photographed by Israel Cohen in 1957 (above); interior with nest boxes and revolving ladder (above right) and exterior today (lower right)

Watkins thought that this design was based on French examples, but there are other buildings in England with strong similarities.[273] It is difficult to date this building because it has little in common with other buildings in this survey. Its first floor form (perhaps to evade the brown rat) and deliberate avoidance of the country house octagonal plan suggest a late 18th or early 19th century date.

HOLMER: Holmer Park (Listed Grade II, Private, but visible from the road)

This curious structure is included in the earlier surveys of pigeon houses as a dovecote, but it could only have been for a decorative purpose because the loft is relatively small and difficult to reach. That Watkins included it in his article has real authority, for he grew up with it. Holmer Park was built by his father, Charles in the 1860s, and the family

Fig. 85 Holmer Park

lived there until 1870, when Alfred Watkins was 15.[274] In his survey of pigeon houses he included it in the table of 'Lofts' and notes that it was 'Over an aviary built of pillars from Hereford old Town Hall' (W20). The Town Hall was demolished in 1862, so the Holmer building must have been built between 1862 and 1870.

The building is open on two sides (Fig. 85), but, in earlier photographs, is shown fully enclosed with timber panels and netting.[275] Also, the louver previously had a pair of pigeon holes at the base of each side. The timbers are impressive – unexpectedly accurate parodies of 13th-century stone piers with engaged shafts – and it needs little imagination to see the magnificence of the Old Town Hall from which they came.

HOPE UNDER DINMORE: Pigeon House Orchard, Bury of Hope

Bury of Hope was one of the granges of Leominster Priory and it is not surprising to find record of a pigeon house. The Orchard is to the south-east of the Bury Farm, where the track crosses the railway line. It might be the site referred to in a survey of 1327, which enumerated a dovecote valued at 2 shillings, but this is not certain. There is greater certainty in an account of buildings in the orchard, compiled in 1818, which refers to 'a Pigeon House, Orchard and Buildings'. The existence of buildings on the site is confirmed by an estate map and recent archaeological investigation. Also, there is an account of £25 being spent on the repair of the pigeon house in 1841, which was, by then, in the hands of the Arkwright estate. It is suggested that the orchard contained a pigeon house with an adjacent barn and stable range. These buildings were converted to cottages, initially for farm workers and later for railway workers, but the close proximity of the railway necessitated their demolition in 1868.[276]

KENCHESTER: The Old Weir, Swainshill (Listed Grade II, Private)

Fig. 86 The Old Weir, Swainshill

The pigeon house, which was probably built in the early 18th century, stands to the south of an extensive range of farm buildings, overlooking the River Wye. It is one of the smallest[277] of the surviving octagonal brick type and similar in detail to that at Credenhill – the next parish. The brick drum is built in English garden wall bond on a stone plinth, and rises to a brick dentil cornice. A curious feature of the cornice is that there is an iron ring, about 3 inches diameter, fixed in the centre of each facet (Fig. 86).

The facets are plain, measuring 6ft 9in (2.05m), and the walls are 1ft 6in (0.45m) thick. The roof covering is slate, topped by a square louver with a tented lead pyramidal roof, which at one time had a ball and pole finial (W19). The faces of the louver had leaded glazing,[278] but this was replaced by wooden slats before 1977 (S.50).

The heavy-framed, north-facing door is full-size, and the interior is octagonal with 475 holes in 17 tiers, each of four courses of bricks, from ground level. In the lowest tier the holes are plain, double-width openings with no enclosed inner space. The holes above are staggered and handed, and have alighting ledges made of pairs of plain brick headers. The plinth stone and beam for the revolving ladder are in place, but the ladder post has been lost since 1977 (S.50).

Within living memory there was a long metal pole which operated a trap.[279]

KENDERCHURCH:

Watkins included a pigeon house of unknown shape at Kenderchurch in his table of demolished buildings (W21).

KENTCHURCH:
Marshall notes that the post mortem inquisition, of 1300, into the estates of John de Tregoz identified in Kentchurch '… a messuage worth 12d, a garden 6d and a dovecot 18d by the year.'[280]

KENTCHURCH: Cart shed at Bannut Tree Farm (Listed Grade II,[281] Private)
This 18th- or 19th-century farm building has an eaves-cote at each end of the west-facing wall (which faces the fields in the next entry). The building is stone but the cotes are formed in brick. The holes are in three tiers (two of five holes under one of three holes). The bricks form a projecting grid which provides alighting ledges.

KENTCHURCH: Pigeon House Hill and Pigeon House Close
The names of fields numbered 398 and 400 on the tithe map of 1839. The former is a narrow wooded strip and the latter a large field, both to the north-west of Kentchurch Court.

KENTCHURCH: Pontrilas Court (Listed Grade II, Private)
The pigeon house stands between the 16th-century Court and the buildings of Court Farm. It is built into a walled bank so that it has a rubble stone basement on the Court side. The Royal Commission survey shows a walled enclosure on the lower side against the north wall, and there is a blocked window in the masonry of the pigeon house on that side.

The upper part is timber framed and probably dates from the 17th century. It is the largest of the timber frames in this survey: 17ft 3in (5.23m) square, six square panels wide and four high (Fig. 87). Most of the panels are formed with brick but this is probably not the original arrangement. The upper panels on the north side still appear to be plaster on daub.[282] At the eaves there is a deep cavetto plaster cornice, which takes up about a half of the top tier of framing. At the east side of the north wall two infill panels are joined together giving the appearance of a door into the upper chamber, however, all early photo-

Fig. 87 Pontrilas Court (Alfred Watkins Collection)

graphs show this to have been panelled in the same way as the walls as a whole. The stone basement, made of the local red stone, is 7ft (2.12m) high on the Court side and 1ft 5in (0.43m) thick. The door to the basement is on the west side, formed by a heavy, pegged and chamfered frame.

The roof is a truncated pyramid covered in stone slates surmounted by a square lantern with wooden louvers and an ogee lead cap. The present finial consisting of a wooden spike with a stone ball pre-dates 1927. In that year the lantern was glazed with six panes on each face, but had no obvious arrangement for birds to come and go;[283] this had been changed to the present arrangement by 1957.[284] The glazed lantern, and possibly the cornice, was probably part of a later 18th-century remodelling when the building had ceased to be used for keeping pigeons. Both the roof structure and the interior of the framed walls show a good deal of modern replacement and strengthening.

The nest boxes were in the upper, timber-framed part, but had been removed by 1977 (S. 27). There was a timber floor set just below the top of the masonry basement which is betrayed by the stub ends of the sawn off joists. A little above the upper floor, and resting on the masonry wall top, are the remains of the foundation timber for the nest boxes. Regularly set rectangular housings can be seen for the feet of the vertical battens which would have supported the tiers of nest boxes and ledges.

KIMBOLTON: Lower Hamnish
Watkins included a square timber-framed pigeon house at Lower Hamnish in his table of demolished buildings (W21).

Fig. 88 Stocktonbury

KIMBOLTON: Pigeon Close Orchard
The name of field numbered 1233 on the tithe map of 1841 to the south-east of the church of St Dubricius and All Saints.

KIMBOLTON: Stocktonbury (Listed Grade II*, Private, but the gardens and pigeon house are open to the public)[285]
Stocktonbury was the most valuable of the granges of Leominster Priory.[286] This presents the possibility that part of the stone drum, at least, is medieval.

The drum is 13ft 6in (4.12m) in diameter inside and the walls 3ft 1in (0.93m) thick. It is difficult to see the stonework outside because of a covering of ivy, but the thin beds of purplish local stone are visible around the low doorway which faces south-west (Fig. 88).

Stainburn (S.7) refers to a step halfway up, but a more obvious change takes place higher up inside. The nest holes start from the rubble stone floor and rise in 20 tiers of 27 holes, giving a total of 510 (the door and windows displace some holes). They are roughly L-shaped on plan and staggered and handed from tier to tier. Between each tier is a continuous, thin stone ledge; these ledges are bare whilst the walling is limewashed. In the lower 14 tiers the holes only take up half the height of the tier but, above that, the wall steps in and the tiers are compressed.[287] This probably marks a major repair scheme, perhaps in 1759 (see date of vane below) when the roof was replaced with the present one of relatively thin, sawn rafters with heavy laths to support the roof slates. Above the level of the step in the wall are four lancet windows. The revolving ladder remains intact inside.[288]

Fig. 89 Stocktonbury's revolving ladder and nests

The roof is a slate cone; in Watkins' photograph 'poverty slating' can be seen, with extra wide joints at the sides of the slates. The louver is hexagonal, open and with a slate roof surmounted by a vane with an arrow. Watkins says that the vane was dated 1759 (W15); the present arrow is decorated with the rebus of the owners.

In the 1887 sale particulars of the Berrington Hall estate,[289] only two of the many farms for sale had buildings for pigeons (see Eye, Lower Farm, Ashton above). At Stocktonbury the 'Dove Cote' is mentioned. In 1933 the Royal Commission surveyor noted: 'The owners fear that the building is deteriorating in condition and while they desire to preserve it as an ancient building do not wish to be put to much expense on repairs. They would be willing to give it into the custody of any recognised society for the sake of preservation. They have been informed that it dates from the 12th century.'[290]

KIMBOLTON: Upper Bache (Listed Grade II, Private, but visible from the Herefordshire Trail)

Upper Bache is high up in the little-visited hills to the north-east of Leominster. It is the most pleasing of the surviving square stone pigeon houses; freestanding, tall and four-gabled (Fig. 90). It is raised up on a 16ft (4.85m) square undercroft at the edge of a terrace. The door, on the north side, is above a short flight of stone steps, the cellar door faces east. Just below half way up each face there is a rectangular opening wooden ventilation slats.[291] In each gable is a sunk plain panel and that facing south holds a date stone. The

Fig. 90 Upper Bache, Kimbolton

Fig. 91 Upper Bache, Kimbolton: Interior

date is eroded away, but Watkins says it was 1747 (W16). The roof is stone slate and the louver square and supported on four corner posts. Until recently this had a four-gabled roof with a modern vane.[292]

The floor structure over the cellar appears to have been raised (there is a lower row of joist holes each side) and the lowest tier of nests is at floor level. The nests, 640 in all, are in regular tiers right up to the gable apexes, each tier has a continuous stone ledge (Fig. 91). The nest holes are placed one over another, but their interiors are handed from tier to tier. Given the relative thinness of the walls (1ft 10in (0.56m)), it is surprising that they are not more riven with vertical cracks. The roof structure follows the common pattern for four gables, with two principal purlins (in this case running north-south) and trimmed purlins spanning to the other gables. The long purlins support bearers for the louver, but the roof has been altered to cover over the entrance, and four ridges now join under the louver. This and the new floor suggest that the building was converted to use as a granary.

There is a central tie beam at the lowest level of the roof which has a hole like the pivot for a revolving ladder seen, quite often, in round and octagonal dovecotes – see Brockhampton Park above for the only extant example in a square dovecote in Herefordshire. As at Brockhampton, the nests in the corners would have been difficult to reach.

Pigeon House Croft and Pigeon House Orchard are the names of fields numbered 975 and 1044 on the tithe map of 1841, to the north and west of the pigeon house.

KINGSLAND: Pigeon House Orchard
The name of field numbered 1022 on the tithe map of 1841 to the west of Street Court.

KING'S CAPLE: Aramstone

The house at Aramstone, of *c*.1730, was 'the most important house of its date in the county'.[293] It was demolished in 1959. Its appurtenances were listed in an advertisement in the *Hereford Journal* of 12 December 1792: 'Two large granaries, a Dove-house, a large garden …'.[294] The early editions of the large scale Ordnance Survey maps show a small square building to the south-east of the house.

KING'S CAPLE: Court (Private, but visible from public road)

This 15ft (4.55m) square pigeon house is built in two stages (Fig. 92). The lower, and larger, part is rubble stone and the upper part is red brick laid in Flemish bond. It is roofless, but Cohen's photograph shows a pyramidal stone slate roof with a square louver with two layers of alighting boards. The top was pyramidal with a claw-shaped vane (W16) and was probably covered with lead. The eaves were formed by a sloping soffit board.

Watkins says there was an upper loft which is marked by the door high up on the south side. The nests were in wooden boxes, since there are no holes in the masonry.

The building's decline began with its conversion to a silo which probably necessitated the addition of the girding of steel tie rods visible today.

Fig. 92 King's Caple Court's dovecote photographed by Israel Cohen in 1957

KING'S CAPLE: Much Fawley

An inventory of 1603 records, 'a garden beneath the parlour, a pigeon house, a cockshoot and a park'.[294]

KING'S CAPLE: Upper Penalt (Listed Grade II, Private)

In the north-east gable of the stables is a blind opening with four tiers of three nest holes. The building is dated 1701.[296]

KING'S PYON: Brook House[297] (Listed Grade II, Private, but visible from the road)

The Brook House pigeon house is 14ft 3in (4.33m) square and consists of a timber-framed structure built over a semi-basement. The basement stage is of stone and the upper stage

Fig. 93 King's Pyon, Brook House

Fig. 94 Interior of King's Pyon Brook House showing the nest boxes

is of closely framed, slender timbers with two long diagonal braces in each stage (Fig. 93). The infilling is of brick. On the north and south sides, the basement has two original doors with ventilation slots. The floor frame over it is formed by a stout, unchamfered spine beam with joists fixed by soffit tenons.

The relatively flimsy, storey height framing is typical of the later 18th century; the RCHM inspector noted: 'The building may be of early 18th century date but this is rather doubtful.'[298] The timber-framed part is reached by an external stone stair under which is a void, with a small door, which was probably the kennel for a terrier. A floor has been inserted into the upper stage leaving headroom of barely 6ft (1.8m) in the middle stage. It is likely that this upper, framed part was previously a single space completely lined with nests. The nest boxes, numbering about 500, are now only in the topmost stage. They are framed up in wood boards with diagonal partitions between the nests (see Fig. 94): the tiers are 1ft 4in (0.4m) deep and 10 inches (0.254m) high.

The pyramidal roof is covered with Welsh slate with lead hip rolls and is surmounted by a square lantern. The lantern is a modern replacement; it repeats the 16 panes of glass on each face seen in earlier photographs but the slot at the bottom, the birds' doorway, has been omitted. The lantern roof is also a slate pyramid; the finial, a turned baluster on earlier photographs, is now decayed.

KING'S PYON: Gate House at The Buttas (Listed Grade II, Private but visible from the end of the public road)

The inclusion of this building in the earlier surveys of dovecotes in amongst the timber-framed pigeon houses is questionable.[299] Pigeons were kept here, that is clear from the survival of a small part of the lining of nest boxes in the upper chamber, but this was first and foremost a gatehouse, similar to that at Lower Brockhampton by Bromyard.[300] The building is dated 1632, only nine years after an inventory of the demesne farm was drawn up which included 'a good pigeon house of stone'.[301] This suggests that there was probably no need to build a pigeon house in 1632. Today, the building stands in isolation – a gatehouse that can be by-passed, but it was previously set in walls that enclosed the house.[302] There are other legends concerning its use as a falconry mews, but no reliable evidence is advanced for this.

Fig. 95 The Buttas, King's Pyon in 1904

It is a very pretty building (Fig. 95); the plan is slightly oblong, 10ft 10in (3.3m) x 11ft 2in (3.4m) at the lower level, with a jetty all round and highly decorative framing on the elevations which hold the doors – it was designed to impress visitors. The date 1632 is found over the entrance with the initials KGE for George and Elizabeth Karver. The floor frame over the entrance way is finely formed by a principal transverse beam into which are jointed four dragon beams which all have chamfers with ogee stops.

KING'S PYON: Pidgeon House Orchard, Wistaston

The name of field number 228 on the undated tithe map (Apportionment dated 1838), to the south-east of Wistaston.

KINGSTONE: Pigeon Close

The name of field 243 on the tithe map of 1840 forming a small narrow strip to the southwest of Whitehouse Farm.

Fig. 96 Lea, Castle End

Fig. 97 Lea, Castle End: Interior

LEA: Castle End (Listed Grade II, Private)
The Castle End pigeon house is the only octagonal stone building in this survey which has nest holes (see Homme House, Much Marcle below); it is also one of the smallest buildings in this survey, with facets of only 5ft (1.52m). It is built of the local red rubble stone with large, dressed quoin stones (Fig. 96). There is a low door on the east side, a blocked doorway on the west, and a door to the upper level facing south, towards the house. This south doorway has a modern arrangement of holes with ledges for the use of the white doves which are the present occupants. On the north side a small lancet lights the lower storey.[303] The roof is covered with clay plain tiles with lead hip rolls. The lantern had already been lost when Watkins photographed it in the 1880s.[304] There are holes about 1ft below the eaves which were probably the seating for brackets supporting a perching ledge.

The interior is circular and lined with brick; the tiers, three courses deep, are separated by continuous stone ledges (Fig. 97); they are staggered and (presumably) handed from tier to tier. There was a floor about seven feet above ground level[305] and a revolving ladder serving the 180 nest holes (W19).

This building has generally been given a late 17th-century date. In this case the two storey arrangement is original; nest holes do not appear in the lower storey and there is a separate entrance to the upper floor.[306] The lower doors do not face the house, or form part of a garden setting, which rules out an intended garden room, although it could have been a gardener's store. These elements suggest this building was built or at least re-lined inside[307] at a much later date, possibly as a response to the spread of brown rats after about 1730.

LEDBURY: Glebe
The glebe terrier of 1616 records a 'pigeon house with wayne house'.[308]

105

LEDBURY: Hilltop

'In 1598 Richard Hooper had been given a licence to build a dovecote but was not listed in the tithe book until 1601, and did not pay birds until 1603, building up to 18 in 1606. Hilltop was later rebuilt without a dovecote.'[309] The numbers of birds suggest a box-cote rather than a pigeon house.

LEDBURY: Mr Biddulph's Lodge (Listed Grade II, Private house)

This oblong 9ft 9in (2.96m) x 12ft (3.64m)) brick pigeon house had been converted to a 'cottage' before Watkins' survey (W18) (Fig. 98). It stands in a prominent position at the north end of Ledbury (Newhouse) Park, on the road frontage. It is made of a dark, rough brick laid in an irregular Flemish bond in which every fifth course is mainly headers. The façades are modelled with sunk panels, edged with chamfered bricks, which give the impression of corner piers. The pyramidal plain-tile roof rises from a strong and unusually elaborate modillion cornice to an ogee lead cap with an arrow vane. These features suggest a late 17th-century date, perhaps just after 1680 when the eponymous Anthony Biddulph acquired the Park through marriage.[310] On the east side is a massive chimney, inserted when the cottage was formed.

Fig. 98 Mr Biddulph's Lodge, Ledbury

LEDBURY: Pigeon Close, Massington Farm

The name of field 169 on the tithe map of 1841 to the south-west of Massington Farm.

LEDBURY: Pigeon Close, Orlham Farm

The name of field 1319 on the tithe map of 1841 to the south-east of Orlham Farm.

LEDBURY: St Katherine's Chapel (Listed Grade II*, Visible from adjacent car park)

The timber-framed west gable has a pedimented wooden box-cote with nine round-headed nest holes. Three of the gable's frame rails have perching boards on brackets.

LEDBURY: Underdown Park

Underdown, to the south of the town, was a gentry estate in the 17th century.[311] Watkins included a pigeon house of unknown shape at Underdown in his table of demolished buildings (W22).

LEINTWARDINE: Pigeon House Close, Heath House

The tithe map of 1847 shows a large field, on both sides of the Hopton Heath to Bedstone lane, to the north and north-west of Heath House. The full title of this field, number 1131, is 'Pigeon House Close with cottage and garden', the 'cottage' being Broadward Cottage.

LEOMINSTER: Barn and Granary at Brierley Court (Listed Grade II, Private, converted to dwellings)

The farm buildings at Brierley Court are numerous and illustrate the evolution and diversity of farming in this part of Herefordshire.[312] Part of that diversity was the keeping of pigeons, not in this case in a pigeon house, but in an eaves-cote and two gable-cotes in the stone walls of farm buildings.

Fig. 99 Brierley Court eaves-cote

To the north of the house is a large barn, which the statutory list describes as 17th and 18th century, made predominantly of the purplish local stone. In the east elevation, under the eaves, are three tiers of nest holes with continuous stone ledges (40 holes in all) (Fig. 99). The stonework around the holes retains lime render, applied to increase the comfort of the occupants exposed to the east wind. This elevation, with its triangular and lancet ventilation slits below the nests holes, has a very pleasing appearance. The south gable of the barn also has nest holes, in eleven tiers (55 holes in all) (Fig. 100). There is no evidence of plaster here, and the stone is much more weathered.

To the east of the house is an 18th-century granary, also built of the local stone, which has nest holes in its south-facing gable.

Fig. 100 Brierley Court gable-cote

LEOMINSTER: Broadward Hall

Watkins missed this now demolished square timber-framed pigeon house. The Royal Commission inspector visited in 1933 and described it (Fig. 101):

When the gardens were remodelled with the building or rebuilding of the house, the east side (of the pigeon house) was re-fronted in red brick as part of the garden wall, and part of the lower storey was adapted for use as a garden house or arbour. The cote is gabled on its north and south sides and is of timber framing on its three unaltered sides (north, south and west), and the east side has also a gable of *c*.1730-40 with a door and, in the head, a bulls-eye window. On the roof is an original hexagonal lantern with segmental arches, open sides and shaped angle posts: it has a curvilinear leaded roof. On a door in the middle of the west side is a burnt inscription HH 1652: the initials may be those of a local carpenter or builder (see also St Oswald's Cholstrey in this parish). In the upper storey are wooden nests against the west wall, later brick nests in the east wall: more on the other walls.[313]

Fig. 101 Broadward Hall, Leominster (National Monuments Record)

The RCHM photograph shows a central door to the upper loft, but it is not clear whether this floor was part of the original design or inserted later. The brick nogging looks uniform, and might well be a feature of the original design.

In 1933 the condition of the building was described as 'poor' and Stainburn suggests it was demolished in about 1938 (S.TII.9).

LEOMINSTER: Cholstrey, Pigeon House Meadow
The name of a long thin field to the east of Cholstrey, numbered 100 on the tithe map of 1850. Primrose Bank is adjacent to the southern end of the field.

LEOMINSTER: Eaton Hall
A 17th-century rental refers to two pigeon houses at Eaton Hall.[314] The field to the east of the Hall, numbered 1354 on the tithe map of 1850 is named 'Pigeon House Orchard'. Eaton Hall Cottages are at the southern end of the field.

LEOMINSTER: Ebnall (Listed Grade II, Private)
The south-east facing elevation of the 17th-century farmhouse has an eaves-cote with ten pigeon holes, some with alighting ledges.[315]

LEOMINSTER: Ivington Court, Pigeon House Meadow
The name of the field to the east of Ivington Court, numbered 712 on the tithe map of 1850.

LEOMINSTER: Knoake's Court, Coldharbour
Watkins included a square timber-framed dovecote (pigeon house) at Knoake's Court in his table of demolished buildings (W21). He gives no details beyond its likely date of demolition *c*.1870.

LEOMINSTER: The Grange
Joe and Caroline Hillaby recorded the presence of dovecotes in the Grange in the fine history of Leominster Priory. 'Here, in what the records refer to as the Grange, were all the buildings one associates with such a place; barns, stables, brewhouse, bakehouse, smithy, wain sheds, pig styes, stock yard, dovecotes, a mill ...'.[316]

LEOMINSTER: The Hyde,[317] Hyde Ash
The site of an octagonal pigeon house in Watkins' table of demolished buildings (W21). The building is not shown on the earliest Ordnance Survey sheet, *c*.1890.

LEOMINSTER: Pigeon House Close
The name of a field numbered 136 on a plan of 1832, to the west of the old course of the Pinsley Brook. Oldfields Close occupies the centre of the field.[318]

LEOMINSTER: Upper Wintercott[319]
Watkins included a square timber-framed dovecote (pigeon house) at Upper Wintercott in his table of demolished buildings (W21). He gave no details beyond the likely date of demolition in 1870.

LETTON: Pigeon House Farm
Watkins records a demolished pigeon house of unknown shape at Pigeon House Farm, Letton and adds the note 'Near the rail is a tump called Pigeon House Tump'.[320] So far, the locations of the farm and the tump have not been found on any edition of the Ordnance Survey.

LEYSTERS: Great Heath (Private, but visible from the road)
Gable-cote of 18 holes in five tiers. Each tier has a continuous ledge formed by a thin slab of the local stone, on which are two courses of red bricks containing the nest holes. Above the brickwork in each tier are three courses of the thin bedded local stone.

LEYSTERS: Pigeon House Meadow

The name of a field numbered 426 on the tithe map of 1842, immediately south of Cinders.

LEYSTERS: Woonton Court (Listed Grade II, Private)

The north-facing stone gable of a late 17th-century range has a gable-cote of seven tiers. The holes are square and have individual stone alighting ledges. A window has been inserted leaving 24 holes.[321]

LINTON BY ROSS: Eccleswall Court (Private)

At first glance the sight of lancet windows in a tall stone tower might indicate an early date for this building. The site is ancient, and it has been suggested that the tower is a remnant of the chapel of Thomas the Martyr which served the (demolished) Eccleswall Castle.[322]

It is, however, more likely that the building is of the early 19th century. It forms part of a group of stone farm buildings, some with similar quoins and coursing, and some which also have Gothic details. The farmhouse is of 19th-century date, and it appears likely that the whole complex was redeveloped at the same time. Added to this, the walls of the building are only 1ft 5in (0.43m) thick, which would be uncharacteristic of mediaeval towers with 'first pointed' windows. The masonry round the windows looks too little weathered, and their detailing, with internal, straight timber lintels, looks too modern to support an early date of building. Old material has been re-used, including a carved man's head in a basinet at the crown of the flat segmental arch over the entrance.[323]

The tower is 13ft (3.94m) square, and the pigeon house is a single volume occupying the two upper storeys as defined by the lancet windows (Fig. 102). There were '640' nests[324] of which about 130 remain. One bank of 100 holes occupies the upper half of the two storeys and is supported off stout timber putlogs (Fig. 103). The tiers are divided by 1 inch thick boards on which battens are planted to form lips (recommended by some 18th-century writers on husbandry to stop the eggs rolling out). The vertical divisions are also 1 inch boards, but the few

Fig. 102 Eccleswall Court, Linton by Ross

110

surviving front panels, nailed to the uprights on one side, are thinner.

The pyramidal roof is covered with corrugated sheets and the lantern, which Watkins unhelpfully described as 'plain', has gone. The roof structure is unusual in that the hip rafters are thin and the principal supports are two crossed open-apex trusses supported at the mid points of the walls. A ring of butt-purlins is formed about two thirds of the way up which supports the rafters spanning from the plate to a thin collar forming the opening for the lost lantern.

Fig. 103 Eccleswall Court, Linton by Ross: Interior with nest boxes

LINTON BY ROSS: Glebe
The glebe terrier of 1615 records: 'There is one dwellinge house with all necessary roomes belonginge thereunto. One stable, iii barnes, a beastes house, sheapcoat and garden; ye pigeon house was decayed in ye owld vicars tyme and is not yet renued.'[325]

LITTLE HEREFORD: Upper House Farm (Listed Grade II, Private)
The north-facing brick gable of a late 18th-century or early 19th-century wing has a gable-cote of six tiers with 21 nest holes. The holes have triangular heads and individual alighting ledges formed by three header bricks.

LLANDINABO: Hoarwithy Mill (Private)
Watkins (W18) recorded a 12ft (3.64m) square brick building with a pyramidal roof and a square lantern, that has since been demolished. The pigeon holes were in an upper loft, which probably denotes a later 18th-century date, which is supported by the large size of the bricks in the illustration by Stainburn (S40). The building stood to the north of the Mill House in a range of outbuildings. Stainburn showed a building reduced in height with a mono-pitch roof, and noted that most of the nest holes were destroyed, but that they still had stone ledges.

LLANDINABO: Llandinabo Court (Listed Grade II, Private)
This is one of the few buildings to which entry could not be obtained in this survey. It is an unfortunate omission because it is not certain whether this building is a pigeon house. It has marked similarities to the nearest standing pigeon house at Pencoyd but this building was not included by Watkins, although its position close to the main Ross to Hereford road means that it is hardly likely that he had not seen it. Marshall's notes include a photograph and the following, '? if a pigeon house but I understand from the

farmer that it had been perhaps a hopkiln or malthouse. Not a pigeon house.'

This omission and later comments are odd because Stainburn (S23) gives a detailed description of a 12ft (3.64m) square stone pigeon house with a brick-lined upper loft with 'approx. 175 holes'. The roof is shown, as now, with a pyramidal slate roof with a square, louvered lantern with a pyramidal top and weathercock. He remarked that 'The roof and lantern are of recent construction. It is said that the original roof was single span without a

Fig. 104 Llandinabo Court photographed by George Marshall

lantern. Access to the loft was by the open lower front (now closed). The building is part of a range of formerly open fronted byres with cylindrical stone columns.'

The statutory list describes the building as a dovecote.[326] The photograph on the ImagesofEngland website shows an arrangement of three external holes on a ledge some distance below the eaves on the north side, which are not visible in Marshall's photograph of 1903 (Fig. 104).

LLANGARRON: Building to the east of Biddlestone Farmhouse (Listed Grade II, Private)
The Royal Commission included this building in its survey as a late 17th-century pigeon house or summer house[327] but it is omitted by Watkins and Stainburn, and the Statutory List describes it as a 'summer house'. The building, of local rubble stone, is rectangular on plan (about 24ft x 15ft) and single storey with an undercroft (Fig. 105). This form must cast doubt on whether it was a dovecote, and when the RCHM surveyor visited in 1930 there was no evidence of nest boxes. Against this, the location of the building, standing alone and in the public view, might suggest a dovecote. The slate roof is modern and without a lantern, which could denote that the building has been lowered and re-roofed. This might also have been a granary with a pigeon loft in the roof (see Figs. 70 and 71).

Fig. 105 Biddlestone Farm, Llangarron

LLANGARRON: Kilreague Farm (Private, but visible from the road)

There are three stages in the construction of this square stone building. It started as a 9ft (2.73m) square single storey privy with gables facing the house and the road (Fig. 106). The outlines of the gables are visible as straight, sloping joints in the masonry. The privy was entered from, and at the level of, the garden. There is also an access hole, which was used for cleaning out, on the road side, below the floor level. The masonry was extended up to form the dovecote. Stainburn says that there were '100 holes in upper loft only, now all blocked' (S.10) but none are visible now. Often there is an upper door to allow access to a loft and to allow the removal of the manure, but none exists here.[328] The decorative intent of the dovecote builders is expressed in a pretty Gothic widow facing the house. The dovecote was subsequently raised a further few courses in very narrow beds and converted to a water tower. The pyramidal slate roof may reflect the form of the previous dovecote roof.[329]

Fig. 106 Kilreague, Llangarron

LLANGARRON: Stable at Little Bernithan (Listed Grade II, Private)

Gable-cote of five tiers with alighting ledges.[330]

LLANGARRON: Llangarren Court (Listed Grade II, Private, but visible from the road)

The pigeon house stands opposite the front of the Court, across the lane to Langstone. It is built from fiery red brick laid in Flemish bond, in contrast to the stone of the Court and farm buildings. The 12ft (3.64m) square[331] brick structure is without orna- ment[332] except for the unusual arrangement of external entrance holes on the south side, facing the house (Fig. 107). Seven brick courses below the eaves there are two tiers of seven holes on continuous stone ledges. These were the entrances for the pigeons, carefully placed to exploit their decorative qualities in the view from the Court.

Fig. 107 Llangarren Court photographed by Israel Cohen in 1958

The slate roof is pyramidal with lead hips. The lantern was elegant, with four panes on each face divided by fine glazing bars.[333] The lead roof of the louver was tented, and surmounted by a ball finial and a vane with a 'huntsman' (S.44). Cohen's picture does not show an entry slit at the base of the louver, which would be typical of others of the lantern type; in this case the holes referred to above made it unnecessary.

The pigeons were confined to an upper loft, which their keepers reached by a stair on the north side. The lower floor was probably used as a store; its door is also on the north side and there is a window low down on the south side (now covered in ivy). There are no nest holes or boxes now. It is probable that this example was built in the second half of the 18th century if only because the upper loft expresses concern about the vulnerability of nest holes near the ground to brown rats.

LLANGARRON: Manse at Llangrove
Stainburn included a two-storey oblong stone building with a lantern and trap in his survey, under the heading of 'pigeon lofts with lanterns projecting above buildings'. He noted that there was no evidence of nest boxes (S.74).

LLANGARRON: Pigeon House Close and Pigeon House Orchard, Treverven
The names of fields numbered 194 and 190 on the tithe map of 1840 to the north of Treverven. On earlier editions of the Ordnance Survey, the more easterly field (190) by the Parkmill Lane is shown as an orchard.

LLANGARRON: Pigeon House Close, Trereece
The name of a field numbered 434 on the tithe map of 1840 to the east of Trereece. The field is bounded on three sides by a meander of the Garren Brook. This is an interesting example of a field name site which is far from the farmstead, and surrounded on three sides by the land of neighbours. The fact that the pigeon house is lost out of memory illustrates the impracticality of unsupervised sites and, perhaps, poetic justice in the possibility that the brown rat put paid to the pigeon houses remotely placed to take as much as possible from the surrounding land of other owners.

LLANROTHAL: Llanrothal Court (Listed Grade II, Private)
The stone-built south-west gable of the house has four tiers of five nest holes on projecting stone ledges. The Royal Commission photograph of 1930 shows an interesting box-cote on the north-facing wall of the same wing.[334] This structure, supported on two large brackets, appears to have two tiers of nests with continuous alighting ledges. Part of the face is plastered. A charming detail is a cat hole in the door below the box-cote.

LLANWARNE: Tower of Church of St John the Baptist (Listed Grade II*, Tower not open to the public)
Marshall notes that:

In the ringing chamber of the tower (14th century) are square holes in the wall; 3 on either side of the window in the west wall, one above another, and two on either side of the windows in the south and east wall, 14 in all, none in the north wall (I think this is correct).[335] They are of about the usual size and enlarge inside, generally a little to the right, very rough inside. They are undoubtedly pigeon holes but rough ones ... There are two in the bell chamber but these are of different character and not pigeon holes.[336] (Fig. 108).

Fig. 108 Llanwarne Old Church:
Some of the 'nest holes' in the ringing chamber

These holes could be for pigeons; there are no alighting ledges, as at Sarnesfield where the arrangement is much more obviously like a dovecote, but there are many examples, outside Herefordshire, of dovecotes without ledges. It does, however, seem odd to have so few holes and to have distributed them so widely, which would have increased the labour of looking after them and keeping the tower chamber clean, and for little return. The holes in the belfry, and the many holes which are visible on the exterior and interior of the church, do not appear significantly different in size and shape, and it is possible that all of the holes were some form of putlog hole.[337]

LLANWARNE: Gable-cote at Lower Monkton
A 19th-century range of pigsties has a gable-cote at its east end. The walling is made of unusually large red bricks built over earlier rubble masonry. The gable has four tiers of nest holes, two courses deep, on continuous, thin stone ledges; there are ten holes (Fig. 109).

LLANWARNE: Pigeon House Field and Pigeon House Meadow, Lower Monkton
The names of fields numbered 212 and 216 on the tithe map of 1840, immediately south and east of Lower Monkton. Lower Monkton was owned by Llanthony Abbey and is described in a valuation in 1535, prior to the abbey being dissolved. In this document there is a field called Culverhouse

Fig. 109 Gable-cote at Lower Monkton, Llanwarne

Furlong. The southern of the two tithe map fields was investigated in 1992 and excavation uncovered the base of a round stone pigeon house: 'Its size points to its medieval monastic ownership.'[338]

LONGTOWN: Pigeon House Meadow

The field north of the Crown Inn (in the V between two roads), so named in the 1840 tithe award and numbered 1045. An archaeological investigation of the area found numerous building platforms but no identifiable remains of a pigeon house.[339]

LOWER BULLINGHAM: Lower Bullingham Farm

Watkins included a square timber-framed dovecote at Lower Bullingham Farm in his table of demolished buildings (W21).

LUGWARDINE: Wilcroft

Wilcroft 'was regarded as a capital mansion', with gardens and a park in the 18th century.[340] Watkins' father died at Wilcroft in 1880, but it is not certain that this is the site of an 11ft 3in (3.43m) square, timber-framed pigeon house listed by Watkins in his table of demolished buildings (W17). It had a pyramidal roof with a square lantern. The nest holes rose from ground level.

It is unlikely that the Royal Commission would have excluded a timber-framed pigeon house, so it must have been demolished before the survey in 1932. Mysteriously, there was reference to an 'ornamental dovecote' in sale particulars of 1976, but it was not illustrated.[341]

LUSTON: Lustonbury

An account of the property of Leominster Priory in 1327 included a 'Dove House eighteen pence.' The exact location cannot be inferred from the text, but Lustonbury must be the most likely place, given that a pigeon house was standard kit at monastic granges.[342]

MADLEY: Canon Bridge House (Private)

The pigeon house stands to the south of the early 18th-century mansion, against the wall between the garden and the farmyard. It is 11ft (3.33m) square and built of brick, laid in an irregular bond with a predominance of stretchers (Fig. 110). A string course deline-

Fig. 110 Canon Bridge House, Madley

ates the level of a floor just under half way up, and the walls are topped with an elaborate corbelled brick cornice with dogtooth decoration. The roof is a simple slate pyramid. There was a door on the south side, now blocked (S.37), and the entrance is now on the north side, towards the house. There are no other openings; the 'square' lantern seen by Watkins was removed when the building was adapted to take water tanks.[343] Watkins also noted that the walls were 1ft 10in (0.56m) thick and that there was a vane with a fox.[344]

The interior was not seen in this survey. Watkins says that the nest holes were 'to the ground' (W17), but the present owner suggested that the holes, with individual brick alighting ledges, were at the upper level only. Stainburn says there were 'approximately 200 with brick ledges', which suggests there was only an upper loft. This is probably a later 18th-century example, but until a detailed survey of the interior can be made any dating must be tentative.

MADLEY: Field's Place Farm (Listed Grade II, Private, converted to a house with adjoining barns)

Fig. 111 Field's Place, Madley photographed by Israel Cohen (undated)

This 20ft square brick building consisted of a granary, with a timber floor five steps above ground level and, at first-floor level, a pigeon house entered by an external stair (S.36) (Fig. 111 and Fig. 71). The exterior brickwork is decorated with over-burnt header bricks forming a pattern at the quoins and on a string/perching course about half way up. There is also a large lozenge outlined with burnt bricks on the upper stage of the east and south elevations.

The roof is a simple pyramid with a square lantern, which also has a pyramidal roof. In Cohen's picture the roofs are covered with stone slate and the lantern is glazed with four panes on each face. Today, the lantern is boarded and the roofs covered in Welsh slate. There is still a vane with a fiery serpent.

The interior had nest holes at first-floor level, which numbered about 500.[345] This is probably a later 18th-century example, but could be a two-storey design for a dual purpose building of an earlier date.

MADLEY: Pigeon House Orchard

There was a corn mill to the north-east of Fields Place, close to the River Wye. Pigeon House Orchard is a small field to the north-east of the mill site bounded by a meander in the leat.

*Fig. 112 Upper Chilstone, Madley
photographed by Israel Cohen in 1957*

*Fig. 113 Webton Court, Madley
(Alfred Watkins Collection)*

MADLEY: Upper Chilstone
Stainburn illustrated a substantial timber-framed and weatherboarded loft which was slung between two barns (S.72)(W20). Cohen's photograph shows more of its form (Fig. 112); it had a square, glazed lantern with eight panes on each face and a pyramidal roof surmounted by a vane.

MADLEY: Webton Court
Watkins recorded a 14ft square pigeon house with a two-gabled, plain-tile roof and a square louver, that has since been demolished (W16) (Fig. 113). He placed this building in his table of square stone dovecotes, but only the plinth was rubble stone and the greater part of the walling was brick. His photograph[346] shows the louver with small-paned glazing. A sloping board sheltered the opening at the base of the louver. The door was in one of the gabled walls; there was a slatted opening in the gable over it. The nests were in an upper loft only. The Royal Commission survey of 1931 does not include this building, which was therefore probably demolished by that date.

MANSELL LACY: Gatehouse at Court Farm (Listed Grade II, Private, but visible from adjacent road)
Watkins photographed this building in the 1890s when it must have been quite new.[347] His picture shows a square, timber-framed structure standing on four massive brick piers. The large windows in the main chamber suggest that intensive production was not an objective.

The pyramidal tile roof is set on a cornice of shaped brackets and carries a square

lantern, which originally had large openings in the faces and smaller holes below the eaves of its pyramidal roof. When Cohen visited in the 1950s the lantern was missing; it has been restored as part of the recent residential conversion scheme. There is no firm evidence that pigeons were ever kept here.

MANSELL LACY: Former Post Office
(Listed Grade II, Private, but visible from adjacent road)

The gable-cote at the Post Office is well known by illustrations inspired by its undeniable rural charm (Fig. 115), but there is also a second building of interest alongside it, which is not so celebrated.

Fig. 114 Gatehouse at Court Farm (photographed by Israel Cohen in the 1950s

The gable-cote is prominently displayed on the south-facing stone cross-wing of the mainly timber-framed cottage. There are three tiers above the ground-floor openings, two further tiers divided by the first-floor window and two further tiers in the gable apex; making 38 holes in all. The alighting ledges are continuous beds of the local stone, and stone slabs set on edge form the fronts of the nests. It is the scale of the elements, the relatively large holes and thick ledges that make a strong impression.

In the garden, to the east, is the 9ft square, stone base of a freestanding pigeon house. The lost upper part was timber-framed and four-gabled.[348]

Fig. 115 Mansell Lacy Old Post Office photographed by Israel Cohen in 1958

MANSELL LACY: Parsonage Farm (Listed Grade II, Private)
The building has 'Thin horizontal slits with three nesting holes to each gable.'[349]

*Fig. 116 Wisteston Court, Marden
(Alfred Watkins Collection)*

Fig. 117 Glewstone Court, Marstow

MARDEN: Amberley Court
Amberley Court is an exceptionally important example of a 14th-century hall house. Watkins recorded a round stone pigeon house that was demolished in about 1840 (W21).

MARDEN: Pigeon House Meadows, Pigeon House Orchard and Pigeon House Orchard, Wisteston Court
The names of three fields numbered 397, 399 and 401 on the tithe map of 1840, to the east of the site of Wisteston Court.

MARDEN: Wisteston Court
The Court, now demolished, was a house of the 15th century and later. In the collection of Watkins' photographs (Fig. 116) is one labelled 'Wisteston Court Dovecote'.[350] It shows an L-shaped brick outbuilding attached to a corner of the Court by its short leg. Over the wide, one and a half storey gable at the end of this short leg of the L is an open louver with a pyramidal roof. This is surmounted by a very grand iron vane with elaborate decoration round the cardinals and a cockerel for the finial.

Watkins also recorded a round stone pigeon house, lined with brick, that was demolished in 1872 (W21).

MARSTOW: (south-west of) Glewstone Court
(Listed Grade II, Private, part of a house)
This 10ft (3.03m) square stone pigeon house was first identified in the statutory list.[351] There is little to betray its original purpose other than its form, and the door at first-floor level (Fig. 117). It has lost its roof and lantern, and also

the entry holes, which are described in the statutory list as being in two rows in the upper window on the east side. It has been altered by the addition of concrete battlements. It is likely that this example had an upper loft only. The statutory list suggests an 18th-century date.

MARSTOW: Holly Mount Farm, Glewstone (Private)
A relatively small square stone tower with a pyramidal roof, but no louver, appears to be a possible pigeon house. It is now converted to a house and is unlikely to yield further evidence. It is not included in earlier surveys.

MARSTOW: Outbuilding south of Marstow Court (Listed Grade II, Private)
Against the gable at one end of this late 18th-century stone building is a lean-to. Just below the point where the lean-to roof meets the gable is a single hole that the statutory list describes as 'a dressed stone triangular-headed opening to a small pigeon loft'.[352] This is probably an owl hole rather than a pigeonhole. Owl holes are much more common in the south of the county; they are more usually seen in the gables of barns.

MARSTOW: Pigeon House and Pigeon House Field
The name of a farm and irregularly shaped field to the south of it, numbered 89 on the tithe map of 1838. These sites are to the east of the Hereford road about half a mile north of Marstow Court. Watkins listed, at Pigeon House, a pigeon house of unknown shape in his table of buildings 'now pulled down' (W22).

MATHON: South Hyde Farm (Listed Grade II, Private)
The barn to the north-west of the house had an attached stable with, presumably, a gable-cote with '3 tiers of 6 holes'.[353]

MIDDLETON ON THE HILL: Moor Abbey (Listed Grade II, Private, but distant views from public paths)
Moor Abbey lies in a deep groove in the high plateau between Leominster and Tenbury. The farmyard is one of the most impressive in this survey, dominated by the big, H-shaped house[354] and enclosed by barns uniformly made of the local stone. Here are mud, muck, cattle, sheep and dogs; it is a working place, a beautiful and inspiring place, and a rare survival of what rural Herefordshire was before the age of barn conversions. At one time this range of buildings was unique in having three kinds of dovecote: the pigeon house, a gable-cote and a box-cote.[355]

The pigeon house is said to have been built in the 17th century, at the end of an oblong range which had an upper floor throughout, reached by a stair at the gable end furthest from the pigeons (Fig. 118).[356] This was extended to form an L-shaped range, and a barn was added to the north-east side engaging it. The four-gabled form is based on a rectangular plan of 18ft 6in (5.61m) x 20ft (6.06m) and has relatively thin, 1ft 6in (0.45m), walls which required the use of wooden nest boxes. The pigeon house appears to have always

been on the upper floor only, and is entered by a fine, heavy-framed door from the adjacent loft. The floor is made of stone slabs which span between six massive logs that are wrought only on their upper surfaces. The principal roof timbers are also unwrought, and consist of two tiers of purlins running parallel with the front (farm-yard wall) crossed by a tier of perpendicular purlins at the upper level. The perpendicular purlins at the lower level are trimmed. There is no evidence of a louver; the plain spike finial has been in place since the 1930s at which time it also had a vane.[357] The mullion windows were clearly the way for the pigeons to come and go.

A significant survival, although now all but derelict, is the lining of timber nest boxes (Fig. 119). They show a different arrangement to other survivals, notably at Brook House, King's Pyon (Fig. 94) and Luntley Court, Pembridge (Fig. 56). The shelves are supported on upright battens, which are housed into the front and back edges of the shelves. The vertical battens are spaced at

Figs. 118 and 119 Moor Abbey, Middleton on the Hill, showing the louver and the box-cote which have been removed (Alfred Watkins Collection), and interior showing nest boxes

half the width of the nest boxes. Horizontal fillets, some of which are triangular in section, are fitted in front of the edge of each shelf, and between these are fitted boards in every other of the rectangles formed by the shelves and uprights. These make, alternately, the nest holes and the fronts of the enclosures, which are divided one from another by thin boards forming partitions. There were probably about 250 nest boxes.

The nesting capacity of the range of buildings was increased by the insertion of nest holes in the gable end furthest from the pigeon house, over the external stair, and by an external triangular wooden box-cote with six nests on the farmyard side of the pigeon house. The wooden cote has gone.[358]

The 17th-century date given to this example is difficult to sustain without any specific dating features and there is nothing to distinguish the stonework from, say, Upper Bache, Kimbolton which is dated 1747.

If anywhere cries out for the revival of adequately funded historic buildings grant schemes it is here. The upkeep of these extensive and exceptionally important buildings must be an impossible task on a farm income.

MIDDLETON ON THE HILL: Nurton Court (Private, converted to a house) and field names

Nurton Court is one of those late Georgian, three-storey, red-brick farmhouses that Herefordshire does so well. The extensive farm buildings to the north of the house may have had earlier origins, and in this group Watkins found one of the largest square stone pigeon houses in his survey (Fig. 120).[359] It was 20ft (6.06m) square with 2ft 8in (0.81m) thick walls and had 850 nest holes. The roof had two gables and a square louver with a serpentine claw finial. The walls had two string/perching courses and three windows. Watkins gave the date of the old house, 1631, as if to suggest that the pigeon house was of the same date.

Stainburn's survey included a picture of a single-storey cow byre which was thought to be the much reduced remains of the pigeon house (S.14). He notes that the nest holes had been obliterated. It is difficult to imagine how Watkins' building was turned into Stainburn's, and now impossible to check, because the farm buildings at Nurton have been converted to a, typically charmless, residential enclave. History is not that easily expunged, however, and the three field names associated with this pigeon house survive in the records of the 1840 tithe apportionment, covering an area immediately to the north and north west of the house (Field 191, Little Pigeon House Field; 192, Pigeon House Field; 193, Pigeon House Field).

Fig. 120 Nurton Court, Middleton on the Hill (Alfred Watkins Collection)

MOCCAS: Home Farm (Listed Grade II*, Private)
One of the gables of the brick estate building, designed by Anthony Keck, and built *c*.1783 to house workshops, stables and a hay loft, has a gable-cote.[360]

MONKLAND AND STRETFORD: Pigeon House Meadow, Wall End
The name of a small field numbered 173 on the Monkland tithe map of 1841, immediately south of Wall End Farm.

MONKLAND AND STRETFORD: Pigeon House Orchard, Moss Hill
The name of field number 11 on the Stretford tithe map of 1838 immediately south of Moss Hill (north of Bainstree Cross). Early editions of the Ordnance Survey show a small building attached to the southern end of a range of farm buildings which could be the pigeon house.

MONKLAND AND STRETFORD: Stretford Court
Watkins included a square timber-framed pigeon house at Stretford Court in his table of demolished buildings (W21). He gave no details beyond its likely date of demolition *c*.1880.

MORDIFORD: Old Sufton (Listed Grade II,[361] Private)
There has been a house at Old Sufton since the 13th century, which allows the possibility that the stone part of the pigeon house is medieval. Its internal diameter is 17ft 6in (5.3m) and the walls are 3ft 9in (1.14m) thick. The nest holes are only visible at the upper level, but there is evidence that they once extended down to the ground. They are 6 inches (0.15m) square on the face, 1ft 5in (0.43m) deep and open into a space about 1ft (0.3m) square. The tiers rise about 10 inches (0.255m) and the holes are staggered and handed from tier to tier (Fig. 122). There are few alighting ledges; two continuous ledges survive, six tiers apart.[362] These dimensions are comparable to those examples known to be medieval, at Garway and Much Cowarne.

It is probable that two factors prompted the repair of the building at some point just before the date of 1764 on the weathervane (which had a double-headed eagle and the initials IHM for James and Martha Hereford).[363] Its condition must have been poor, considering the distortions in the masonry which are betrayed by the uneven brickwork. That was also the time of creating the great walled garden in which the pigeon house makes such a strong visual statement and serves the purpose of a summer house. It is interesting that the brick garden wall wraps round the front of the drum and not the back – so that appearance was probably more important than preservation as a motive.[364]

The brickwork is in Flemish bond and finished below the eaves with a dentil cornice. Inside, a broad band at the top of the wall is formed of brick, and also one or two large patches down to the level of the inserted floor. Nests were formed in the brick-work, broadly in the same pattern as the stone part, with individual alighting ledges

Figs. 121, 122 and 123
The pigeon house at Sufton as illustrated in Watkins' article of 1890 (top left); as recently repaired (left) and the older nest holes showing some of the brick repairs (above)

made of pairs of projecting headers. A floor was inserted and three doors were formed facing the magnificent view over the city towards the Black Mountains. The ground floor of the interior was plastered and fragments of Georgian wallpaper were still visible recently.[365] There are nine tiers of nests (Fig. 122) with a total of 360 holes but it is doubtful whether they were ever used intensively after the brick casing was applied.

The conical roof is covered in clay plain tiles. The lantern has recently been rebuilt (and most of the roof timbers have been renewed). In earlier illustrations (Fig. 121) the lantern was exceptionally tall, elegantly corniced and surmounted by an ogee-shaped lead cap with a magnificent vane. The facets were glazed and a narrow gap was left at the base, protected by a sloping board (as at Canon Frome), for entry and exit. Watkins' picture shows semi-circular arches at the heads of the glazed panels; Stainburn's photograph (S.2) shows straight tops. In the recent repair these details have been simplified. It is possible that this tall glazed structure was used as a belvedere when the pigeon house became a gazebo.

MUCH BIRCH: Pigeon House Orchard, Bigglestone
The name of an irregular shaped field numbered 356 on the tithe map of 1842, alongside the track to Bigglestone to the south of the farm.

MUCH COWARNE: Cowarne Court (Listed Grade II*, Private, but distant views from public paths)

The pigeon house at Cowarne is slightly smaller than that at Garway, but the remains of the springing for a vault within, and the projection outside which, at Garway, heralds the corbelling-in over the vault suggest that the two buildings are of similar date.

The plan is a circle of 16ft 3in (4.92m) diameter inside, and the walls are 3ft 8in (1.18m) thick. There is a low door, 4ft 6in (1.36m) x 2ft 8in (0.81m), facing west (Fig. 124). The walling is well-coursed local red stone, the base of which is made up of large boulders. The roof is a truncated cone; the lower part is covered with stone slates and the upper part with machine-made clay tiles. The roof of the louver is also a cone, covered in wood shingles, and supported on a ring of stout posts. This visually pleasing arrangement was part of the restoration carried out early in the last century, but could be based on earlier evidence.[366]

Inside, the nest holes are in 17 tiers, from ground floor level, each about 10 inches (0.24m) deep, with about 500 nests in all. They are 6 inches (0.15m) square at the opening, widening to about 10 inches within the wall, and are 1ft 9in (0.53m) deep on average. They are staggered, and their skews handed from tier to tier, and there is a continuous alighting ledge at every third tier. Around most of the circumference, immediately above the highest tier of nests, the springing of the vault remains (Fig. 125).

The present roof structure consists of a grillage of tie beams across the wall pate and evenly spaced common rafters spanning between the plate, the louver collar and an intermediate ring purlin. There are many modern timbers in this structure.

Figs. 124 and 125
Much Cowarne. The dark stones in the photograph of the interior are the remains of the springing of the vault

On the wall, almost opposite the entrance and about 5ft (1.52m) from the floor, is an iron shackle which was probably part of the mechanism for operating a trap.

The pigeon house stands in isolation, but it was not always so, for immediately to the north is the site of Cowarne Court,[367] another of the lost great houses that left behind a pigeon house. The medieval house was replaced by a house in Tudor style in the 1870s, and that later house was demolished in the 1960s.[368] Elgar was a visitor to the Court, to see his friends, the Bournes, and is known to have been there during the time he was composing 'Pomp and Circumstance No. 1'.

The tithe map of 1847 shows a group of buildings close to the pigeon house, and the field to the south, numbered 418, is called Pigeon House Orchard.

English Heritage has included the pigeon house in its list of buildings and monuments 'at risk'.[369]

MUCH COWARNE: Loft at Cowarne Mill (Private, but visible from public footpath)
A quirky modern pigeon loft over a rustic pergola.

MUCH MARCLE: Chandos (Listed Grade II*, Private)
The listing description notes that the 'North side of the main range has heavy closely set studs to west of tallet[370] stairs and nesting ledges of rear parallel block'.[371]

MUCH MARCLE: Hellens (Listed Grade II*, the house is open to the public in the summer)
The pigeon house at Hellens is second only to Garway in the extent to which it has been cited and illustrated in national surveys. It is not difficult to understand why; its form is delightfully proportioned and decorated, its brickwork has a rich patina of age and it is gloriously signed and dated (Fig. 126 overleaf). It is surprising therefore to learn that it was not built as a dovecote, but is the result of converting part of the defences of the house. Malcolm Munthe in his *Hellens, The Story of a Herefordshire Manor* tells the story,

> … young Fulke and Margaret (Walwyn) … had employed the local 'king's carpenter' – overseer of the public buildings in Herefordshire – John Abel to carry out the modernisation of Hellens … They raised the level of the little yard in front of the Audleys' stone door on the north front and reduced the old tower to a pleasant, unfearsome dovecote. On this tower walls they had their initials inset: F. M. W. 1641. By clever use of plaster quoins all traces of the medieval aspect gave way to the new Jacobean look.[372]

The old tower was built in the 16th century. Its brick drum, with 7ft 4in (2.22m) facets, stands on a stone plinth and is divided into three stages by lower stone and upper brick string courses. The brickwork is laid in English bond. There are a number of openings, but it is the exceptionally low door framed by massive blocks of the local red stone that sticks in the memory (Fig. 11c).

Not all of the roof structure is visible. The principal members forming the hips, two tiers of purlins, the plate and the collar can be seen, but the areas between them are now finished with new plasterwork – part of a recent adaptation of the building to office use.

The roof covering is plain tile with five courses of stone slate at the eaves.[373] The octagonal louver is glazed with four panes on each facet, and is roofed with tiles. The present appearance is similar to that photographed by Watkins,[374] although the horizontal slit, sheltered by a sloping board, for entry and access has been lost. At some point prior to the most recent restoration the louver facets were covered with sloping slats.[375] The vane is a flag with the inscription, EW 1783.

Figs. 126 Hellens, Much Marcle

Inside, a very fine brick ground floor survives. Watkins found a 'middle floor supported by post in centre with joists radiating', an arrangement repeated in the restoration. The only visible evidence of the wooden nest boxes is provided by tiers of vertical grooves cut into the brickwork above the upper floor level. These are roughly staggered from tier to tier, and must have held the ends of the vertical partitions between the boxes.[376] There is a pair of crossed beams at eaves level with a hole in the underside of their crossing; this suggests that there was a revolving ladder in the upper part as at Holme Lacy.[377]

MUCH MARCLE: Homme House Gazebo and Pigeon House Field (Listed Grade II*, Private)

It is suggested, but not in the previous surveys of pigeon houses, that this gazebo is a 16th-century pigeon house, which was altered to make a summer house in the 18th century.[378] This possibility is strongly supported by the name of the field immediately to the south-west, called Pigeon House Field on the tithe map of 1839 (and numbered 541) and by its location close to a significant manor house.

The rubble stone octagon, with 7ft (2.12m) facets, has convincing proportions for a pigeon house and retained a square glazed lantern, with a tented metal roof and timber finial, when Cohen photographed it in 1957 – his picture leaves little doubt (Fig. 127). There is no evidence of nest holes because internal plastering formed part of the later works, but wooden nest boxes would probably have been unusual in this thin-walled stone building.

Figs. 127 and 128 Homme House, Much Marcle (left) photographed by Israel Cohen (undated) and (right) today

The alterations included the addition of a stair tower and a fireplace and chimney. The most eye-catching work is however the formation of a continuous arcade of Gothic windows, two per facet, at the upper level (Fig. 128).

The building is in very poor condition which has led Herefordshire Council to use its powers to protect listed buildings by undertaking compulsory purchase.

MUCH MARCLE: former Vicarage (Private, converted to a house, but visible from the road)
This 18ft (5.45m) square brick building was one of the outbuildings to the unusually splendid late 17th-century Vicarage (now Phillips House). It was converted to a house in the late 1970s (Fig. 23). The brickwork, in Flemish bond, is undecorated and the pyramidal slate roof rises from a plain eaves with a flat plaster soffit. The louver and the nest holes had gone by the time of Watkins when it had been 'added to stables' (W18).

NORTON: Buckenhill Manor (Listed Grade II, Private)
The pigeon house at Buckenhill is octagonal, with 8ft (2.42m) facets, and typical of those associated with country houses. Its brick drum is laid in English bond and divided at about mid height by a string/perching course, above which there is a large sunk panel on each facet. The embellishment is completed with a dentil cornice. The roof was covered with clay plain tiles with lead hips. Cohen's photograph shows that the louver was square with a pyramidal roof, and had a row of arched pigeon holes on each side (much like the nearby example at Thornbury, Netherwood) (Fig. 129). The interior is circular and

Figs. 129 and 130 Buckenhill Manor, Norton
(photographed by Israel Cohen in 1957 (left) and today (right)

reached through a low door on the north side. The wall is 2ft 4in thick at the doorway. There are 440 L-shaped nest holes in 16 tiers, starting just above the ground. They are staggered and handed from tier to tier and have a single, plain brick header as an alighting ledge. The ruins of the roof and revolving ladder litter the floor including the iron pivot from one end of the ladder shaft.

The Manor was brought up to date and re-fronted in 1730,[379] which is a likely date for the pigeon house. In 1973 the louver had 'partly fallen';[380] today, the building is roofless and the brick drum riven with vertical cracks (Fig. 130).

NORTON CANON:
Watkins included a square timber-framed pigeon house at Norton Canon in his table of demolished buildings (W21).

OCLE PYCHARD: Lyvers Ocle
Watkins includes a square timber-framed dovecote at Lyvers Ocle in his table of demolished buildings (W21). He gives no details beyond a likely date of demolition c.1885. Lyvers Ocle is the site of a priory, 'Benedictine founded c.1100 and granted to Sheen Priory c.1414'.[381]

ORCOP: Pigeon House Farm
Watkins recorded a 12ft (3.64m) square stone pigeon house, since demolished, with a single span roof and upper loft. The louver had been demolished (W16). Stainburn found a building 'much altered and probably reduced in height' with 'approximately 50 holes, upper loft only.' (S.12)

A poem by Lettie Cole, written in 1917, and called 'The Song of the Bread Cart Girl' refers to the pigeon house:

Fig. 131 Orleton: The small building behind The Boot

Oh! Its down to Orcop and up to the Globe
And up and down the lane,
Past the Pigeon House, through the ruts
And up the hill again.[382]

ORLETON: Small building behind The Boot (Private)
This timber-framed building is normally celebrated as a remarkably small cottage, but it looks more like a pigeon house which has had the top range of frame panels removed. With its full height restored, it would appear very like the small pigeon house at Pump House Farm, Hanbury, Worcestershire.[383]

Fig. 132 Pembridge:
Unidentified thatched pigeon house

PEMBRIDGE: Unidentified thatched pigeon house

Among Marshall's papers is a printed article which has a sketch of a square, timber-framed building with a pyramidal thatched roof (Fig. 132), said to be in Pembridge. This is the only record of a thatched building in this survey.[384]

PEMBRIDGE: Broxwood Court (Private, converted to holiday accommodation)

The stable range of the, now demolished, house designed by Charles Hansom was completed before his death in 1891. The gateway is surmounted by a clock tower with a steep pyramidal roof. Each face of the roof has a gabled dormer, and these each have three pigeon holes, with wooden alighting ledges, arranged in a triangle. Here, the common pigeon is engaged in High Gothic Revival drama.

PEMBRIDGE: Clearbrook Farm

A timber-framed barn at Clearbrook had a wooden gable-cote (Fig. 133) with about 60 round-headed holes in eight tiers.[385] In the centre of each tier were pairs of closely spaced holes. Each tier had a continuous alighting ledge. Had it survived this would have been one of the most pleasing gable-cotes in the county.

Fig. 133 Clearbrook Farm, Pembridge illustrated by Parkinson and Ould in 1904

PEMBRIDGE: Manor of Marston

An undated document at Longleat records that the Manor of Marston contained 18 messuages, 6 cottages, 4 tofts, 2 mills, 4 dove houses, 20 gardens, 20 Orchards, 600 acres of land, 400 acres of meadow, 600 acres of pasture, 100 acres of wood, 500 acres furze and heath.[386]

There is a sham timber-framed pigeon house attached to the 'Old School' (which is not very old).

PEMBRIDGE: Pigeon House Orchard, Byletts

The name of a field to the south-east of Byletts, numbered 422 on the tithe map of 1842. The present modern house was preceded by a 17th-century, or earlier, house which may have had a pigeon house in the named field.[386]

PEMBRIDGE: Pigeon House Orchard, The Leen

The two fields, numbered 371 and 372, immediately to the east of the farm buildings at The Leen, are both called Pigeon House Orchard on the tithe map of 1842. The railway line cut off the southern end of these fields.

Fig. 134 Barn at Lower Marston photographed by George Marshall in 1926 (Woolhope Club Library)

PENCOMBE: Barn at Lower Marston, Marston Stannert (Listed Grade II, Private)

A low barn with a gable-cote and an eaves-cote. The gable-cote is in seven tiers with continuous alighting ledges (Fig. 134). The eaves-cote is on the adjacent wall and has five holes on a continuous ledge. This is a very pretty and neatly made example.

PENCOMBE: Court Farm outbuilding[388] (Listed Grade II, Private, converted to an office, but visible from the churchyard to the south)

This stone building has a raised floor and undercroft, which suggests that it may have been a granary.[389] The principal range has gables to the east and west, and a third gable in the centre of the south side of the two-gabled roof (Fig. 17). The south and west gables have gable-cotes. The south side is typical with 16 tiers with continuous stone alighting ledges but, unlike the other gable, the lowest two tiers extend sideways under the eaves of the main range. There is a central loft door high up in the apex of each gable. The nest holes are roughly staggered from tier to tier. This example had the highest number of external nest holes in this survey, about 280 in all, but many are now blocked.

PENCOYD: Pencoyd Court (Listed Grade II, Private)

Fig. 135 Pencoyd from the churchyard

This oblong (11ft (3.33m) x 13ft (3.94m)) stone pigeon house stands at the boundary between the yard of the Court farm and the churchyard. It was previously embraced by lean-to stock shelters on the farm side.[390] Its distinctive pyramidal slate roof with elegant, oversailing eaves and the carefully proportioned, louvered lantern with its tented lead roof and weather vane are clearly meant for show (Fig. 135). So too is the pointed arch over the doorway to the upper loft which has holes for entry and exit. There is a door below this which serves the room at ground level. The roof structure is sawn timber of relatively thin sections forming hips and trimmed common rafters supporting stout battens. The upper storey is plastered and limewashed and contains a wooden box on the north wall with just two tiers of nests. The underside of the box carries the marks of the angled partitions between the nests of another tier which shows that there were more nests, although there are putlog holes at the same level in the adjacent wall for supports which indicate that the present arrangement, with the nests raised above the floor, was probably used throughout. Those nests that remain have square holes on the face. The holes are staggered, and the angle of the partition boards is handed from tier to tier.

The listing[391] gives an early 19th-century date which seems sound given the use of an upper loft and the Regency roof form with its low pitch, lead hips and plastered eaves soffit.

PETERCHURCH: Pigeon House Field, Hinton
The name of field number 845 on the tithe map of 1843 on the north side of Long Lane west of Hinton Cross.

PETERCHURCH: Pigeon House Fields, Mowbage
A group of three fields numbered 147, 148 and 149 on the tithe map of 1843 to the west of Mowbage (previously Mowbach) Farm, all of which are called Pigeon House Field.

PETERCHURCH: Urishay

The remains of a deserted medieval village are visible to the south of Urishay Castle. House platforms and hollow ways have been identified, and the base of a circular stone structure that might be a dovecote.[392]

PIPE ASTON: Halfway House (Private, but visible from the road)

The gable of a small stone and brick shed has arched nest holes with shaped brick ledges. Probably 19th century or later.

PIPE ASTON: Manor

The manor of Pipe Aston was recovered in 1782. It is described as, 'The Manor of Aston with appurtenances, 15 messuages, one dovehouse, one water cornmill ...'.[393]

PIXLEY: Eaves-cote and Pigeon House Meadow, Poolend Farm

This granary and cart shed has a timber-framed upper storey built on rubble stone walls. The framing is two panels high with infill panels of red brick; five pairs of panels on the south-east elevation have been formed into an eaves-cote, with four tiers of holes in each pair of panels (in four pairs the central timber rail has been removed) (Fig. 136). The nest holes are two courses high; in Cohen's picture they sit on continuous stone ledges, only a few of which now remain.

Fig. 136 Poolend Farm, Pixley photographed by Israel Cohen in 1956

The field numbered 105 on the tithe map of 1838, to the north of Poolend, is called Pigeon House Meadow. The A438 now runs through this field. In the north corner a small close is shown on earlier editions of the Ordnance Survey that could denote the position of a pigeon house.

PRESTON WYNNE:

Watkins includes a square timber-framed pigeon house in Preston Wynne in his table of demolished buildings (W21). Unfortunately he gives no details beyond its likely date of demolition in 1887. It was probably associated with one of the field names described below.

PRESTON WYNNE: Pigeon Close, Court Farm
The name of a field split into two ownerships, numbered 90 and 91, on the tithe map of 1839, east of Court Farm. It is likely that this is the site of the square timber-framed pigeon house which Watkins says was pulled down in 1887.

PRESTON WYNNE: Pigeon House Orchard, Lower Town
The name of field number 134 on the tithe map of 1839 to the south-west of Lower Town.

Fig. 137 Putley Court
(Alfred Watkins Collection)

PUDLESTONE: Pigeon House Close, Lower Whyle
The name of field number 238 on the tithe map of 1842 to the east of the site of the chapel at Lower Whyle.

PUTLEY: Putley Court
The demolished timber-framed pigeon house photographed by Watkins (Fig. 137) was 10ft (3.03m) square on plan. It had the four-gabled form of Luntley, but had a door at first-floor level reached by a wooden external stair serving an 'upper loft only' (W17). The roof was slate and the lantern was octagonal and arcaded with semi-circular arches. The top, which can just be made out in the picture, appears to have been a tented lead cap with a ball finial. The timber frame was clad in ugly timber boarding. The nest boxes had been removed before Watkins visited.

RICHARD'S CASTLE:

Richard's Castle is remarkable for having records and standing fabric from three round stone pigeon houses.[394] The very fine example at Court House Farm had been admired and illustrated for more than a century[395] before two more structures, associated with the castle and town wall, were discovered in archaeological excavations in 1962-64 (Fig. 139).[396] In the report on the excavations it is suggested that, 'It is extremely unlikely that the lord inflicted the pigeons from more than one dovecote on his tenants simultaneously', and that they were therefore built consecutively, culminating in the building at Court House Farm in the 17th century.

From the broader survey in this gazetteer, it is apparent that a parish, or even a single manor, could contain a number of dovecotes, and that the landscape in parts of the county was quite densely populated with pigeons. It is possible that they were of similar date, reflecting their similar construction, and that competition between them led to the demise of the less favourably placed dovecotes on the higher, less hospitable ground. The only distinguishing feature of Richard's Castle that supports consecutive dating is the close proximity of the three sites. In other concentrations such as in Dilwyn parish the buildings are much further apart.

RICHARD'S CASTLE: Tower in castle wall (Scheduled Ancient Monument, Listed Grade II, Accessible but not visible)

Little can be seen of the tower on the steeply sloping north-east side of the motte. There is a discernible mound, but it is entirely overgrown, even in the winter.[397] The excavation uncovered a tower with an internal diameter of 10ft 6in (3.18m) (the smallest of the three pigeon houses in the parish) (Fig. 139C). The remnants of four tiers of nest holes showed some clear characteristics, notably in the provision of a stone perching ledge below each tier, and the alternation of the holes. In this example pairs of tiers have their holes vertically aligned and it is the pairs, not the individual nest holes in every tier that are staggered. This is a unique arrangement of holes in a round stone building (Fig. 138). The nest holes here are of similar dimension and form to those in the other two pigeon houses, penetrating the wall at an angle and broadening with depth. The angles are alternated from course to course, again, a common feature in all three.

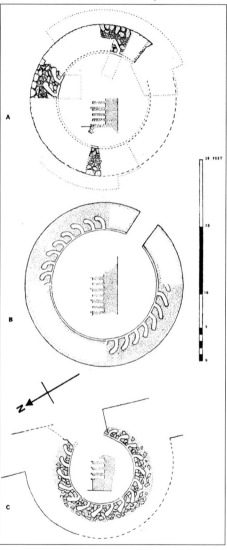

Fig. 138 Interior of the Castle Tower (by kind permission of the Archaeological Association)

Fig. 139 Comparison of the plans of the three round pigeon houses at Richard's Castle (by kind permission of the Archaeological Association)

The castle walls were probably built in the late 13th century.[398] They had become redundant by the 'later Middle Ages', at which time the castle was used as a farmyard. It is thought that the pigeon house was 'inserted' at that time.[399] It is, however, possible that it was part of the first building. In other cases where dovecotes have been inserted, the construction has been carried out in a different material.[400] To 'insert' the dovecote in this case would have required the dismantling of, at least, the inner leaf of the wall, which must surely have been a discouragement. There are examples of castles which were built with pigeon houses; that in the Norman tower at Rochester Castle is thought to be the oldest dovecote in Britain.[401] That history must surely be a possibility at Richard's Castle.

RICHARD'S CASTLE: Court House Farm (Listed Grade I, Scheduled Ancient Monument, Private)
There are few buildings that give greater pleasure to the eye than this pigeon house (Fig. 140). Its 17ft (5.15m) internal diameter (Fig. 141) and 4ft (1.21m) thick walls impart

Fig. 140 Court House Farm, Richard's Castle

Fig. 141 Interior of pigeon house at Court House Farm, Richard's Castle

impressive scale, which is emphasised by the proportions arising from the masons having made the height from the floor to the top of the masonry drum the same 17ft as the internal diameter (Fig. 139B). There is a real sense of the building having been designed with visual aptitude (although it is likely to be of more than one build). The drum has a marked entasis, and the conical roof has, unlike any other similar building in this survey, three gabled dormers, which add immense interest to its outline. The louver also has three little gables which are carefully oriented to face between the dormers. The design is dressed in beautifully laid stone and stone slate.

There is a low doorway with an old plank door facing west. Inside, the nest holes start just above the floor and rise in 18 tiers to the underside of the timber wall plate, with a perching ledge every second tier (Fig. 141). There are 580 holes which are precisely staggered and handed from tier to tier. The revolving ladder is still *in situ*, its pegged frame with big curved braces is pivoted in a single tie beam at eaves level.

The walls might well be medieval, but the roof structure is not. It is a conical form of the butt purlin roof, which, in its axial form, is not normally found before the early 17th century. In this impressive structure there are six principal rafters spanning between the wall plate and the collar which supports the louver. The bases of the principals have vertical ashlar posts resting on hammer beams projecting from the plate. The purlins form the sills to the dormers, above which there are two further staggered tiers. The common rafters are laid over this framework.

Stainburn found a trap at the base of the louver, which is no longer there (S.4). He also refers to the dormers being fitted with shutters rather than the present fixed panels of sloping slats.

RICHARD'S CASTLE: Town wall (Scheduled Ancient Monument, Private, not visible)
Excavations in the field to the east of the group of buildings around the old church revealed, on the line of the town wall, the foundations and lower wall of a dovecote of very similar form to that at Court House Farm. This example is the second largest of the three in the parish, with an internal diameter of 14ft 6in (4.39m). Its stone drum and nest holes are similar in all respects except that the perching ledges are provided only at every third tier of nest holes (Fig. 139A).

ROSS ON WYE: Alton Court (Listed Grade II, Private)

There is not much to show that this building was a pigeon house.[402] The louver is reduced to the size of a ventilator, although probably still accessible to pigeons, and there are no nest holes or boxes inside (Fig. 142). The upper floor has been raised above the sill of the upper door, and the roof trusses form an obstruction to free flight towards the louver. It was, however, included by Watkins as a pigeon house with an upper loft; he also described it as 'modern' (W16).

This is one of the largest of the square stone buildings, with 19ft 3in sides. There is a stone stair externally on the south-east side giving access to the loft, and a door and window at ground level on the north-

Fig. 142 Alton Court, Ross on Wye photographed by Israel Cohen (undated)

east side. The roof is covered with Welsh slate. There has been no change since Cohen visited in 1957.

ROSS ON WYE: Bishop's Palace

Marshall notes, 'South of the Pound House Ross "was a Dovecote of curious appearance but pulled down in the last [18th] century or earlier" – vide *Ariconensia* by The Rev. Dudley Fosbroke – 1821 p.82.' This round stone building was part of the Bishop's Palace. A lease of 1612 described it as 'A pigeon house being neare the church yard of Rosse.'[403]

ROSS RURAL: Pigeonhouse Farm

The site of a round stone pigeon house which Watkins included in his table of demolished buildings (W21). (The site is to the east of the town and south of the M50 roundabout.)

ST MARGARETS: Parish Church (Listed grade II*)

The church has a weather-boarded, timber-framed belfry. There is a local insistence that there was a dovecote in this structure but no evidence is visible now. It may have been removed in the first modern restoration scheme in 1852.

ST MARGARETS: White House

An indenture securing a loan refers to 'out houses, buildings, barns, stables, dove-houses …'.[404]

ST WEONARDS: Outbuilding at Trippenkennett (Listed Grade II, Private)
The north-east gable has a brick panel with six tiers of three nesting holes with continuous ledges to each tier.[405]

SARNESFIELD: Church tower (Listed Grade I, Interior of tower inaccessible)
George Marshall,[406] the antiquary whose notes and photographs illuminate a number of entries in this survey, lived at Sarnesfield Court.[407] He published an account of the Sarnesfield 'columbarium'[408] in 1904[409] in which he described it as follows:

> Some months ago, being in the church tower, my attention was attracted by a number of holes in the wall just below the belfry stage. At first I thought that they were only old apertures in which the timbers of an earlier belfry stage had rested, but on looking closer I saw that they were evenly distributed in all four walls, in two tiers, and further inspection disclosed four more tiers above these, partially hidden by the belfry timbers (Fig. 141). They proved to be true pigeon holes of the usual dimensions, viz., 6 inches by 6 inches at the entrance, slightly enlarging inside, and entering the wall at an angle to a depth of 15 to 18 inches. Each tier has four holes, and in a few cases five, in each wall face. In addition to the six tiers, which commence just below the belfry windows, are two holes in each angle about half-way up these windows. There are about 108 nesting holes in all … between each tier is an alighting ledge of stone from two to four inches thick.

Fig. 143 The nest holes in Sarnesfield church tower seen between trusses of the bell frame

His manuscript notes add: 'The holes slope inward to the right and left in alternate tiers, this is not quite regular throughout, enlarging little if at all. The holes in the different tiers are not directly under each other but alternate though not regularly.'

The tower was probably added 'in the second half of the 13th century',[410] and, by a strange co-incidence, its pyramidal roof gives it a familiar pigeon house profile (Fig. 4).[411] If the pigeon holes are part of the original building, this is the oldest pigeon house in Herefordshire (Fig. 4). Examination of the masonry reveals no crudely executed alterations or junctions, which suggests that the columbarium is original. The two pit, king post bell frame, which is superimposed on the pigeon holes, indicates a *terminus ante quem* of some time in the 15th century. The tenor bell is thought to date from *c*.1300.[412]

George Marshall was keen to find other ecclesiastical examples nationally, two of which are in this survey at Llanwarne Church and St Katherine's, Ledbury.

SARNESFIELD: Pigeon House Field
Stainburn listed a pigeon house of unknown shape in his table of demolished buildings at 'Sarnesfield Court' (S.TI), and earlier editions of the Ordnance Survey show a small square building between the Court and the church tower.[413] It is however likely that Stainburn had seen Watkins' reference to a pigeon house and assumed it was at the Court, whereas Watkins links the missing dovecote to field names in the parish which are some distance to the south-west of the Court at Woodmanton Farm.[414] These fields are numbered 70 and 71 on the tithe map of 1844.

SELLACK: Caradoc
In 1308 '... the property consisted of a messuage, garden, dovecote, 2 ploughlands of 80 acres each ...'. There was still a 'dovehouse' there when the property changed hands in 1594.[415]

SHOBDON: Shobdon Court (Listed Grade II, Private)
Shobdon Court was one of the greatest of the now lost country houses of Herefordshire. The seeds of that greatness were sown at the purchase of the estate by Robert Chaplin in 1690. Ivor Pfuell says that the estate 'came with all the usual ... gardens, dovehouses ...'.[416] Chaplin built the stable block which stands next to the present pigeon house c.1700, and it is likely that he replaced the old dovehouses with the present one at the same time.[417] The building of the big house had to wait for his successor, James Bateman. It was during his time, probably about 1710, that John Harris, a leading cartographer, drew an aerial view of Shobdon Court which shows a pigeon house in the present position,[418] although his pigeon house is rather different from the one that stands today. The big sunk panels on the upper part of the brick octagon are accurately shown but appear to be glazed, while the roof and lantern are much more elaborate. The latter is shown as being tall and thin with an ogee cap[419] and tall vane, accompanied by dormers on every facet of the octagonal roof. As ever with topographical prints the questions hang – is Harris' drawing accurate and was the pigeon house rebuilt? It has been suggested that the foundations of the present building date from the 16th century.[420] There are two distinct types of stone, and the lower masonry looks rougher and older. Perhaps, then, the prettier, less productive building of Harris' print was rebuilt to achieve a higher level of production, or was the roof with its massive lantern and dormers too heavy to be held up?

This is one of the largest of the octagonal pigeon houses with facets measuring 9ft 9in (2.95m) (Fig. 6). The upper part is brick, raised up on a ground storey of dressed stone. The brickwork is of high quality, laid in Flemish bond, with burnt headers decorating the segmental arches over the sunk panels. The later replacement of the roof is suggested by eaves which have a marked overhang but lack decoration, and by the roof covering of Welsh slate with lead hips. The roof structure is also relatively flimsy with principal rafters at the hips and two rings of butt purlins below the collar which supports the lantern. The lantern is octagonal with arched, glazed openings on each facet and a lead cap surmounted by a blunt finial.

The site, at the north side of a very large walled garden, gives use to the lower storey, which is fitted out as a gardener's shed with shelves still labelled for the roots and fruits that were stored. The gardener's door is marked by a simple stone doorcase which is dated 1832. The dovecote floor, over the gardener's room, is made of lime and ash. It was probably inserted at the same date, 1832. Before that, the nest holes extended further down the walls as can be seen by surviving alighting ledges within the lower chamber, but the full extent of their original layout is now obscured by plaster. When the upper floor was inserted a new external doorway had to be formed at the higher level, possibly in an existing window opening. The old door and frame from the garden front was re-used in the new opening.

Fig. 144 The interior of Shobdon

The walls are 2ft 4in (0.71m) thick and plastered inside. The nest holes, as at Eardisley Park and Burghill Grange, are slots, three courses high (Fig. 144). They rise in eleven tiers to the eaves, being both staggered and handed. Each of the 424 remaining holes has a stone perch with a rounded edge. The post and beams of a revolving ladder remain, as do the supporting masonry column in the basement storey and the cross beams with a wrought iron cross bracket which form the socket for the top pivot of the post.

It is from Shobdon that we have one of very few contemporary accounts of the eating of pigeons. Lady Bateman's diary for 29 August 1788 refers to 'Mr Dunne who ate for his dinner a very large piece of salmon, 3 pork stakes, five bones of lamb glaced, a pigeon with pie crust, a leg and wing of a large chicken, a large piece of plum tart and two marrow round puffs.'[421]

In the Second World War the walled garden was the local Home Guard training ground and it is probable that the pigeon house, as the only building within the walls, was their HQ.[422]

SOLLARS HOPE: Court (Listed Grade II, Private)
Stone and timber-framed barn with a gable-cote in a south-facing stone gable. There are eight tiers of nest holes on continuous stone alighting ledges.[423]

STANFORD BISHOP: Hope House Farm

In her history of the Stanfords, Phyllis Williams illustrates a modest farm building consisting of a privy, hen house and pigeon house.[424] The building, which appears to be of 19th-century date, still stands.

STANFORD BISHOP: Pigeon House Orchard, Boyce Farm

The name of field number 16 on the undated tithe map relating to the apportionment of 1838, immediately east of Boyce Farm. An inventory of Boyce farm in 1727 records a 'dovehouse'.[425]

STAUNTON ON ARROW: Staunton Park (Private, gardens open to the public Thursdays mid-May to mid-September)

The Staunton dovecote is primarily a landscape feature rather than a building for food production. It stands on a knoll overlooking the Park and the surrounding landscape, in probably the most beautiful setting of any of the buildings in this survey. This ambivalence of purpose is captured in sale particulars of 1884 which describe it as 'an observatory or dovecote'.[426] There is some difficulty in dating this example; the character is of the first half of the 18th century, but it is difficult to relate this early date to the building of the house and the laying out of the Park, which were probably happening much later in that century.[427]

The Staunton dovecote is one of only two hexagonal buildings[428] in Herefordshire, the other is at Foxley, Yazor (see below) (Fig. 145). The hexagonal plan is rare: a search of the ImagesofEngland website reveals only 20 listed hexagonal pigeon house, with a significant proportion (about a third) in Yorkshire and Northumberland. Peter and Jean Hansell, in their magnificent survey, say there is 'a handful'. They illustrate an example not far from Herefordshire's borders, at Golding Farm, Cound, Shropshire.[429]

The brick drum at Staunton stands on a plinth of the local thin-bedded stone. The facets are 8ft 2in (2.44m) and the wall 1ft 7in (0.48m) thick. This seems dangerously thin, given that the nest holes are not staggered from tier to tier; but the brickwork is of very high quality and there are, surprisingly, no vertical cracks. The bond is Flemish bond, but every fifth course is made of headers.[430] The quoins are a slightly different shade which gives a pleasing effect, but the wall tops are decayed so that it is impossible to

Fig. 145 Staunton Park, Staunton on Arrow

tell whether there was some form of cornice. There is a low door on the south side, and, facing the house, on the north side, high up, there are three triangular-headed flight holes, and the brackets for an alighting ledge. In Cohen's picture of 1958 the ledge is intact.

The roof and lantern have gone; it is perhaps possible that they were removed to make an 'observatory'. This might explain the timber cross beams inside the building, which indicate the relatively recent addition of floors.

The nest holes, about 300 in number, are in 13 tiers from ground level. The tiers are four courses high, while the holes are only two courses high on the wall face (which assists the stability of the drum). They are 1ft 3in (0.38m) deep, L-shaped, handed from tier to tier, but, as noted above, not staggered. Each hole has a separate ledge made of two projecting brick headers. There is a staple driven into the north facet, inside, which may have been for tying a cord operating a trap.

STAUNTON ON WYE: Letton Court
Watkins included a pigeon house of unknown shape at Letton Court in his table of demolished buildings (W21).

STOKE EDITH: Home Farm
Watkins recorded a round stone pigeon house that was demolished in about 1870 (W21).

STOKE LACY: Pigeon House Orchard
The name of field number 203 on the tithe map of 1842 to the south-east of Nether Court, alongside a lane. The barn to the north is called 'Dovecote Barn' but this is a modern name.

STOKE PRIOR: See Ford and Stoke Prior above

STRETTON GRANDISON: Barn at Stretton Court
Stainburn illustrated a gable-cote on a barn attached to an 18th-century hop kiln (S.69). This was destroyed in the recent residential conversion. There were 29 holes with continuous alighting ledges.

STRETTON SUGWAS:
Marshall noted in his paper on the manor of Sugwas that there 'was a dovecote on the manor in the time of Bishop Swinfield, and one was specifically mentioned in the leases of 1503 and 1533'.[431]

TARRINGTON: Aldersend
Stainburn says that the round stone pigeon house at Aldersend was destroyed in 1943 as a result of enemy action (S.TII.1), presumably in a raid on the Rotherwas munitions factory

about five miles to the west. It is not, however, included in the Royal Commission survey of 1932 (even though the house is) and must have been demolished before then.

The pigeon house is clearly shown on early editions of the Ordnance Survey. The adjacent fields, numbered 108a, 110 and 111 on the tithe map of 1841, immediately east of Aldersend, are called Pigeon House Road, Pigeon House Pool and Pigeon House Orchard respectively.

Fortunately this is one of the lost pigeon houses photographed by Watkins (Fig. 146).[432] The exterior was rendered and there was a string course or perching ledge just over three-quarters of the way up the wall. The roof was a truncated cone covered in stone slates laid in more or less regular coursing. The lantern was octagonal with leaded glazing, at the base of which was a slit for entry and exit sheltered by a projecting board. The lantern roof was conical and had a ball finial. The interior was 16ft (4.85m) in diameter and the walls 2ft 9in (0.83m) thick. The holes were 'irregular' and 'bottle shaped', and numbered 576 in tiers starting at the ground level. The revolving ladder and trap were extant when Watkins visited.

Fig. 146 Aldersend, Tarrington (Alfred Watkins Collection)

TARRINGTON: Little Tarrington
Cohen photographed the stone plinth and lower panels of a square timber-framed pigeon house at Little Tarrington Farm. Watkins recorded it as 15ft square and made of brick with a pyramidal roof, a square lantern and wooden nest boxes in an upper loft (W18).

THORNBURY: Netherwood (Listed Grade II*, Private)
The last thing one expects to see these days when visiting a dovecote is doves! But there are doves here and, although few relative to the number of

Fig. 147 Netherwood, Thornbury

nest holes, they give a very powerfully mucky idea of what a working dovecote would have been like.

The plan is circular, 15ft (4.55m) diameter internally, and has 2ft 6in (0.76m) thick walls. The Royal Commission illustration of 1932 shows rubble stone of relatively thin course depth, and fragments of external render, which have been taken as precedent for the fully rendered finish seen today (Fig. 147).[433] There is a low doorway on the north side with wooden lintels. The roof is a truncated cone covered in stone slates which supports a square louver with a boarded pyramidal roof (Fig. 148). The louver sits on a lead-clad collar: at the bottom there are four pigeon holes on each face over a continuous wooden alighting ledge. Above the holes the louver is slatted, with gaps left between the horizontal slats for light and air.

The interior wall rises 15ft (4.55m) to the eaves plate with 20 tiers of 35 nest holes (Fig. 149). There were 698 originally (the doorway displaces some) but the lowest tier at floor level has been blocked. The pattern of alighting ledges is unusually complicated. Tiers (not counting the blocked lowest tier) 1, 3, 5, 7, 9, 11 and 15 have continuous ledges, that below the third tier being of double thickness. The holes in the other tiers all have ledges formed by individual stones, but the top two tiers have no ledges at all. In the 16th tier the stone has been almost completely replaced with red brick and there are brick patches above that tier and in the blocking up of the lowest tier. This brickwork indicates an extensive repair scheme and possibly the insertion of a ring beam to contain the roof thrust.

The holes are roughly 6 inches (0.15m) square and 1ft 4in (0.41m) deep; they are only slightly enlarged within the wall depth. They are only slightly skewed in alternate directions from tier to tier and not carefully staggered. This arrangement is inherently weak and accounts for the large vertical crack on the south side. There are remains of lime plastering which indicate that the whole of the interior was plastered and limewashed. The revolving ladder is still in use.

Figs. 148 and 149 Netherwood, Thornbury: a close up of its louver and the interior

The roof structure consists of 24 common rafters, many of which have been strengthened with modern sawn sections. There are no purlins

147

but every fourth rafter is trimmed by a trimmer spanning between the adjacent rafters. The collar is braced by three inserted cross pieces.

THORNBURY: Westwood Farm (Private)

This is a good example of the later alteration of a stone barn to form a gable-cote. The south-facing gable apex has been rebuilt in brick with continuous stone ledges for each tier of nest holes. These are arranged around a loft access door in six tiers.

TITLEY: Eywood (Unlisted, Private)

Eywood House was the seat of the Harleys, Earls of Oxford and Mortimer. The house was demolished in 1956[434] but the stables, gardener's cottage, icehouse and many of the walls and bridges of the formal gardens survive, making a fascinating setting for the pigeon house.[435] Lord Byron visited here numerous times in the winter of 1812, during his court-ship of Lady Oxford. He almost certainly ate squabs from the pigeon house.[436]

This building has been roofless since before 1979 (S.57). It stands within a walled pasture at some elevation above, and to the south-west of, the site of the great house. It is made of red brick, in Flemish bond, laid on a stone footing and topped with a dentil eaves cornice. On the outside there are patches of stucco which has been ruled with mock joints. This was the original finish, perhaps intended to assist the impression of a hillside temple in the landscape of the park.[437] Watkins' photograph (Fig. 150) shows the roof (probably) covered in heavy stone slates laid to diminishing courses with lead hips. The louver was a most elegant design; an ogee lead cap held on an arcade of posts with shouldered arches. Above all was a tall spike with a ball finial.[438]

Fig. 150 Eywood, Titley: The great house in the background no longer stands
(Alfred Watkins Collection)

The exterior is octagonal, with 9ft 6in (2.88m) facets. The interior cylindrical with a radius of 10ft (3.03m), and the nest holes go down to ground level. These features suggest a date in the first half of the 18th century, which is consistent with the development of the house from *c.*1705.

There are 760 nest holes, which are roughly staggered, and have their L-shaped plan handed, from tier to tier. The lower part of the interior has been limewashed. The alighting ledges are formed from two projecting brick headers. In 1979 the door with its wrought iron hinges remained, but now all of the timber elements of the building have been lost.

TITLEY: Pigeon House Orchard

The name of a field number 201 on the tithe map of 1843, immediately west of Titley Court, on the other side of the Kington to Presteigne road. Early editions of the Ordnance Survey show a small square building adjacent to the road.

TYBERTON: Tyberton Court

Early editions of the Ordnance Survey show what was an octagonal brick pigeon house on the north shore of the middle pond of the park, just west of the Lodge (and south of the church). Cohen's picture, of the 1930s, shows a gentry dovecote; an octagonal brick building with slightly projecting corner piers, already in declining condition and bereft of its lantern.[439] Watkins' record says that the facets were 8ft 6in (2.58m) and it was three storeys with an upper pigeon loft (W20). He also, not very helpfully, described the louver as 'plain', but his photograph (Fig. 151)[440] shows a very squat structure with a slit at the bottom, for entry and exit, sheltered by a sloping board. Cohen's picture shows that the brick drum stood on a stone plinth and there were windows in the middle storey, which may have been used as a gazebo. Stainburn suggested that the basement was an ice house, and the location, close to a body of water supports this (S.TII.17). However there is an 'Ice House Plantation' in the park, on the other side of the pond, which suggests that ice for the estate was stored elsewhere.

Fig. 151 The demolished pigeon house at Tyberton Court (Alfred Watkins Collection)

The big house, associated with the early career of the architect John Wood, of Bath, who was working there in 1728, was demolished in 1952 and the pigeon house with it.[441]

ULLINGSWICK: Glebe

The glebe terrier for 1589 has no pigeon house,[442] but that for 1619 refers to 'The parsonage house, pigeon house, the barne and sheepinne'.[443]

ULLINGSWICK: Lower Court

Lower Court is one of the finest of the county's large, rambling, timber-framed farmhouses. A survey of 1649 refers to 'one Dove House' among the farm buildings. This had gone by the time of an inventory taken towards the end of the following century.[444]

UPTON BISHOP: The Beeches (Private)

The pigeon house is part of a range of stone outbuildings close to the house of *c*.1830, and is probably of similar date. It is oblong on plan, 10ft 3in (3.11m) on the narrower side with 1ft 6in (0.45m) thick walls built of the local rubble stone with dressed quoins. The 'nests' are in an upper storey reached by a metal ladder on the north side. The ground floor is divided into a privy and a gardener's room. The roof is pyramidal, covered with Welsh slates and supports an oblong glazed lantern with a sheet metal roof and an arrow weather vane. It is glazed with small panes 5 high x 4 wide on the narrow side and 5 x 6 on the wider, but has no provision for entry.

The upper storey has three tiers of shelves on the upper half of the walls. The tiers are 9 feet deep and divided by stout wooden boards supported on brick piers. Each wall is two shelves wide so that there are 24 in all. The roof structure is of uniform hip and common rafters with stout battens for the slating.

The arrangement of 'nests' is unique in this survey (Fig. 153) and appears to go against all the published advice on the keeping of pigeons and their need for their own nesting space. The open shelves may have

Figs. 152 and 153 Upton Bishop and its unique 'nest ledges'

150

been subdivided by wooden partitions, but no evidence of this can be seen now. Given the lack of any means of entry for pigeons and the unusual arrangement of shelves, it must be asked whether this was a pigeon house at all.

Upton Bishop: Pigeon House Orchard
The name of field numbered 17 on the tithe map of 1839, immediately south of Coldborough Park Farm.

Upton Bishop: Pigeon House Field
The name of the field north of Rudhall House, numbered 709 in the tithe award of 1839. This field is split between two parishes. Another part appears (field 539) in the 1838 tithe award for Brampton Abbots.

Vowchurch: Poston Court (Listed Grade II, Private, but visible from public footpath)
This is a relatively grand building in a part of the county where dovecotes, of all kinds, are thinly spread. The form and details of this building suggest an early 18th-century date in common with the majority of country house octagonal pigeon houses.

The brick octagon stands on a low rubble stone plinth (Fig. 154). The facets are 9ft 9in (2.95m) wide and almost entirely occupied by single sunk panels, leaving the appearance of thin corner piers. The walls are 2ft 2in (0.65m) thick at their thinnest point. A shallow three course string course divides the panels at mid height and the wall top is finished with a three course deep cornice with dogtooth, a plain fascia and dentils; over burnt bricks are used alternately on the string, cornice and piers. The walling follows no bonding pattern, even the courses with a majority of headers seem unrelated to the pattern of nest holes inside. On the south-east side is a low doorway under a segmental brick arch. Modern openings have been made in three other facets. The octagonal slate roof, with plain mitred hips, is finished with a modern, low, octagonal slate cap.[445]

The interior is circular with holes to the ground.[446] There are 20 tiers, the full ones with 39 nest holes; the holes in the lower ones much reduced in number by the doorways. The tiers are four courses deep and the holes are two courses deep each with a pair of brick headers for alighting; they are L-shaped on plan and arranged alter-

Fig. 154 Poston Court, Vowchurch

nately and handed from tier to tier. The holes in the eight lowest tiers have had their alighting ledges broken off. Pigeons manage without ledges, but this is probably a deliberate change after the keeping of pigeons ceased.

The roof structure consists of stout hip rafters with short collars and purlins butted between. This framework supports a modern array of sawn rafters and battens for the slating. There are crossed ties at eaves level and the surviving pivot for a revolving ladder.

WALFORD: Hill Court (Listed Grade II, Private)

The pigeon house stands to the south of Hill Court, which was started in 1695 and extended in the 1720s. The brick octagon rises from a low brick plinth; it has 9ft 9in (2.95m) facets and the 2ft 3in (0.68m) thick walls are faced in Flemish bond (Fig. 155). There is no cornice or other decoration of the exterior. The pyramidal roof is covered with plain tile, with lead hip rolls, and is surmounted by an octagonal, glazed lantern which has an ogee lead cap with a simple wooden spike for a finial. On the west side, the lower pane of one facet of the lantern is replaced by three tiers of arched entrance holes with wooden ledges. This corresponds with a wooden ledge on iron brackets set just below the eaves of the main roof which encouraged the birds to perch in a sheltered place in view of the house.

The interior is circular and of two stories. The ground storey appears to have been used as a garden room with the door (of normal height) facing the house, and windows (now blocked) on the adjacent facets of the octagon. The interior is also plastered so that it is impossible to see if the nests once extended down to the level of the rather nicely made brick ground floor, but the upper floor frame is of some age, with the joists pegged at the spine beam, which could be consistent with an early 18th century date. The domestication of the interior is further enhanced by the provision of a bench all round, for which evidence exists in the form of holes for brackets. There is no access to the upper level other than a trap, which must have made mucking out difficult.

The upper part is fully lined with nests in the wall thickness, each with a single brick header for alighting. The entrance holes are slots, three courses deep; they are staggered and handed from tier to tier and there are 15 tiers of 42 holes, with a few losses for a small window. The roof structure is almost entirely modern but probably follows the old pattern of heavy hip rafters with a ring of butt purlins and a collar to support the common rafters.

Fig. 155 Hill Court, Walford

The Royal Commission gives a date of *c.*1700, contemporary with some of the garden walls,[447] and the brickwork, with relatively narrow bricks (4 courses rise 11.5 inches (0.29m)), could be of that date, but is by no means certainly so. If 1700 is accepted, the plastered walls of the lower storey, which may conceal blocked nest holes, leave the question unanswered as to whether the two-storey arrangement was part of the original design, or a later alteration.[448]

WALFORD: Upper Wythall

The survey of historic parks and gardens in Herefordshire[449] notes:

> The 1" Ordnance Survey plan of 1831 is uninformative but the last piece of information available is some hand-written sale particulars for 1813, which describe an 'old family mansion house with walled garden well planted – two dove cotes – a fish pond full stocked with trout.'

WALTERSTONE: Allt yr Ynys

A conveyance of 1597 refers to '2 dove cots' in 'Alterynnys, Walterstone, Cloddock and Longtowne.'[450]

WELLINGTON: Kipperknoll (Listed Grade II, Private, part of a residential conversion but visible from public footpath)

The 15ft 6in (4.7m) square pigeon house is attached to a four-bay stone barn. The whole range is built of local stone, and probably dates from the 18th century. A pyramidal slate roof is surmounted by a square louver, also with a pyramidal roof finished with a ball finial.

The walls are 2ft 6in (0.76m) thick but only the upper storey has nest holes. These number about 380 and are both staggered and handed between tiers. There is a continuous stone alighting ledge below each tier of holes. The pigeon house appears to have been reached by a ladder to a small door.[451]

As at Moor Abbey (see Middleton on the Hill above) the attached barn also has nest holes. Both the east and west elevations have eaves-cotes with two rows of nine holes.

Fig. 156 Kipperknoll, Wellington

153

WELLINGTON: Pigeon House Croft and Pigeon House Orchard

The names of fields at Wootton, to the north of Wellington village. Pigeon House Orchard, numbered 291 on the 1843 tithe map, is immediately south of Wootton. Pigeon House Croft, numbered 110, is the triangle between the lane and the track to the east.

WELLINGTON: Stocks House (Listed Grade II, Private but prominent in the village street)

There are no pigeon houses more prominent than this one – it dominates the village street (Fig. 7). In form it is similar to, for example, Eywood (see Titley above) which also has an octagonal exterior and a cylindrical interior – but Wellington is the work of a much more modest level of gentry, and displays a showiness which must have been desperate to keep up with the Burghill Joneses (it is probably more or less contemporary with the date of 1717 at Burghill Grange). It is smaller than Eywood, with 7ft 9in (2.35m) facets, but the quality of the Flemish bond brickwork is very fine, and a diaper pattern is embroidered on each facet with over-burnt headers. The slates overhang the eaves, betraying the previous existence of a deep plaster cornice. The roof is covered in slate as is the roof of the octagonal louver. Earlier photographs show arcading just below its eaves, boarding down to an entrance slot and a copper ball on top of the finial spike (W19).[452] The roof structure consists of hip rafters with common rafters and horizontal laths of the same section.

There is a low door with a heavy, pegged frame on the farmyard side, at which point the wall is 2ft 8in (0.51m) thick. The nest holes, numbering about 550, rise in 19 tiers from ground level (Fig. 157). They are irregularly staggered and handed from tier to

Fig. 157 Interior of Stocks House Farm, Wellington

tier, and have alighting ledges formed by two brick headers. Watkins found a two tier revolving ladder (W19) standing on 'a circular mass of brickwork, with nesting holes',[453] but all that remains of it is the pivot in the crossed beams at eaves level.

WELSH NEWTON: St Wolstans Chapel
'The remains of this chapel and associated garden, dovecote and other buildings stood above St Wolstans Farm. The chapel was extant in 1313, and the site was in the possession of the Knights Templar of Garway.'[454] Marshall says that in the year 1312-1313 the Garway pigeon house yielded nothing but that at Welsh Newton earned 3s 0d.[455]

WEOBLEY: Pigeon House Orchard, The Ley
The name of a field immediately west of the Ley numbered 344 on the tithe map of 1838.

WESTON BEGGARD: Pigeon House Farm
(Listed Grade II, Private)
It is the scale of Weston Beggard that impresses. Its 9ft 4in (2.84m) facets make it one of the largest surviving octagonal farmyard buildings in this survey (Fig. 158). The brick drum is built in English garden wall bond with a row of headers every fourth course (reflecting the tiers of nests inside). Each facet has a tall recessed panel, except for the east-facing facet which has the original, now disused, door. That facet and three others are decorated with lozenges made from over-burnt headers. The building has been underpinned with hard red engineering bricks – possibly during the tenure of William Pitt, died 1870, 'Late of Pigeon House Farm' and resting in the churchyard (Fig. 159). He may also have formed the present west-facing door. Watkins (W19) said that the nest holes were 'to ground'. If this is taken literally, the underpinning in fact happened after about 1890, the time of Watkins' survey, because, as noted, the first row of nests is now 3ft (0.91m) above the floor.

Fig. 158 Pigeon House Farm, Weston Beggard

Fig. 159 The tombstone of William Pitt of Pigeon House Farm

At the top of the wall there is a simple, sloping wooden soffit above which is the plain tile roof with its unusual pressed iron hip flashings. The octagonal lantern has six panes in each facet; previously there was an entrance slot at the bottom sheltered by a sloping board.[456] The roof of the lantern is covered in slate and finished with a ball finial. The roof structure consists of stout hip rafters with staggered butt purlins, into which jack rafters are joined. Some of the weight of the lantern was carried, via posts, to a pair of parallel beams at eaves level, which have been reinforced by a pair of steels at right angles.

Inside there are 18 tiers[457] of nests with a total of 720 holes. The tiers occupy four courses; the entrances are two courses and the nests are three courses high inside, with one course forming the horizontal divisions. The holes are staggered and handed from tier to tier, and have individual alighting ledges formed by two projecting headers. Watkins found a revolving ladder but there is no evidence of it now.[458]

The fields adjacent to the pigeon house, numbered 226 and 228 on the tithe map of 1839, are called Pigeon House Homestead and Pigeon House Orchard respectively. The tithe map shows the pigeon house as a circular outline.

Fig. 160 Bollitree Castle photographed by Israel Cohen (undated)

WESTON BEGGARD: Pigeon House Orchard
The name of field number 135 on the tithe map of 1839, immediately north-east of Hill End.

WESTON BEGGARD: Tithes
The lesser tithes for 1535 included four pence for doves.[459]

WESTON UNDER PENYARD: Bollitree Castle (Listed Grade II, Private)
The Bollitree Castle pigeon house is more for show than commercial food production; every part of its exterior has been carefully designed to be stylish. It is a modest, 9ft (2.73m) square, brick and stone building which has been built as part of a walled enclosure. Today the setting is very much a garden one, part of the Rococo landscape of the Castle, but this was not always so; Cohen's picture has a more agricultural appearance (Fig. 160).

The lower storey is built of the local red stone and the upper part, containing the nest holes, is made of red brick rendered on the outside. This was recently re-coated and finished with rather ugly scallop decoration on the surface. The roof is a stone tiled pyramid on a boxed timber eaves with ogee iron guttering. The lantern, clearly designed as an eye catcher, is eight-sided with fine timber glazing bars forming eight well-proportioned panes on each facet. At the base is an entrance slot sheltered by a projecting, sloping board. The crowning glory is a splendid ogee lead cap with a bold spike.

Inside there are less than 150 nest holes. The tiers are four courses high, the holes two courses, and the staggered and handed holes each have an individual brick header for an alighting ledge.[460]

Bollitree was developed in the second half of the 18th century by the Merricks and there is nothing to suggest an earlier date for the pigeon house.[461] The upper loft, probably a response to the spread of the brown rat, and the modest scale of the building are consistent with pigeon houses of that period.

Weston under Penyard: Dairy Cottages, Bollitree (Private – converted to a water tower for the adjacent houses – but visible from the road)[462]

The pigeon house is in the background of one of Watkins' most charming photographs (Fig. 161).[463] The foreground subject is the timber-framed Dairy Cottage which stood prior to the present houses. A woman wearing a long skirt, an apron and a bonnet, stands in the doorway. The lantern of the pigeon house can be clearly seen to be worryingly out of plumb.

The ground plan is a relatively small oblong, 8ft 6in (2.37m) x 10ft 6in (3.18m). The walls are rubble stone in two distinctly different stages (Fig. 162). The upper third is made of bigger, purpler blocks of stone suggesting some later enlargement of the building. The nest holes

Figs. 161 and 162 Dairy Cottages, Bollitree (Alfred Watkins Collection) (above) and today (right)

were confined to the upper two thirds so that there are two doors – one at ground level (facing north-west) and one above (facing north-east). Watkins says that there were 'plates of sheet iron bent round outside angles of walls 18ft[464] up to keep rats from climbing'. It is noted above in the introduction that this purpose is doubtful, and that the iron sheets were more likely to have been for the pigeons to alight on. At '18ft' (5.45m) the metal would have been immediately under the eaves. The roof is covered with plain tiles; the lantern it supported was an open structure with four posts and an ogee cap with a flag vane.

WHITBOURNE: Gaines (Listed Building Grade II and Scheduled Monument, Private)
This is an important dated (by the vane) example, made more significant by the ice house in its foundations (Fig. 22). It stands close to the back of the rather dull big house, between it and the lakes, in 'a textbook example of mid-18th century landscaping by a minor gentry family.'[465] It predates the nearest wings of the house and must have had greater prominence and landscape significance when it was first built. Preserved inside is a wrought iron vane inscribed IF 1718; the initials standing for John Freeman[466] who was the second Freeman at Gaines.

The exterior is 15ft (4.55m) square on plan with four gables (Fig. 163). The walls are made of relatively thin brick (four courses rise 10.5 inches (0.27m)), laid in Flemish garden wall bond. The roof is tiled, so too is the modern four-gabled louver which is partly glazed and partly boarded. There are iron brackets on each wall, at the base of the gables, which supported sloping wooden boards for perching.

On the north side, at ground level, is a low, arched door which gives entry to the ice house. This is of typical, cylindrical form tapered towards the bottom (Fig. 165).

Figs. 163 and 164 Gaines,
exterior and interior

The pigeon house floor, above, is supported by an almost flat brick vault. The upper part, from ground level to the vault, is lined with squared stone blocks, the rest is lined with brick. The 4ft thickness of masonry, visible at the doorway, provided insulation for the ice which would have been hauled up from the nearby lakes.

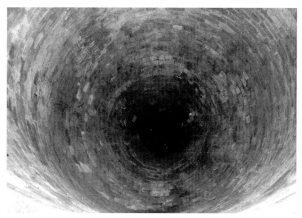

Fig. 165 Ice House at Gaines

On the south side is a doorway for the pigeon house: 4ft 6in (1.35m) x 2ft 8in (0.81m) with the sill 5ft 9in (1.74m) above the ground. The nest holes in the walls below the gables resemble those at Eardisland, except that each tier has a continuous brick ledge (Fig. 164). They are three brick courses high (four including the ledge course) and neither staggered nor handed from tier to tier. The lowest tier has open nest boxes. The walls are only 1ft 8in thick, and the weak arrangement of nest holes accounts for extensive brickwork repairs visible outside. The holes in the gables are two courses deep, roughly staggered and handed from tier to tier, and have continuous brick header alighting ledges. There are 490 holes in all. The roof structure is typical of the four-gable form with two long[467] and two trimmed purlins supporting the valley and common rafters. There is additional cradling for the corner posts of the louver and an additional tie has been inserted to carry the preserved vanes.

WHITCHURCH: Barn at Lewstone Farmhouse (Listed Grade II, Private but visible from the road)

This magnificent example of an eaves-cote is dated to the late 18th century by the listing inspectors (Fig. 166).[468] There are 50 square nest holes along the whole of the south side of the barn, divided into two by the threshing bay opening. Each group has a continuous alighting ledge.

WHITCHURCH: Old Court Hotel

Stainburn included this in his list of lofts with lanterns. 'Part of the building, now the dining room of the Hotel, is said to have contained a pigeon loft in the roof space, and was surmounted by a lantern.' (S75)

Fig. 166 Eaves-cote at Lewstone, Whitchurch

WIGMORE: Pigeon House Orchard
A field name in the 1840 Wigmore tithe award, numbered plot 137 under the ownership of Greenhill Farm.[469] The plot is very narrow and fronts on to Ford Street, near the present day Compasses Hotel. It is at some distance from Greenhill Farm, which is between the castle and the church.

WITHINGTON: Glebe
The glebe terrier of 1638 records: 'one Dwellinghowse in the tenure and occupation of Magdalen Kenwen and one Orchard thereunto belonging One Pigeon howse, one barne conteyning three bayes of building'.[470]

WITHINGTON: Outbuilding south-east of The Lawns (Listed Grade II, Private, converted to a house)
The Statutory List description refers to 'wooden pigeon nesting boxes above the ground floor door'.[471]

WOOLHOPE: Pigeon House Orchard
The name of field number 184 on the tithe map of 1845, immediately south of the Crown Inn.

WORMBRIDGE: Pigeon Close
The name of field number 123 on the tithe map of 1839, on the corner immediately west of the Crown Inn.

WORMBRIDGE: Wormbridge Court Farm (Listed Grade II, Private)
This red brick pigeon house was described by Watkins as 'a tall building' (W18). It is the most attenuated and elegant of the brick towers in the county, 13ft 5in (4.06m) square on plan and rising from a 3ft (0.91m) high stone plinth to a height of 27ft (8.18m) at the eaves (Fig. 167). The brickwork is laid in Flemish garden wall bond with a row of headers every fourth course, corresponding with the nests inside. The wall tops are finished with a dentil cornice which supports a pyramidal, stone slate roof. The square lantern is also relatively tall. The sides are louvered and the cap takes a distinctive double curved form which was finished with a ball finial. The tower is built against, or rather partly within a barn; the nests are in an upper loft entered from a doorway below the lower part of the cat-slide roof of the barn.

It is unsafe to enter the upper floor, but it is possible to see through a hole that there are 14 tiers of nest holes each with an alighting ledge of two brick headers.[472] The 390 nests are unevenly staggered from tier to tier. There is also a central post, with a mortice low down, which may be the remains of that rare thing – a revolving ladder in a square pigeon house.

Fig. 167 Wormbridge Court (Alfred Watkins Collection)

WORMSLEY: Wormsley Grange

The field name 'Pigeon House Orchard' appears in Plot 4 of the 1846 tithe award map. The field is shown immediately south of the Grange, although it is not clear that it belonged to it. Watkins recorded a dovecote of unknown shape at the Grange which had been demolished before 1890 (W22).

YARKHILL: Green Lanes (Private, but visible from the road)

This 18th-century house has a chimney-cote at the east gable just above first-floor level (Fig. 21). The cote is in a lean-to extension to the side of the stack. Seven nest holes face south in three tiers on continuous stone ledges. There are two holes in the east side.

YARKHILL: Monksbury Court, Monkhide

Duncumb notes, 'Monksbury Court and Moat, the remains of a Convent Chapel and Columbarium are to be seen here'.[473] A 'pigeon house' is found in an inventory of 1649 and again in 1790 when it was described as 'A dove house timber built and thatched in bad repair'. It had gone by 1910.[474]

YARKHILL: Showle Court

Watkins recorded this round brick pigeon house, the only example of its type in the county. (Old Sufton in Mordiford is brick-cased not brick-built).[475] It had an internal diameter of 17ft (5.15m) and 2ft 2in (0.66m) thick walls. The lowest tier of nest holes was near ground level and the nests had brick alighting ledges. The lantern was 'round' (W16).

Fig. 168 *Showle Court photographed by Israel Cohen (undated)*

*Fig. 169 Whitwick Manor
(Alfred Watkins Collection)*

By 1957 the building had been almost completely demolished (Fig. 168).[476] Stainburn found even less remaining and adds little to Watkins, but says the alighting ledges may have been 'projecting bricks or oak boards let into the brickwork.' He suggests a 17th-century date for the brickwork (S9). Certainly the existence of nest holes to ground level suggests a date in the earlier 18th century or before.

YARKHILL: Whitwick Manor

Site of octagonal brick pigeon house, demolished *c.*1927.[477] If Whitwick had survived it would, according to previous surveys, be the largest octagonal brick dovecote in the county, with 13ft 4in (4.04m) facets (W19). Watkins' photograph (Fig. 169)[478] shows a magnificent structure built in English bond brickwork. The walls are divided into two 'storeys' by an interrupted string/perching course. Each storey has a segmental arched sunk panel and the wall top is finished with a brick dentil cornice. This all amounts to the showiest brickwork of any of the octagonal pigeon houses of the first half of the 18th century. It is, however, unlikely that the building was as big as previously suggested. The sunk panels are 12 brick headers wide, and each of the pilasters one stretcher and a three-quarter bat. This is unlikely to add up to more than 7ft 3in (2.2m).

The roof was probably of clay tiles and supported an octagonal lantern that took the relatively common form of glazed panels over an entry and exit slit protected by a sloping board. The eight-pane panels had segmental arched heads. The lantern roof was unusual in form, with a tented outline.

This pigeon house had some other unusual features. It stood over an ice house which suggests that it was sited close to the medieval fishponds to the south-west of the Manor

House.[479] The interior was equipped with a double revolving ladder in two tiers, and a trap. There were 432 nest holes starting at ground level.

YATTON: Rock's Place[480]

This building was included in Watkins' list of square stone dovecotes, but no details were given. It must have been demolished prior to the Royal Commission survey of 1932; the barns at Rock's Place are described in that survey but the dovecote is not included.

YAZOR: Foxley (Listed Grade II, Private)

This was said to be the only hexagonal pigeon house in Herefordshire, but the recounting of the sides of the one at Staunton on Arrow means that it no longer has that distinction. It is, nevertheless, a rare type; the nearest parallels are at Golding Cound near Shrewsbury, Pipe Ridware Hall, Staffordshire and Offchurch, Warwickshire. A search of the ImagesofEngland website reveals only 20 listed hexagonal pigeon houses, with a significant proportion (about a third) in Yorkshire and Northumberland.

Yazor is a further example of a country house dovecote that has outlived the building it served. The big house was a work of Smith of Warwick, begun in the second decade of the 18th century and 'tricked up'[481] by John Davenport, who acquired it in 1856. These two dates are significant for the pigeon house. The early 18th-century date is probably the

*Figs. 170 and 171 Foxley photographed by Israel Cohen 1958 (left)
and the upper entrance (right)*

Fig. 172 Foxley
(Alfred Watkins Collection)

time of its building, whilst the change of ownership brought alterations, notably in the form of a fountain and trough in an arched opening which is dated 1866 (Fig. 170).

This building is designed to serve a number of needs of the big house, which stood about 200m to the south. It is in three storeys; the lowest is an ice house, the middle a game larder and the top a pigeon house (S61). It is part of the stable range and cleverly built against a retained bank so that the upper level is entered from the higher ground without need of stairs or ladder (Fig. 171). The lowest storey forms a rubble stone plinth above which the brick drum rises in English garden wall bond to a plain, closed eaves, with 11ft (3.33m) facets (S61). The pyramidal roof is covered in clay tiles with lead hip rolls and is surmounted by an open louver, similarly roofed and finished with a ball finial.

The upper storey contains 200 nest holes. Outside, on one of the facets, about 3ft (0.91m) below the eaves are four holes above a wooden alighting ledge (Fig. 172). This is similar to the three holes facing the house at Staunton on Arrow.

YAZOR: Pigeon House Close, Yarsop House
A long thin field, number 62 on the tithe map of 1841, immediately south of Yarsop House.

YAZOR: Pigeon House Bank
The name of a field, number 191 on the tithe map of 1841, immediately south of the church (by Yazor Court). The field is listed as part of the Foxley estate but is remote from the Foxley pigeon house described above.

If you know of sites, records or illustrations of dovecotes that are missing or not illustrated in this gazetteer please let the author know at rwalkercam@aol.com.

Notes and References

1. There are other examples of pigeon house imitation in Herefordshire, notably an octagonal tower in Bridge Street, Leominster and an oil tank container in Dilwyn.
2. My wife, Meredith, who deserves at least a footnote, was brought up in Leominster. Her aiding and abetting made this book possible.
3. The Woolhope Club was founded in 1851 as the Woolhope Naturalists' Field Club. Its interests nowadays cover the local history, archaeology and architecture of Herefordshire as well as natural history and geology. Its headquarters and Club Library are in the Woolhope Room in Hereford Library.
4. For the life of Alfred Watkins see: Shoesmith, R. *Alfred Watkins: A Herefordshire Man*, Logaston Press (1900).
5. It was also published in: Watkins, A. 'Pigeon Houses in Herefordshire and Gower' *Archaeological Journal* (1891), 48, pp.29-41 and Watkins, A. 'Ancient Dovecotes' *Trans. Birmingham Archaeological Society* (1893), 19, pp.8-21.
6. Ferguson, R.S. 'Culverhouses' *Archaeological Journal* (1887), 44, pp.106-116; Ferguson, R.S. 'Pigeon Houses in Cumberland' *Transactions of the Cumberland and Westmorland Antiquarian Society* (1888), 9, pp 412-434.
7. Webb, J. 'Notes upon a Preceptory of the Templars at Garway' *Archaeologia* XXXI (1846), pp.182-197.
8. Marshall, G. 'The Discovery of a Columbarium in the Tower of Sarnesfield Church, Herefordshire' *TWNFC* (1904), 18, p.263. His manuscript notes record that he made the discovery on 29 May 1903.
9. Micklethwaite, J.T. 'On Pigeon Houses in Churches' *Archaeological Journal* (1888), 45, pp.374-378.
10. Israel Cohen published important articles about the Wye navigation and about the Jewry of medieval Hereford.
11. Arthur Cooke's book is available, with modern annotations, at the website www.pigeoncote.com. The chapter on churches begins, 'About twenty years ago George Marshall, the owner of Sarnesfield Court …'.
12. McCann, *Somerset*, p.22.
13. See for example the account of glebe records below where the word 'dovecote' is very rare.
14. Pole mounted pigeon houses are not included in this survey.
15. Hansell p.40.
16. Marcus Terentius Varro's (116 BC -27 BC), *Rerum Rusticarum Libri III* (or *Agricultural Topics in Three Books*) is the most often quoted – See Hansell and Stainburn.
17. Recent archaeological investigations at the Prospect in Ross on Wye uncovered the base of a small masonry tower of the Roman period.. It has been suggested, in preliminary consideration, that this may be a pigeon house. If so it would be unique.
18. Hansell p.40. '*Peristerion*' is the Greek word for a dovecote. The analogy breaks down with '*testudo*' which means tortoise; but Varro may have been referring to the rectangular, not round, defensive shield formation used by the legions.
19. See the gazetteer entry below for this and other references to Herefordshire buildings.
20. Webb, J. 'A Roll of the Household Expenses of Richard de Swinfield, Bishop of Hereford' *Camden Society* 59 & 62 old series (1854 and 1855).
21. A relatively high number (13) of churches in the diocese of Hereford are dedicated to St Mary Magdalene, which may explain the special occasion at this date. The missing summer accounts might however have shown that the numbers of birds consumed was not exceptional.
22. McCann (1991), p.93. The Durham accounts begin about 25 years after Bishop Swinfield's.
23. A penny in 1290 was roughly the equivalent of £5 today.
24. A pair of pigeon houses, built in the 12th century as part of the first castle at Allington in Kent, survive as considerably altered circular stone buildings. They have been described as the earliest dovecotes in England. See www.imagesofengland.org.uk.
25. McCann (2000), p.27. See also McCann *Suffolk*: Appendix for extracts from manorial account rolls showing both rental income, income from the sale of pigeons from demesne dovecotes, and expenditure on maintenance.
26 Williams, P. 'The Tenure of the Bishop's Manor of Whitbourne', *TWNFC* (1972).

27. For example: Lord Ernle *English Farming Past and Present,* Longmans (1927), p.18.

28. In this matter Herefordshire is greatly wanting a Victoria County History, and to be included in the National Archives Manorial Documents Register.

29. This figure only counts field names associated with a house called 'Manor' or 'Court'.

30. The distribution in Fig. 13 could simply show the limit of incursions by the Welsh; that pigeon houses were there but destroyed, and only rebuilt at Garway and Wigmore.

31. VCH p.411.

32. Samuel Hartlib writing in 1653 quoted in McCann (1991), p.99. This figure is probably very high. Pigeons eat things other than grain and modern pigeon keepers would not expect to feed a pair as much as 4 bushels.

33. McCann (1991).

34. Pinches, S. *Ledbury: A Market Town and its Tudor Heritage,* VCH (2009), p.17.

35. J. Grundy, looking at 70 documents from 43 parishes found 17% of documents mention pigeon houses – the proportion of parishes is not given. In some parishes more than one terrier mentions a dovecote, Grundy J. 'Herefordshire Farmsteads in their Agrarian Context' *TWNFC* (2006), 54, p.75.

36. Watts, S. *The Glebe Terriers of Shropshire Part 1 Abdon – Llanfair Waterdine,* Keele University (2001) and *The Glebe Terriers of Shropshire Part 1 Llanybodwel to Wroxeter,* Keele University (2002). The parishes with pigeon houses are:

Donington	1612: '… cowhouse, barn, cote, dovehouse, orchard …'
	1693: '… new built dove house …'
Egmond	168 : '… dove house …'
Hodnet	1701: '… pigeon house …' Not mentioned in 1685.
	1705: '… old pigeon house 1 bay now used to lay coals and other fuel …'
Ludlow	1625: '… house with garden and pigeon house …'
Onibury	1607: '… house with barn, ox house, dovehouse …'
Pitchford	1612: '… cote …'
Rushbury	1589: '… house with pigeon house …'
Shawbury	1689: 'There was formerly, some have heard, a pigeon house but decayed long since.'
	1801: '… dove house over the granary …'
Stanton Hine	1612: '… dovehouse …'
Upton Magna	1612: '… pigeon house …'
	1705: ditto
Withington	1682: '… dove house …'
	1699: '… pigeon house …' Not mentioned in 1841.
Wrockwardine	1612: 'House with barn and dove house …'
	1698: '… dove house …'
	1718: '… dove house …'

37. McCann (2003), p.220.

38. Stephen Podd has looked at aver 200 terriers in Suffolk and found seven 17th-century references to dovecotes, including one 'over a stable'.

39. Capes, C. *The Register of Bishop Richard de Swinfield,* Hereford (1909), p.283. He also had one on his manor at Bishops Castle in Shropshire. This proportion, 2 out of 21 or 9.5% is little removed from the proportion of parochial and manorial builders.

40. John McCann points out that the second half of the 16th century was a time when there was discontent, and even rioting, against 'the increasing number' of pigeon houses, McCann (2000), p.31. At Meppershall in Bedfordshire, the glebe terrier records the taking down of the pigeon house in 1706. Perhaps this expresses a wider disinclination on the part of the clergy to keep a source of luxury food, Bedfordshire Record Office P/29/1/7. Against this, there are records of other parishes, for example Bubwith, near York, which still had a pigeon house in 1778. I am grateful to Trevor Cooper for drawing my attention to the following declaration of scruples, which bears directly on parsons' attitudes to pigeons, from the community at Little Gidding in about 1620: 'Then the young children, the youths with their masters, went down to breakfast, and, that ended, to their school-house, which was near adjoining to the house, having been formerly a fair dovehouse. There being an ancient large

dove-house that belonged to the lordship near adjoining to the house, it was by Nicholas [Ferrar] and his mother's contrivement dispigeoned, not chiefly for that intent [the school], for happily they might have found some other place for that use of schooling in some remote part of that great house, but the main cause was that they thought it (though a very great accommodation to the necessary provision of housekeeping) not to be fitting for them, seeing they had no corn in their own lordship to maintain the flight and breed (for it was turned all into pasture upon an hundred years before these times), to keep up a dove-house to devour as so many thieves and to steal away the corn from their neighbouring corn fields which encompassed them about, and that it was more decent for them to want pigeons than to have them kept at other men's cost. So that from a house of pigeons it was turned into a school ...'. Muir, L. & White, J. 1996 *Materials for the Life of Nicholas Ferrar,* Leeds (1996), pp.81-2.

41. There is no exhaustive list of cotes in churches. I have found the following in published sources: From Micklethwaite, J. 'On Pigeon Houses in Churches' *Archaeological Journal* (1888), 45, pp.374-78:

Selby Abbey	Possible wooden nest holes in north-west tower.
Great Yarmouth	Documentary evidence.
Marlborough	Above chancel vault.
Elkstone, Gloucestershire	ditto.
Overbury, Worcestershire	ditto – entered by a small door under the eaves on the north side.
Stanley, Gloucestershire	In the roof of the north transept.
Birlingham, Pershore	Tower.

From Arthur Cooke:

Collingbourne Dulcis, Wilts	Has a unique square flight hole with an alighting ledge.
Monk's Bretton, Yorks	Tower.
Gumfreston, Pembs.	Tower.

From ImagesofEngland:

Ugley, Essex	Tower (probably no physical evidence remaining).
Strumpshaw, Norfolk	Upper level of tower contains a 17th-century dovecote, lined with brick nesting boxes.
Erth Barton, Saltash	In east gable.
St Priam, Tintagel	In west gable.
Padley Chapel, Hathersage	in gable apex.
Upton, Newark	In former priest's room in tower – 'gypsum plaster nest boxes'.
Tewksbury Abbey	North porch parvis.

From McCann, J. *et al* 'A Columbarium at Compton Martin Church' *Somerset Archaeological and Natural History Society Proceedings* (1999), p.143:

Compton Martin, Somerset	Above chancel vault.

[There is now, since the time of writing, a comprehensive study of columbaria: It examines the examples listed above and adds a number of lost columbaria from secondary documentary sources. McCann J. and Pexton F. 'Keeping Pigeons in Parish Churches' *Transactions of the Ancient Monuments Society* (2010), pp.51-82. At John McCann's suggestion that there might be more surviving examples along the Welsh Border further research yielded an example at Meifod near Welshpool. 'In the bell-chamber is a double row of pigeon nesting boxes, twenty four in all', Eisel J. 1986 'Bells of Montgomeryshire' *Archaeologia Cambrensis* (1986), p.190.]

42. McCann (2000), p.37 points to a court case in 1694 which established that pigeons raised for sale were tithable.

43. *Oxfordshire*, VCH, Vol. 8, p.99.

44. Hillaby, J. *St Katherine's Hospital Ledbury*, Logaston Press (2003) p.66; Pinches, S. *Ledbury: A Market Town and its Tudor Heritage,* VCH (2009), p.17.

45. Also not far outside the county, at Llanthony Priory, where the buried remains of a pigeon house were excavated and photographed by Alfred Watkins in 1908. This is a unique find, in that the structure was designed to be subterranean, and therefore only had a good stone face on the inside of the walls. In Watkins' photograph it can be seen that the nest holes are staggered from course to course, and every course has a continuous stone alighting ledge. The roof was missing but there was evidence of a vault or dome. Watkins, A. 'Discovery of a Dovecote at Llanthony', *TWNFC* (1908), p.80.

46. Hillaby, J. & C. *Leominster Minster Priory and Borough*, Logaston Press (2006), p.206 notes that '…each bury had a dove house'.
47. *ibid*, p.211.
48. McCann (2000), p.31.
49. *ibid*, p.35.
50. One of which was built prior to 1619.
51. It could be argued that these 'hot spots' are simply the places where evidence has survived, and that they were typical of the whole county. This would overturn the assertion that there were generally fewer pigeon houses than previously thought.
52. Considering pigeon houses in Shropshire: Atcham (2), Lydbury North (2), Chirbury (2), Wrockwardine (2), Bicton (3), Pimhill (3), Pontesbury (3). In Worcestershire: Cleeve Prior (2), Huddington (2), Himbleton (2), Wichenford (2), Chaddesley Corbett (2), Bredon (2), Dormston (3), Bretforton (4), Pebworth (4). In Gloucestershire: Ashworth (2), Bitton (2), Daglingworth (2), Driffield (2), Frampton (2), Kings Stanley (2), Painswick (2), Saperton (2), Stoke Orchard (2), Bibury (3).
53. Taylor, E. *Kings Caple in Archenfield*, Logaston Press (1997), p.214.
54. There is a distinction in law between the wild creature confined in a pigeon house but free to leave, and a tame bird, such as a messenger or racing pigeon, which has the quality of *animum revertendi*. The latter was thought to remain the property of the owner.
55. McCann (2000), p.41.
56. Reid, P. *Burke's and Savills Guide to Country Houses: Vol.2: Herefordshire, Shropshire, Warwickshire and Worcestershire*, Burke's Peerage (1980).
57. Of the 35 buildings whose form of construction is known 19 were, or are, built of brick.
58. Hansell p.185 has drawings by James Wyatt for Badger Hall, Shropshire based on the design of the Tower of the Winds, which stands below the Acropolis in Athens.
59. VCH, pp.408-409: It yielded the fourth lowest assessment for the wool tax in 1341.
60. Jackson, N. 'Some Observations on the Herefordshire Environment in the Seventeenth and Eighteenth Centuries' *TWNFC* (1958), p.31.
61. VCH, p.410.
62. HRL: Bound extract from 1695 translation of William Camden's *Britannia* of 1586, p.69.
63. VCH, p.411: 20 bushels per acre was achieved on good land in 1805.
64. Samuel Hartlib writing in 1653 quoted in McCann (1991), p.99. This figure is probably very high. Pigeons eat things other than grain and modern pigeon keepers would not expect to feed a pair as much as 4 bushels.
65. Is it possible that the Revolution in France, where pigeons were considered a real grievance, was avoided here because the social checks and balances and the limited privileges meant that the capacity of the land to support pigeons without causing hardship was never exceeded?
66. In this comparison of the statutory lists only pigeon houses are included; dovecotes in barns and other buildings are excluded.
67. It is realised that this is not a very sound assumption. It is probable that, for example, the rate of survival would be higher in more pastoral areas where dovecotes 'survived in use longer', McCann (199), p.89.
68. Fox, C. and Lord Raglan *Monmouthshire Houses: Part III: Renaissance Houses*, National Museum of Wales (1954), p.124. The Welsh lists of listed buildings are not on a computer database that can be searched from the Internet.
69. 71% of England's area of 243,000 km^2 is in agriculture about 90,000 km^2 of which is upland grazing. This leaves 82,530km^2 of land in lowland agriculture, broadly similar to Herefordshire: 82,530/2180 x 300 = 11,300.
70. Watkins (1890), p.31.
71. McCann (1991), p.97.
72. By 1794 an exceptional 2/3rds of Herefordshire was freehold, VCH, p.411.
73. McCann (1991) p.98.
74. Duncumb, J. *General View of the Agriculture of Herefordshire*, The Board of Agriculture (1805), p.135.
75. VCH, p.414.
76. Clerk, John *View of the Agriculture of the County of Herefordshire*, The Board of Agriculture (1794).
77. The subject of another proverb, 'a bean to catch two pigeons'.

78. Moore, John *Columbarium*, London (1735) in the reprint by W.B. Tegetmeier of 1897, p.4.
79. Hansell p.57.
80. Hansell p.55 but here modernised.
81. Doves dung is referred to in the Old Testament (2 Kings 6.25) when one-fourth of a kab load was bought for five silver shekels during the siege of Samaria. The 'doves dung' in this story is the bulb of the plant *Ornithogalum umbellatum* or Star of Bethlehem. The white flowers appear like pigeons droppings on the ground, hence its biblical name. The bulb is eaten throughout the Middle East.
82. About ten times as rich as pig manure.
83. Fussell, G.E. 'Crop Nutrition in Tudor and Early Stuart England' *Agricultural History Review* (1955), 3.2, p.101.
84. Hansell p.25.
85. McCann (1991), p.127.
86. Davis, E. 'Dovecotes of South Cambridgeshire' *Proceedings of the Cambridge Antiquarian Society,* 75 (1986), p.89.
87. Hansell p.54 says that the birds were captured with a net on a pole.
88. McCann (1998), p.28.
89. Davis, E. 'Dovecotes of South Cambridgeshire' *Proceedings of the Cambridge Antiquarian Society* (1986), 75, p.89 refers to a newspaper report of 1823 in which two men were convicted of stealing 11 dozen pigeons and taking them to London to be sold in a shop. One of the two offenders was transported for seven years; the other got a year's hard labour.
90. Other surveys have found a variety of forms including cob and lath and plaster. See Hansell pp.47-53 for illustrations of other forms of nest.
91. Moore, John *Columbarium*, London (1735) in the reprint by W.B. Tegetmeier of 1897, p.4. Moore was an apothecary, and salesman of a famous worm powder, who died shortly after publication of the *Columbarium,* prompting Pope to write, 'Oh learned friend of Abchurch Lane, Who sett'st our entrails free, Vain is thy art, thy powder vain, Since worms shall eat e'en thee', *Gentleman's Magazine* (1737), p.252.
92. Watkins (1892), p.48.
93. Another very good example is found at Kinwarton in Worcestershire.
94. McCann (1991), p.142, notes that pigeons manage perfectly well in cotes with no ledges.
95. McCann (1991), p.145.
96. McCann (1991), p.145 gives another example of a plinth with nest holes at Whitton Hall, Shropshire.
97. McCann, *Somerset*, p.45 illustrates and example at Dunster.
98. Watkins p.13 says that they are 'quite useless in a square building and never found in it.'
99. The extant ladders seem flimsy to a 15-stone architectural historian and I wondered whether they suggested that the keeping of pigeon houses was women's or children's work.
100. HRO E23.
101. McCann (1991), p.107.
102. Plummer, D.B. *Tales of a Rat-hunting Man* Boydell (1978)
103. Stainburn, p.9.
104. The idea of the rat ledge is persistent, even in Booker Prize winning fiction. In Michael Ondaatje's 1992 novel *The English Patient* the death of Patrick is described, 'Patrick died in a dove-cote in France. In France in the 17th and 18th centuries they built them huge, larger than most houses. The horizontal line 1/3 of the way down was called the rat ledge – to stop rats running up the brick, so the doves would be safe. Safe as a dove-cote. A sacred place. Like a church in many ways. A comforting place. Patrick died in a comforting place.'
105. The under-building at Weston Beggard may be a protection against rats but appears to have been done for structural reasons.
106. Davis, E. 'Dovecotes of South Cambridgeshire' *Proceedings of the Cambridge Antiquarian* Society (1986), 75, p.70.
107. The buildings with oblong plans are included in 'square'.
108. There must be some doubt about this dimension which is unusually thin for the diameter of the building.
109. McCann *Somerset*.

110. It was there in 1979 (S.55), but access was not obtained in this survey. It is the 'policy' of the tenants to deny access.

111. See the gazetteer entry which casts doubt on this measurement.

112. John McCann proposed the idea that the raised loft was a dating feature in his 1991 paper but drew back from firmly stating it in his 1992 addendum because there are early 18th-century buildings with raised lofts. However the striking difference between the octagonal and square buildings in this county may suggest that it is generally true even if not in every case.

113. McCann *Somerset*, Fig.127.

114. I am grateful to Alan Stoyel for drawing this example to my attention.

115. At the time of writing planning permission exists to convert the loft to residential use.

116. McCann (2000), p.40. He also describes the 1829 case of Rex v. Brooks which concerned theft from a box-cote. The defendant claimed the birds were wild and thus not personal property. His case was lost because the birds were tame and came home to roost every night, which made them personal property.

117. McCann (1991), p.94. The fireplace at Eardisland was probably more for the benefit of humans than pigeons.

118. Such statements invite contradiction. This conclusion was reached searching www.listedbuildingsonline.org for 'dovecote' with 'ice house'.

119 Faraday, M. *Herefordshire Taxes in the Reign of Henry VIII*, Woolhope Club, Hereford (2005): Refs 46B27 and 47B4. The spellings Pigeon, Pygyn, Pygyon, Pyggyn, Pegyn, ap Pyggyn and Pejon are listed.

120. This includes the 100 'pigeon house' names.

121. Simpson, J. and Roud, S. *A Dictionary of English Folklore*, Oxford University Press (2000), p.278.

122. Leather, E. *The Folk-lore of Herefordshire* (1912), p.25.

123. *ibid.* p.64.

124. *ibid*, p.99.

125. Unfortunately English Heritage plays the part of grandparent in conservation today – its officers have all the fun but hand the babies to the local authorities when the nappies need changing.

126. Administered by Natural England.

127. The term used by George MacLeod for the work of rebuilding the monastic quarters at Iona Abbey. The abbey tower has a loft with white doves – much to the delight of the local peregrines.

128. Many of these images are illustrated in: Thurlby, M. *The Herefordshire School of Romanesque Sculpture*, Logaston Press (1999).

129. The church is thought to have been completed before 1135.

130. Demesne land was land retained by a medieval manorial lord (in this case the abbey) for his own use. Such land was initially worked by serfs, but later, and almost certainly by 1540, paid workers were hired. Demesne land was also leased out, but it would be reasonable to suppose that the dovecotes at Dore were retained by the abbey for the monks' own use.

131. A township or vill was a small unit of civil administration. Sometimes a parish was a township.

132. Williams, D.H. 'The Abbey of Dore' in Richardson, R. & Shoesmith, R. (eds), *A Definitive History of Dore Abbey*, Logaston Press (1997), p.30.

133. This may be an unusual location in that pigeon houses are not generally found close to or within monastic complexes. Bury St Edmunds is the only example found by searching ImagesofEngland. They were a common feature of granges, and the smaller rural settlements – all of Leominster's granges had them – but not, it seems, wanted close to great monastic houses.

134. Bannister, A.T. *The History of Ewyas Harold*, privately published (1902), Appendix p.125.

135. *Gentleman's Magazine* LVII (1787), p.949.

136. Statutory List of Listed Buildings signed on 19 February 1987.

137. Watkins (1890), frontispiece.

138. RCHM III (1934), p.1.

139. Pound Farm Holme Lacy was thought by Watkins to exhibit French influence. LeVeux's drawing looks more like Pound Farm than Watkins' photograph of Wigmore Abbey.

140. Dingley, T. *History from Marble. Compiled in the reign of Charles II by T. Dingley. Volume 1 with an introduction and descriptive table of contents by J.G. Nichols,* Camden Society (1867), f.ccxi.

141. Whitehead, D. *A Survey of Historic Parks and Gardens in Herefordshire*, Hereford and Worcester Gardens Trust (2001), p.29.

142. Grant F. and Patton J. *The Walled Gardens of Herefordshire,* Logaston Press (2009), p.53.
143. Williams, P. *Avenbury and the Ruined Church of St. Mary*, privately published (2000), p.162.
144. *ibid.* As at The White House, St Margarets, this list may be a lazy lawyer's coverall rather than a site specific inventory.
145. Statutory List of Listed Buildings signed 4 December 1985.
146. SMR Record 46275
147. At that time Upper Hill was in Hope under Dinmore not Birley.
148. Probably a good example of a response to the coming of the brown rat.
149. RCHM II (1932), p.11
150. Statutory List of Listed Buildings signed 23 September 1987.
151. This past is captured in the pictures of Watkins Ref. 62 (*c*.1890), The Royal Commission Surveyor's notes in the NMR (1931) and by Cohen (1955). In all of these pictures the roof and lantern are intact. Stainburn Ref. 52 (1977) shows the building without its lantern but with the cornice still in place. The photograph posted on ImagesofEngland (2003) shows the upper part of the cornice removed.
152. Bentley, S. *History and Description of the Parish of Bosbury*, privately published (1891), p.23; Robinson, C.J. *The Mansions of Herefordshire and their Memories*, Longmans & Co. (1872), p.32.
153. Statutory List of Listed Buildings signed 20 August 1991.
154. Cooke, W.H. *Collections towards the History and Antiquities of the County of Herefordshire in Continuation of Duncumb's History: Volume 3*, (1882), p.159.
155. I am grateful to the Architect, Malcolm Harrison for this information and sight of his photographs.
156. Statutory List of Listed Buildings signed 26 March 1987.
157. Hurley, H. (ed) *Landscape Origins of the Wye Valley: Holme Lacy to Bridstow*, Logaston Press (2008), p.55.
158. HRL Watkins Collection Ref. 1456 is the photograph which is the basis for the drawing in Watkins' article of 1890.
159. The Statutory List of Listed Buildings signed 12 April 1973 has an entry headed 'Stables north west of Brockhampton Park'. It implies that the courtyard with the dovecote is listed by stating that 'ranges at rear form enclosed yard'.
160. Whitehead *A Survey of Historic Parks, op.cit.,* p.63.
161. Phyllis Williams *Bromyard: Minster, Manor and Town*, Bromyard and District Local History Society, (1987), Plate 91 shows the ladder in a derelict state prior to its restoration.
162. Whitehead *A Survey of Historic Parks, op.cit.,* p.63.
163. *ibid,* p.159.
164. Phyllis Williams *Bromyard: Minster, Manor and Town, op.cit,* p.176.
165. *ibid.*
166. *ibid,* p.157. 'We are fortunate that in Winslow the survey of 1575 is compiled in a way that makes it possible to consider the common field system of the settlement ... Each of the territories had a chief or manor house with the appurtenances of pigeon house, barn and farm buildings ...'
167. Cave, E.L. 'Discovery of Foundations of an old Pigeon House at Instone, near Bromyard', *TWNFC* (1894), 13, p.264.
168. Phyllis Williams *Bromyard: Minster, Manor and Town, op.cit.,* p.176.
169. *ibid.*
170. Phyllis Williams *Bromyard: Minster, Manor and Town, op.cit.,* p.176.
171. *ibid.*
172. Watkins p.19. Watkins gives the alternative name 'The New Manor House'.
173. Stainburn Ref. 53, Watkins p.19. Watkins named this 'Burghill Vicarage', Stainburn used the alternative name given by Watkins, 'Old Manor House'.
174. Pexton, F. & McCann, J. 'An Early 18th-century Dovecote at Burghill' *TWNFC* (2006), 54, pp.15-24.
175. *ibid,* p.20. The lantern roof is incorrectly described as being tiled. There is also confusion about Watkins' descriptions of the Burghill pigeon houses. This article says that Watkins recorded that the lantern was covered with a lead dome, but Watkins recorded this feature against the building at Burghill Court. His record for the Grange simply says 'octagonal' (Watkins p.19).
176. *ibid.*
177. Whitehead *A Survey of Historic Parks, op.cit.,* p.359.

178. *ibid*, p.378.

179. The plinth oversails by 4 inches all round. Even with this addition the building is rather smaller than the 18/0 square given in Watkins p.17 and repeated by Stainburn Ref. 25.

180. HRL Watkins Collection Ref. 145B. Also in Cohen's photograph of 1957.

181. The dimensions given in this entry are based on earlier accounts. The dovecote is still standing but could not be surveyed; Watkins p.20, Stainburn Ref. 55.

182. Listed by the curtilage rule under the Grade II listing of the Court.

183. Hopton, M. *Froma Cannonica; or, the History of Canon Frome and the Hopton Family*, privately published (1902), p.171 refers to the mention of a dove-house in Michael Hopton's lease.

184. B & S, p.13. The SMR record 1093 suggests a late 17th century date.

185. HRO CD 53.

186. This is also seen in Watkins' photograph HRL Watkins Collection Ref. 148B. The louver was replaced with a less elegantly detailed 'replica' in 1978, while the building was still owned by Herefordshire and Worcester County Council.

187. Stainburn Ref. 55 says it was 'replaced' in 1978.

188. HRL Watkins Collection Ref. 148B.

189. Herefordshire Council: Application for listed building consent NE05/1658/L. The application to coat the underside of the slates with rigid chemical foam was, understandably, refused.

190. Statutory List of Listed Buildings signed 9 February 1988.

191. RCHM II, p.47

192. Cohen's collection includes a photograph of Lawton's Hope. The timber frame in this picture is not obviously a dovecote but could be part of the building recorded by Watkins.

193. Statutory List of Listed Buildings signed 22 October 1986. The building was demolished at some unknown time and subsequently de-listed in January 2009.

194. B & S, p.47. A water tower and three obelisks remain in the landscape that comprised the park.

195. Taken on 5 May 1958.

196. Watkins p.20 included this building in his table of 'Pigeon lofts with lanterns projecting above main buildings.' He mistakenly described it as 'stone'.

197. B & S, p.5.

198. For example Cohen's photograph of 1957.

199. HRL Watkins Collection Ref. 188.

200. *TWNFC* (1921), p.181.

201. NMR Record Card from RCHM Survey (dated 3/3/31).

202. Grundy 'Herefordshire Farmsteads in their Agrarian Context' *TWNFC* (2006), 54, p.81. HRO AT51.

203. HRO HD2/1/31 & 32.

204. Hunt, W. *Cradley: A Village History*, privately published (2002), p.51.

205. Both Watkins p.19 and Stainburn Ref. 51 place this under the heading 'Credenhill Court'. The Statutory List of Listed Buildings signed 12 August 1987 describes 'Dovecote approximately 50m east of Town Well'. This has led to confusion, and to a number of records in the SMR for the same building. Confusion is not eased by the inaccuracy of the measurements in the previous surveys and the change in the design of the louver. What is the point of listing if the louver can be changed from square to octagonal for no good reason?

206. The Statutory List of Listed Buildings signed 9 December 1986 gives the date of the stable block, of which the pigeon house forms part, as 'Late C18 to early C19'. The dovecote is probably earlier. One wall is in Flemish bond with a string course typical of the earlier 18th century, and the stone building which forms the larger part of the range is clearly butted up to it and later in date.

207. Also an undated but probably earlier picture at HRO CD61.

208. RCHM III (1934), p.43.

209. There is also a possibility that the small square building shown to the west on the tithe map is the dovecote in an intermediate position.

210. It will be suggested that the other highly decorated example at Butt House, King's Pyon, is probably not a pigeon house.

211. Watkins p.19. HRL Watkins Collection Ref. 240A. Stainburn did not include this in his table of demolished buildings. The date of demolition is not known.

212. A common problem of brick buildings weakened by the nest holes. The extensive alterations probably explain why this pigeon house is not listed.

213. Watkins omitted this pigeon house from his original survey but included it in the 'Additional Notes'.

214. A floor beam with empty mortices is used at the upper storey level between the pigeon house and the attached barn.

215. It may be that the stone plinth and heavy floor frame were also later alterations.

216. Marshall's photograph.

217. Stainburn Ref. 22, Watkins p.17.

218. HRL Watkins Collection Refs. 242-244.

219. *TWNFC* (1901), p.125.

220. The terrier hole appears, with a lady in crinolines, in Marshall's photograph *c*.1900.

221. Statutory List of Listed Buildings signed 10 November 1987. The pigeon house was first listed in 1953.

222. Murray, Richard Hollins *Dinmore Manor and the Commandery of the Knights Hospitaller of St John of Jerusalem at Dinmore, Herefordshire*, privately published (1936), p.23.

223. Hermitage-Day, E. 'The Preceptory of the Knights Hospitaller at Dinmore' *TWNFC* (1927), p.59.

224. Statutory List of Listed Buildings signed 29 September 1952.

225. HRL Watkins Collection Ref. 280.

226. Farm water mills were relatively common in Herefordshire in the 19th century. Most appear to have been built to drive farm machinery such as root cutters for animal feed. This one is unusual in having a pair of stones for grinding feed. A similar mill exists at Court of Noke in Pembridge. I am grateful to Alan Stoyell for pointing out this example.

227. *pers. comm.* Barry Freeman of the Eardisland Dovecote Trust.

228. SMR 9319.

229. The 1933 survey notes of the RCHM kept in the National Monuments Record.

230. *ibid.*

231. John Ruskin (speaking of Rouen Cathedral in 1859). Quoted from publicity material of the Society for the Protection of Ancient Buildings.

232. Watkins p.18 called this *Porch House.*

233. Watkins recorded the walls as being 2/6 (757) thick.

234. The opening was attended by Peter and Jean Hansell. They donated the model of a dovecote, illustrated in their own books on the subject and gave a generous sum towards the project. Planning permission and listed building consent were recently granted to establish a village shop in the ground floor room.

235. SMR 1626.

236. *pers. comm.* of the present owner.

237. The house was almost completely rebuilt following a fire in 1999.

238. Watkins p.18: the vane 'bears a defaced coat of arms'. Stainburn, entry 39: notes a copper ball and flag vane.

239. Lemore Manor is called Lower Moor on the tithe map and Campbell Manor on the current Ordnance Survey.

240. HRO Glebe Terrier transcripts.

241. Watkins p.16. Stainburn Table II Ref. 5 puts this pigeon house in Upton Bishop by mistake.

242. Watkins p.17 (He incorrectly describes the louver as 'octagonal'). Stainburn Ref. 32 embroiders the story: 'Said to have been moved on rollers from Berrington Hall (Pigeon House Orchard) by several yoke of oxen.'

243. Statutory list prior to 1989. The building is not listed now.

244. In shape, finish, form and roof type it is, perhaps, more reminiscent of East Anglian buildings. One at Clare in Suffolk has almost exactly the same dimensions, McCann, J. *The Dovecotes of Suffolk*, Suffolk Institute of Archaeology and History, (1998).

245. HRO M5/8/49.

246. There is evidence in, for example, empty mortices in the rails, of re-assembly. An accurate measured survey would address this possibility.

247. Watkins p.15. Stainburn Table II Ref. 2 says it had a revolving ladder, but Watkins says it had 'none'. HRL Watkins Collection 944a (which was wrongly labelled 'Stocktonbury'. HRL Pilley Collection 351.

248. Stainburn Ref. 42 suggests that the building may be an older stone building cased in brickwork, but that is not the case.

249. *ibid.*

250. Statutory List of Listed Buildings signed 9 July 1976. This building was not included in Watkins' paper or in the first edition of Stainburn, but in an addendum to the latter work of 1979. It was probably assumed to be a pigeon house because it has a louver.

251. Stainburn Addendum.

252. Previous surveys missed this fragment. Stainburn included it in his Addendum a year later.

253. Hurley *Landscape Origins, op.cit.,* p.57.

254. Fleming-Yates, J. *The River Running By,* privately published (2005), p.108.

255. RCHM III (1934), p.72. This is based on: Webb, J. 'Notes upon a Preceptory of the Templars at Garway' *Archaeologia* XXXI (1846), pp.182-197.

256. Fleming-Yates, *The River Running By, op.cit.,* p.108.

257. See Much Cowarne for the largest – but only by 6 inches.

258. Photograph at HRO CD61.

259. This probably comes from Watkins' *Summer Among the Dovecotes.*

260. The recent television series 'Bonekickers' explored some of these fanciful ideas. As the BBC website reported, 'We were led inside. The curved walls were lined with stone nesting boxes. We counted 666. This time, the number of the Beast. Mark informed me that these were 666 doves to counter the power of Satan. I vowed to give this line to Hugh Bonneville who plays Dr Mark's fictional incarnation: Professor Gregory 'Dolly' Parton. What stunned us most was the huge stone block in the middle of the room. Mark was certain it was there to cover a well mouth. Perhaps a well leading down into an underground chamber. And whatever was placed down there, the Knights wanted nobody ever to find it. A shiver scuttled up my spine and I realized I had a new ending for episode one and a new location. We would have to come here and film inside the real dovecote. We had our tonal philosophy for the show – to include as many real places as possible. An audience could watch our team in action, then visit the place where it happened and perhaps have a slightly greater understanding of its significance. Garway would no longer be a dot on the edge of a map. It would be a secret Templar outpost filled with mystery.' If the internal diameter of the building is divided by the wall thickness the result is 4.6666666666666666 66666666666666r. - Very troubling!

261. Statutory List of Listed Buildings dated 30 April 1986.

262. The English Heritage website, www.ImagesofEngland.org.uk has a photograph Ref ImagesofEngland Number 153808.

263. Illustrated in Stainburn Ref. 66.

264. Statutory List of Listed Buildings dated 22 August 1996.

265. Watkins p.18. HRL Watkins Collection Ref 419.

266. RCHM original inventory notes at NMR.

267. Watkins p.18 says that the string course was 'against rats' but current thinking is that such projecting courses were for perching (see the Introduction). HRL Watkins Collection Ref. 419, also RCHM I, p.84.

268. Watkins additional notes. Stainburn Table II Ref. 6 says that it was 'Thought to have been demolished about 30 years ago' but this must be wrong as he was writing in 1978.

269. HRL Watkins Collection Refs 1457 and 1458 A-C.

270. Watkins p.21 and HRL Watkins Collection Ref 1503.

271. There is some confusion about the location of this dovecote. The Statutory List signed 21 May 1987 describes it as being 35 yards north-west of Pound Farmhouse, but the name of the house has been changed by the agricultural college to Wilsly House. The Images of England website illustrates this listing with a picture of the ugly concrete silo at Bower Farm! The SMR has two records, one at Holme Lacy Farm (23878) and one at Pound Farm (20638). Stainburn Ref. 6, after Watkins p.15, puts the dovecote at Home Farm, which is the old name for Pound Farm – see 1909 sale particulars of the Holme Lacy Estate at HRL PC2344.2, p.33.

272. HRL Watkins Collection Ref. 452A shows it intact, Cohen's picture of 1958 shows the loss of some of the balustrade of the gallery, Stainburn's picture of 1977 shows only the supports of the gallery – the stitch delayed with ruin paid.

273. The ImagesofEngland website has a number of examples of round stone pigeon houses with deep eaves and steep conical roofs. A 17th-century example at Walcot Hall, Lydbury North is only 40 miles away.

274. Shoesmith, R. *Alfred Watkins: A Herefordshire Man,* Logaston Press (1990), pp.17 & 73. The Statutory List of Listed Buildings signed 8 October 1988 wrongly says it was built for Alfred Watkins.

275. For example Cohen's picture of 6 May 1958.

276. The whole of the forgoing is based on a detailed report on excavations: Children, G. & Priestley, S. *Archaeological Excavation: Pigeon House Orchard, Hope Under Dinmore, Herefordshire,* unpublished report BA0425LUHDP2 by Border Archaeology, Leominster, (2004).

277. Bishopstone was a mere 6/0 (1818) but is now demolished.

278. Cohen's photograph for example.

279. The owner, who kindly allowed me to visit, told me about this trap.

280. Bannister, A.T. *The History of Ewyas Harold*, privately published (1902), Appendix, p.120.

281. Statutory List of Listed Buildings signed on 20 May 1987. This building is illustrated on the Images of England website Ref. 155548.

282. In the photograph taken by the Royal Commission investigator in 1927 the whole of the north side has plaster panels. The original survey notes are held in the National Monuments Record.

283. *ibid.*

284. Cohen's photograph.

285. Open April to October in 2010. See www.stocktonbury.com.

286. Price, J. *An Historical and Topographical Account of Leominster* (1795), p.78. Here quoting an account by the bailiffs of Henry VIII.

287. In Watkins' picture the ivy has not taken hold. There is a distinct change in the external masonry at the level of the window sills which is not a step but a change in silhouette. The lower part has a bulging curve (entasis see Garway and Richard's Castle) but from the line below the windows the wall is taken up straight.

288. Stainburn Ref. 7 refers to a trap but there is no sign of one now.

289. HRO M5/8/49.

290. NMR Record Card from RCHM Survey. The '12th century' date was probably designed to impress the owners, 'the Misses Williams', because in the same record card the surveyor, J.W. Bloe, notes 'The building is probably medieval but has little distinctive evidence of the date except for the fact it is circular.'

291. Examination of these during repair work revealed that the slats are a later alteration.

292. Stainburn Ref. 13 shows these features. Watkins p.16 said the vane had 'gone'.

293. B & S, p.4.

294. Whitehead *A Survey of Historic Parks, op.cit.,* p.6.

295. *ibid*, p.159.

296. Statutory List of Listed Buildings signed 19 June 1987.

297. Watkins p.17 and Stainburn Ref. 29 give the address as 'White House'.

298. Royal Commission survey record of 3/3/1932 held at the National Monuments Record.

299. Watkins p.17, Stainburn Ref. 24. Watkins (1892), p.46 suggests that the middle level above the gateway was a falconry and the pigeons were in the attic. This seems an odd idea given that pigeons would surely be nervous in the presence of birds of prey.

300. RCHM III, p.87 describes the building as a gatehouse and makes no mention of the nest boxes.

301. HRO LC Deeds 6129(I) cited in Thirsk, J. *The Agrarian History of England and Wales Vol IV 1500-1640*, Cambridge CUP (1967), p.106.

302. Parkinson, J. & Ould, A.E. *Old Cottages, Farm Houses, and Other Half-Timber Buildings in Shropshire, Herefordshire, and Cheshire*, Batsford (1904), Plate LXVI and RCHM III, Plates 118 and 119 show the hard boundaries. See also Watkins' photograph in *TWFNC* (1924), p.xcii.

303. This was the author's only view of the interior, achieved by inserting a camera.

304. HRL Watkins Collection. Cohen's picture shows a finial listing heavily.

305. RCHM II, p.100.

306. This upper door has a massive stone sill but no external lintel, which casts some doubt on it being original. However, the internal wooden lintel does not appear to be modern.

307. John McCann (*Somerset*, p.32) gives examples of the re-lining of stone buildings at Norton sub Hamdon and Montacute.

308. HRO HD2.

309. Pinches, S. *Ledbury: A Market Town and its Tudor Heritage,* VCH (2009), p.17.
310. Whitehead *A Survey of Historic Parks, op.cit.,* p.243
311. *ibid*, p.386.
312. The statutory list signed 15 March 1996 describes this as a 'remarkably complete complex'.
313. NMR Record Card from RCHM survey, RCHM III, p.131.
314. SMR 12007.
315. Statutory List of Listed Buildings signed 24 July 1954.
316. Hillaby, J. & C. *Leominster Minster, Priory and Borough*, Logaston Press (2006), p.123.
317. 'Upper Hyde' in Watkins' table and on early editions of the Ordnance Survey.
318. *TWFNC* (2004), p.37.
319. South of Ivington.
320. Watkins p.22. Stainburn incorrectly attaches the note about the 'Tump' to Kenderchurch in his Table I.
321. Stainburn Ref. 67 for illustration.
322. SMR 800.
323. The carving is mentioned in RCHM II p.121 but the building was not considered suitable for listing. This probably means that the listing investigator also thought the building is modern.
324. Watkins p.16. Stainburn Ref. 19 repeats this number. It is probably incorrect. At present only the upper half of the walls has evidence of nests; this area would provide 400 nests. If the whole height were used, with nests supported from the floor, there would be room for at least 800 nests.
325. HRO HD2.
326. Statutory List of Listed Buildings signed 30 April 1986. No nests are referred to in the list description.
327. RCHM I, p.171.
328. This might indicate that the timber floor to the loft is later and part of the change to water tower and garden room.
329. But see Bollingham House, Eardisley where the roof shape was changed when a water tank was inserted. The plastering of the interior of the ground floor may indicate, as at Bollingham, the conversion to a garden room or gazebo when the water tower was made.
330. Statutory List of Listed Buildings signed 3 July 1985.
331. 10 headers and 11 stretchers = 45 + 99 inches = 144 inches = 12 feet.
332. There is the hint of a pattern of over-burnt headers on the lower part of the south elevation which is not carried over the whole surface.
333. All this fine detail has been lost.
334. RCHM I, Plate 21.
335. This is broadly correct, but there is no window in the east wall. On the south side there are only two holes to the east of the window.
336. Marshall.
337. I was told that a fox had made its home in this tower, gaining entry through the low west window and sleeping in the very top, among the bells.
338. *Herefordshire Archaeological News* 58; *TWNFC* (1992), p.38
339. Smith, N. and Field, F. *Longtown Herefordshire: A Medieval Castle and Borough,* English Heritage (2003), p.21. The field is misnamed in this report.
340. Whitehead *A Survey of Historic Parks, op.cit.,* p.413.
341. SMR Record 2418.
342. Price, J. *An Historical and Topographical Account of Leominster*, Hereford (1795), p.151.
343. Stainburn found that the holes had been blocked (1976).
344. Watkins p.18.
345. Stainburn Ref. 36. Stainburn found that the holes had been blocked before his visit in 1976.
346. HRL Watkins Collection 721A.
347. HRL Watkins Collection 729C. Cohen also photographed the building in 1957. Statutory List of Listed Buildings signed 4 September 1988 suggests a date of *c.*1870.
348. Watkins p.17. He also describes it as the smallest he had seen. Stainburn Ref. 30. Part of the frame was still standing in 1978 but is now utterly lost to ivy.
349. Statutory List of Listed Buildings signed 9 February 1988.
350. HRL Watkins Collection 753B.

351. Statutory List of Listed Buildings signed 26 March 1987.

352. *ibid.*

353. Statutory List of Listed Buildings signed 19 September 1984.

354. RCHM III, p.148 suggests that the main block and south cross-wing are of the 16th-century and that the north cross-wing was added in the next. The dour stone casing was done in the 18th century.

355. There is also a remarkable bell tower to the north-west of the house.

356. Note the dormer with cusped framing in its gable which would suggest a pre-Classical date. This range was later adapted for hop drying and the machine for compressing the hops in the pockets survives.

357. RCHM III, Plate 40.

358. *ibid.*

359. Watkins p.16 and HRL Watkins Collection 773C.

360. Statutory List of Listed Buildings signed 23 September 1987.

361. The item in the statutory list is headed 'dovecote and garden wall'.

362. It is difficult to be certain about this feature when so much rebuilding has taken place. In one small area near the top of the stone walling there are ledges two tiers apart.

363. Watkins p.15. and HRL Watkins Collection 792A and 792B. The vane was not in place at the time of writing.

364. Grant F. and Patton J. *The Walled Gardens of Herefordshire,* Logaston Press (2009), pp.31-45.

365. Whitehead *A Survey of Historic Parks, op.cit.,* p.300.

366. In Watkins' illustration there is no louver, the roof is wholly stone slate and the building looks to be in a sorry state. In his undated photograph, HRL Watkins Collection 196A, the, possibly, circular collar remains but the louver is missing. The photograph in RCHM II (1932) Plate 36 shows a newly restored roof with the existing details.

367. Impressively portrayed as a backdrop to the dovecote in Watkins' picture HRL 196A.

368. B & S, p.18.

369. English Heritage *Heritage at Risk: West Midlands* (2008), p.278.

370. A tallet is a loft, usually for storing hay.

371. Statutory List of Listed Buildings signed 18 November 1952.

372. Munthe, M. *Hellens. The Story of a Herefordshire Manor,* London (1957), p.87.

373. This arrangement dates back to Watkins' photograph HRL 738 and 739.

374. *ibid.*

375. Photograph by Angela Stanger-Leathes on www.imagesofengland.org.uk.

376. Watkins p.20 says of the nest boxes 'None left upper storey'. This implies that nests were left lower down but no grooves for the partitions exist there. The Statutory List of 4 December 1985 provides other evidence. The floor was missing at that time and the description says, 'remains of bottom part of potence [revolving ladder]', but this must be the bottom of the post that previously supported the floor. It also refers to 'about 20 rows of sawn-off tenons (which) indicate that there were projecting nesting ledges rather than hollowed out nests.' These tenons are not visible now.

377. Although Watkins gives a categorical 'No' in the revolving ladder column of his table of octagonal pigeon houses.

378. SMR 4891.

379. B & S, p.10.

380. Statutory List of Listed Buildings signed 12 April 1973.

381. SMR 6535.

382. Thomas, J. & B. *Garway Hill Through the Ages,* Logaston Press (2007), p.52.

383. See the Images of England website.

384. The article that includes the illustration comes from the Cyclists' Touring Club Gazette.

385. HRL Watkins Collection 833. Parkinson, J. & Ould, A.E. *Old Cottages, Farm Houses, and Other Half-Timber Buildings in Shropshire, Herefordshire, and Cheshire,* Batsford (1904), Plate LXVIII (wrongly captioned 'Middlebrook').

386. HRO Harleian Catalogue Bundle 60.

387. Whitehead *A Survey of Historic Parks, op.cit.,* p.87. This puts the pigeon house to the north-west of the house, but the tithe map is clear that the field named for the pigeon house is to the south-east.

388. Stainburn Ref. 65. Statutory List of Listed Buildings signed 12 April 1973. Images of England Number 410191.

389. It is also suggested that a hop kiln was inserted. Herefordshire Application for Listed Building Consent NC01/2128/L.

390. Photograph shown to me by the owner.

391. Statutory List of Listed Buildings signed 30 April 1986.

392. *TWNFC* (1983), VLIV, p.257.

393. HRO Downton Estate Papers, T.74 Bundle 691.

394. The neighbouring town of Ludlow in Shropshire, which was also a planted Norman town with a castle also had pigeon houses within its bounds. 'Pigeons were also kept, despite their depredations on cultivators. Culverhouse Close, next to the [river] Corve at the north end on Linney, had an early dovecote ... There were others like Ellis Evans's pigeon house in Corve Street', Faraday, M. *Ludlow 1086-1660*, Phillimore (1991), p.107.

395. For example in Bradley, A. *In the March and Borderland of Wales*, Constable (1905), p.172.

396. Curnow, P.E. & Thompson M.W. 'Excavations at Richard's Castle, Herefordshire, 1962-1964' *Journal of British Archaeological Association* (1969), 32, pp.105-121.

397. The County SMR article notes, 'Although the excavations [*ibid*] have provided us with useful information on the foundation and subsequent periods of rebuilding of the castle, they unfortunately left many of the foundations of the walls uncovered, which resulted in the subsequent collapse of remaining structures.'

398. *ibid*. The date suggested in the Statutory List of Listed Buildings is 14th century. RCHM III (1934), p.172 does not hazard a guess.

399. *ibid* County SMR.

400. At Herstmonceux's the brick lining of the tower which holds the nest holes is more obviously a later insertion. At Tattershall, the Statutory List notes that, 'A garderobe chamber on the south side has been converted to a dovecote having side walls lined with mud and lath construction containing circular nesting boxes.' Thornham, Caister, Kirby Muxloe and Conisbrough have a variety of adaptations.

401. Rochester and Dunster are similar to Richard's Castle while Herstmonceux's brick lined tower is more obviously a later insertion. Thornham, Caister, Tattershall, Kirby Muxloe and Conisbrough have a variety of adaptations.

402. The Statutory List of Listed Buildings signed 4 August 1972 expresses some doubt about the purpose of the building. It says, 'In farmyard is a small square building with a hipped slate roof and low open lantern that may have been a dovehouse.'

403. Hughes, P. and Hurley, H. *The Story of Ross,* Logaston Press (2009) p.43. This includes a conjectural reconstruction of the appearance of the Palace precincts.

404. This unpublished history of the White House estate by Arthur Wood is held on the estimable Ewyaslacy.org.uk website. Wood suggests that the list is a standard, cover-all list used by solicitors of the day, rather than being a site-specific inventory.

405. Statutory List of Listed Buildings signed 30 April 1986.

406. I was conducted up the tower by his great nephew.

407. The house was demolished in 1957 leaving only a service wing and part of the walled garden.

408. A modern use of the word 'is the name given to a place reserved for a dignified and worthy resting place for cremated ashes' (Website of St John's Cathedral, Norwich), which frustrates searching on the internet.

409. Marshall, G. 'The Discovery of a Columbarium in the Tower of Sarnesfield Church, Herefordshire' *TWNFC* (1904), 18, p.263. Marshall's manuscript notes record that he made the discovery on 29 May 1903.

410. RCHM III, (1934), p.177.

411. There is no evidence of a louver but the roof shape suggests there should be one.

412. Sharpe, F. *The Church Bells of Herefordshire*, privately published (1972), Vol. 4, p.445.

413. The Court was demolished in 1955. B & S, p.56.

414. Watkins Additional Notes – he refers to information given to him by George Marshall but says the building stood in 'Pigeon House Meadow' not 'Pigeon House Field'.

415. Hurley *Landscape Origins, op.cit.,* p.65.

416. Pfuell, I. *A History of Shobdon*, privately published (1994), p.31.

417. Whitehead *A Survey of Historic Parks, op.cit.,* p.335 from HRO G39/97/690. 'When Sir James Bateman purchased Shobdon in 1705 he acquired "A large new built seat with outhouses and barns, stables, malt kilns and other offices, pigeon's house, gardens, orchards ...".'

418. There is a small photograph of this John Harris print at HRO AA17/199. The British Library holds an original print at BL.004931950. The Hereford Museum has the print in its collection.

419. See Bolitree House, Weston under Penyard.

420. Ordnance Survey topographical record card. Held in the Sites and Monuments Record: Source Number 7805

421. Pfuell *History of Shobdon, op.cit.,* p.51.

422. *ibid*, p.143.

423. Stainburn Ref. 68 and ImagesofEngland 154317 for illustration.

424. Williams, P. *The Three Stamfords*, Bromyard Local History Society (undated), pp.109-110.

425. *ibid*, p.105.

426. Whitehead *A Survey of Historic Parks, op.cit.,* p.339 from HRO M5/30/14.

427. *ibid*.

428. Watkins p.19 and Stainburn Ref. 54 say it is 'octagonal'.

429. Hansell pp.152 & 161.

430. Four courses rise 11.75 inches.

431. Marshall, G. 'Notes on the Manor of Sugwas' *TWNFC* (1921), p.117.

432. Watkins p.15. The article includes a line drawing of Aldersend. There is a photograph at HRL Watkins Collection 966A.

433. RCHM II (1932), Plate 36. Cohen's photograph of 1953 also shows bare rubble stone.

434. B & S, p.24.

435. The stables, gardener's house and icehouse are listed, Grade II, but the dovecote is not; presumably because it was incomplete when the listing survey was carried out. The whole park is included in the list of Historic Parks and Gardens at Grade II.

436. Whitehead *A Survey of Historic Parks, op.cit.,* p.156.

437. The Tower of the Winds, in the Roman Agora in Athens, was the inspiration for many English park buildings. James Wyatt designed just such an octagonal dovecote for Badger Hall, Shropshire which was, unfortunately, never built. (Hansell p.185).

438. HRL Watkins Collection 977B. The roof of great house is clearly seen in this picture.

439. A later picture by Cohen shows a bare roof with the timbers showing.

440. HRL Watkins Collection 992.

441. B & S, p.62.

442. Transcript at HRO BP 64.

443. HRO HD2/1/73.

444. The owner of Lower Court kindly showed me the typed transcripts of these surveys but did not know the original sources.

445. Unfortunately Watkins p.29 simply reports this as 'lately restored'.

446. See Eywood, Titley and Hill House, Walford. Stainburn Ref. 56 wrongly gives this as 'upper loft only' and also gives incorrect measurements.

447. RCHM II, p.247.

448. The blocking up of the two ground floor windows has been roughly done so that it is not possible to establish if they were original or inserted.

449. Whitehead *A Survey of Historic Parks, op.cit.,* p.391 from HRO, RC/IV/E/959.

450. HRO AW/28/41/1 which is also held on the estimable Ewyaslacy.org.uk website.

451. *ibid*.

452. RCHM II, Plate 10. The roof is derelict in this picture and a brick shed stands alongside. Repairs had been carried out by 1957 when Cohen visited.

453. McCann (1991), p.145 gives another example of a plinth with nest holes at Whitton Hall, Shropshire.

454. SMR 6392.

455. Marshall, G. 'The Church of the Knights Templar at Garway' *TWFNC* (1927), p.88.

456. Cohen's photograph of 1957. Watkins left no picture of this pigeon house.

457. At the top of the wall the brickwork has been rendered. In places the ledges for a nineteenth tier are visible.

458. In the cradle below the lantern there is a short length of what may have been one of the timbers holding the top bearing of a revolving ladder.

459. Hillaby, J. *St Katherine's Hospital Ledbury,* Logaston Press (2003), p.66.

460. I am grateful to Chris Partrick for this information.

461. The Statutory List of Listed Buildings signed 17 March 1987 suggests a date of *c.*1700.

462. It was not possible to get inside this building because it is securely boarded up. The descriptions of Watkins p.16 and Stainburn Ref. 17 throw little light on the interior.

463. HRL Watkins Collection 1099D.

464. At Watkins p.13 he says they were 15ft up.

465. Whitehead *A Survey of Historic Parks*, op.cit., p.168.

466. *ibid.* There were successive Johns in the Freeman line. John II was not born until 1731.

467. One of which has been replaced by a new square baulk.

468. Statutory List of Listed Buildings signed 3 July 1985.

469. HFNS Vol. 139. This field name is not included in the County SMR.

470. HRO HD2 Transcripts.

471. Statutory List of Listed Buildings signed 15 July 1985.

472. Statutory List of Listed Buildings signed 26 January 1967 says that there are no nests.

473. SMR 7186. Watkins, M. *Collections towards the History and Antiquities of the County of Herefordshire in Continuation of Duncumb's History: Hundred of Radelow*, Hereford (1902), p.161.

474. Grundy 'Herefordshire Farmsteads in their Agrarian Context' *TWNFC*, (2006), 54, p.79.

475. It is shown on early editions of the Ordnance Survey to the east of the house and north of the pond (remains of the moat).

476. Cohen's photograph.

477. Stainburn Table II Ref. 14. Previous surveys put this in Much Cowarne parish. It is disappointing that it has not been possible to identify the exact location on earlier editions of the Ordnance Survey.

478. HRL Watkns Collection Ref. 196B.

479. SMR 11894.

480. Watkins p.16 puts this dovecote in Much Marcle and gives no details beyond including it in the table of square stone dovecotes.

481. B & S, p.26.

Index

Entries in italics refer to illustrations

183

Also from Logaston Press

Around and About Herefordshire and the southern Welsh Marches
by Graham Roberts

First published in 2004 and updated in 2010, this book of twelve road-based tours cover south-east Powys, east Monmouthshire, north-west Gloucestershire, west Worcestershire, south Shropshire and — at their heart — Herefordshire (320 pages with 380 black and white photographs and maps, price £12.95).

Castles & Moated Sites of Herefordshire
by Ron Shoesmith

This book is in two parts. The first gives an overview of the early history of the county in relation to its castle building, the second is a gazetteer that includes details and history relating to any site that may have been an individual defensive work (320 pages with over 130 black and white illustrations, price £10).

Arthur, Louise and the True Hound of the Baskervilles
by Margaret Newman Turner

The debate as to whether the Hound of the Baskervilles originally haunted Dartmoor or whether it was the disguised Black Hound of Hergest Court near Kington in north-west Herefordshire has raged for many years. Margaret Newman Turner is well placed to shed new light on the matter, her father, Cecil Philip Turner, having corresponded with Conan Doyle himself about it. Their letters, and statements collected by Cecil Turner from people who had experienced the Hound, form an important part of this book (110 pages, 25 black and white illustrations, price £10).

Merrily's Border: The Marches share their secrets
with novelist Phil Rickman & photographer John Mason

This book reveals the sources and inspiration behind Phil Rickman's addictive Merrily Watkins series about the diocesan exorcist for Hereford (112 pages, over 90 colour and 60 black and whte photographs, hardback price £20, paperback price £12.95).

Herefordshire Folklore
by Roy Palmer

Roy Palmer presents the folklore of the county as a series of themes that embrace landscape, buildings, beliefs, work, seasons and people (230 pages, copiously illustrated, price £12.95).

Herefordshire Bricks & Brickmakers
by Edwin Davey & Rebecca Roseff

An account of the brick industry in Herefordshire which locates and explains many hollows in the ground as old brickworks (160 pages, 70 lack and white and 25 colour illustrations, price £9.95).

Also from Logaston Press

Orchard: A year in the life of a Herefordshire cider orchard
photographs by Gareth Rees-Roberts

This is a visual contemplation of a year in the life of a mature sixty-acre cider orchard (144 pages with 138 colour photographs, price £20 hardback, £15 paperback).

Roses round the door? Rural images, realities & responses: Herefordshire, 1830s-1930s *by* Tim Ward

Tim Ward's collection of postcards includes many images of Herefordshire's past rural life: harvesting and hop-picking, cidermaking and cattle breeding, blacksmiths, beekeepers and basketmakers. Behind these photographs lay the working lives of men and women (168 pages with 135 black and white illustrations, price £12.95).

Haunted Herefordshire
by Rupert Matthews

With tales of exorcism, buried treasure and much besides, this is a book full of mysterious happenings (96 pages with 48 black and white photographs, price £7.95).

Herefordshire Churches through Victorian Eyes
by Sir Stephen Glynne, with watercolours by Charles F. Walker, *edited by* John Leonard

Glynne was the original 'church-crawler' and during his lifetime (1807-74) he visited over 5,000 churches. He provides an excellent description of the churches, and often describes features (or, indeed, churches) which have now vanished. The paintings by Charles Walker were executed in 1849-51, and many are roughly contemporaneous with Glynne's notes (176 pages, over 100 watercolours, price £12.95).

Herefordshire Place-Names
by Bruce Coplestone-Crow

This book seeks to explain the place-names of Herefordshire — not just those of the major settlements, but also of districts, hamlets and even old farmsteads (268 pages with 7 maps, price £12.95).

Knights Templar & Hospitaller in Herefordshire
by Audrey Tapper

This book provides a brief history of the knights and delves into their grants of land and property in the county. It also discusses issues such as right of sanctuary, the honesty of the bookkeepers and quality of the estate staff in general (80 pages, 30 black and white illustrations, price £4.95).

The Walled Gardens of Herefordshire
edited by Fiona Grant and Jane Patton

A gazetteer lists the gardens and summarises their condition, whilst seven are selected for detailed study (112 pages, 55 mainly colour illustrations, price £10).